The Female Voice in *The Assembly of Ladies*

The Female Voice in *The Assembly of Ladies:*
Text and Context in Fifteenth-Century England

By

Simone Celine Marshall

Cambridge Scholars Publishing

The Female Voice in *The Assembly of Ladies*: Text and Context in Fifteenth-Century England,
by Simone Celine Marshall

This book first published 2008 by

Cambridge Scholars Publishing

15 Angerton Gardens, Newcastle, NE5 2JA, UK

British Library Cataloguing in Publication Data
A catalogue record for this book is available from the British Library

ISBN (10): 1-84718-570-3, ISBN (13): 9781847185709

TABLE OF CONTENTS

ACKNOWLEDGEMENTS

I would like to acknowledge the assistance of several individuals and institutions during the research and writing of this book: Diane Speed, Margaret Rogerson, Geraldine Barnes and Penny van Toorn from the Department of English at the University of Sydney, Alexandra Barratt from the University of Waikato for her suggestions that instigated this work, and Ruth Evans from the University of Stirling for allowing me to discuss several issues with her. In particular I would like to thank Carole Cusack from the Department of Studies in Religion at the University of Sydney, and Vrasadis Karalis from the Department of Modern Greek at the University of Sydney, for their encouragement. I would like to thank the librarians at Fisher Library, University of Sydney, the Wren Library, Trinity College, Cambridge, the University Library, Cambridge, the British Library, London, and Longleat House, Warminster.

LIST OF ABBREVIATIONS

EETS e.s.	Early English Text Society extra series
EETS o.s.	Early English Text Society original series
IMEV	Index of Middle English Verse
MED	Middle English Dictionary
MLN	Modern Language Notes
MP	Modern Philology
NM	Neuphilologische Mitteilungen
NQ	Notes and Queries
OED	Oxford English Dictionary
PMLA	Publication of the Modern Language Association
PQ	Philological Quarterly
RES	Review of English Studies
Suppl.	Supplement to the Index of Middle English Verse

CHAPTER ONE

THE ASSEMBLY OF LADIES:
TEXT AND CONTEXT

The story of *The Assembly of Ladies* begins with its composition sometime in fifteenth-century England. Who wrote it, for whom and why, are questions about which we can speculate, but never ultimately answer–the poem itself gives us few clues. Yet the poem has had a remarkable shelf-life; in subsequent centuries the poem has continued to be noticed, read, and debated, as a small but significant artefact from fifteenth-century England.

The history of its reception is as remarkable as the poem itself, and is perhaps one of the reasons we still read the poem today. Early in the life of the printing press in England, the poem was included in collected editions of Chaucer (along with nearly every other poem written during this period!). The shadow of Chaucer loomed large over fifteenth-century English literature, so much so that in collected print-editions editors frequently included "newly discovered" works and attributed them to the great poet. In some ways, this is the starting point for our story here, as the attribution to Chaucer carried *The Assembly of Ladies* along for many centuries, until 1810 when it was finally removed forever from the Chaucer canon.

Yet I want to step back to an earlier starting point for this story, to the three extant manuscripts in which *The Assembly of Ladies* exists. The three manuscripts, London, British Library Additional MS 34360, Cambridge, Trinity College MS R.3.19, and Warminster, Longleat MS 258, are all witnesses to an earlier record of literature in the fifteenth century, and it is this record that this book will attempt to tap into. This book will consider *The Assembly of Ladies* in terms of its fifteenth-century English literary context. From the contents of the poem, and from the contents of the manuscripts in which it exists, we can catch glimpses of a past time, we see a late medieval view of the world. The poem opens up for us a world of architecture, social etiquette, law, science, art, and literature to present a story that is deeply embedded in the knowledge of its day. The poem provides us with a view of fifteenth-century English society and culture, but what marks it as different from other texts of its time is that it is the world-view of a woman.

Since its exclusion from the Chaucer canon in 1810, *The Assembly of Ladies* has remained on the edge of scholarly attention because of its female narrator. A female narrator was not unheard of in medieval literature, although it was particularly rare. The anonymity of the poet exacerbated the speculation–was the poet, also, a woman? Who was she? Why did she write this poem? What were the circumstances in which she wrote it? Such are the questions that scholars raised about her. Walter Skeat suggested the poet was the Countess of Oxford, Margaret Neville,[1] and later Ruth M. Fisher suggested she must have been a woman associated with the court of the Duke of Suffolk.[2] Not all scholars have accepted the theory of a female author, however; Ethel Seaton has suggested Sir Richard Roos as a possible author[3] and G. L. Marsh has suggested John Lydgate.[4] Most recently, Alexandra Barratt, has argued in favour of female authorship.[5]

It is fair to say that much of the scholarship concerning the authorship of *The Assembly of Ladies* reflects the time in which it was written. Skeat, writing at the turn of the twentieth century, famously suggested that *The Assembly of Ladies* and another fifteenth-century English poem with a female narrator, *The Floure and The Leafe*, must have been written by the same poetess, as surely there could not have been two female poets in fifteenth-century England. This is very much a comment of its time, as is Barratt's argument, at the close of the twentieth century, that one cannot automatically rule out female authorship. *The Floure and The Leafe* is certainly a poem that features closely with *The Assembly of Ladies* in previous scholarship. It, too, was attributed to Chaucer, and has a female narrator, but its success has overshadowed *The Assembly of Ladies*, resulting in *The Assembly of Ladies* receiving limited scholarly attention.

The previous scholarship on *The Assembly of Ladies* certainly offers a distinct position for this book, one that has clearly grown out of the concern of previous scholarship on the authorship question, and yet one that also reflects the concerns of twenty-first century scholarship in gender and society. This book sets aside the debate on female authorship, because it is a debate that, unless further evidence comes to hand, can never be concluded. Yet what as been overlooked in this debate is that, while we may never know the identity of the author, we know that the narrator is a woman and that she offers us her poetic world as a reflection of fifteenth-century English society.

This book investigates how fifteenth-century English social conventions impact upon gender relations in *The Assembly of Ladies*.[6] The book's focal aim is to show the poet's correlation of social conventions with literary conventions, with an aim to highlighting that gender constructions in society are replicated in literary conventions. The poet of *The Assembly of Ladies* demonstrates to the reader that female participation in the production of literature is always limited and restricted, just as female participation in fifteenth-century English society in general is limited. The restrictive literary conventions are used by the poet in such a way as to show that the female voice cannot be expressed fully in the poem. *The Assembly of Ladies* is a secular love poem that adheres closely to conventional poetic structures but throws these conventions into relief as it presents the narrative from a woman's point of view, a rare occurrence for poetry of this period.[7] The immediate effect of a female narrator is to draw attention to the way gender is presented within the poem, and subsequently gender becomes a defining issue throughout the poem.[8] A useful definition for the female voice in *The Assembly of Ladies* is Luce Irigaray's definition of woman as *incontournable volume*–volume without contours–an entity that cannot be contained by either social or literary boundaries.[9] Here in *The Assembly of Ladies* we will see a woman's view of a society that attempts to restrict and confine the pursuits of women. It is a very personal view that is sometimes in conflict with the views of other women, and our narrator frequently struggles to express herself. Yet despite her difficulties, our narrator succeeds in presenting us with a specifically female view of fifteenth-century England and its literature.

A synopsis of the poem follows. The narrative begins in September with the narrator wandering aimlessly through a garden maze with her companions. Her companions are four ladies (with the narrator describing herself as "I, the fift, symplest of alle" (7)) and four gentlewomen. As an afterthought, the narrator mentions that they are also accompanied by a number of knights and squires, one of whom asks the narrator why she is in the maze. She is rather evasive in her answer, but the inquisitive knight pressures her to explain more. Eventually she relents and begins her tale, which is the recounting of a dream that took place on a previous occasion in the same maze. In her account, the narrator, the four ladies, and the four gentlewomen negotiate their way through the maze on a spring afternoon. The narrator reaches the centre of the maze before her companions, and sits down to wait for them. On falling asleep, she dreams of a woman who summons the narrator and her companions to an all-female assembly to be held by Lady Loiaulte at her castle Pleasaunt Regarde. It is a long journey and the narrator-dreamer will have to leave immediately, but she is concerned about her companions, who have not yet arrived. Reassured that they will be provided with a guide, however, she sets off with Perseveraunce as her own guide, and journeys for most of the day before arriving at a "hospital." Here she is met by a gentlewoman who provides her with the appropriate attire for an audience with Lady Loiaulte, a blue dress. She arrives at Pleasaunt Regarde and awaits the arrival of her companions. When they have all arrived and are likewise in blue, they attend the court of Lady Loiaulte, where they each present a bill of complaint against unfaithful lovers. Lady Loiaulte defers her judgment on the bills until another date, and the company of women leaves, content to have been heard. The narrator-dreamer awakens from her dream and writes the events down for posterity. Back in the opening scene, her listener commends her on the tale and asks what she will call it. Her reply: "La Semble des Dames."

Literature by Women, for Women, and about Women

Clearly this book responds to the current trend in literary studies and in medieval studies of examining the ways in which women participated in the production and consumption of literature. As such it is useful here to offer some comment on the impetus to consider women in literature to indicate the assumptions underlying this book. This book does not attempt an overtly feminist reading of *The Assembly of Ladies*. There are specific reasons for this, outlined below, but the book does participate to a certain extent in the feminist act of recovering women's literature. The two issues I wish to deal with at this point suggest the reasons for not offering an overt feminist reading of *The Assembly of Ladies*, and it is hoped that these issues will point towards an expansion in understanding of the ways we define and categorise women's literature, particularly literature of the medieval period. The first issue is how to approach texts whose authors are unknown, when feminist theory, and in particular Gynocriticism, places such a large emphasis on the impact of the gender of the text's author.[10] The second issue, related to the previous, is how to define the writing process with respect to medieval literature, when so many texts are known only through scribal copies, translations, recensions, and altered versions. Manuscripts, as they have survived, are often the result of the efforts of numerous people who have each contributed in some way to the product, and are not necessarily the result of a single author.[11]

The Anonymous Author

Feminist critical analysis often relies on prior knowledge of an author's gender and Gynocriticism is essentially founded on this knowledge. Knowing the author's gender prior to analysis has resulted in the issue of an author's anonymity being neglected, yet *The Assembly of Ladies*, I will argue, demonstrates that a poet's anonymity can be a significant means of elevating gender as a defining literary issue.

The Assembly of Ladies is an anonymous poem and, as already mentioned, there is little circumstantial evidence to indicate the poet's gender. Towards the conclusion of *The Assembly of Ladies*, however, the narrator of the poem says: "With that anon I went and made this booke," indicating emphatically that she is the author of a book which she entitles "La Semble de Dames." Recent scholarship by Alexandra Barratt has argued that this internal reference to authorship is a legitimate argument for considering the poem to have been written by a woman.[12] It is certainly fair to say that the presence of the character Geoffrey Chaucer in *The Canterbury Tales*, who claims to have written down the stories he has been listening to, is accepted as one of the means of determining authorship of that text. Similarly, the character of Will in *Piers Plowman* is generally accepted to be a fictional persona of the author William Langland. Following such logic, it is entirely acceptable to suggest that the narrator of *The Assembly of Ladies* represents the poet.

There is further internal evidence in the poem to support this theory. As will be seen, the poem clearly elevates for the reader the notion of women's participation in literature. In particular, one of the poem's narrative frames specifically contains two central characters, the narrator and the inquisitive knight, and in this frame, the knight is positioned as the audience for the narrator's story. This seems to me to be an overt attempt at offering for the reader a scenario of female authorship, in which the narrator is positioned as the authority behind the text, which is then presented to the inquisitive knight for reception. His response to her story is disappointingly indifferent, which, I will argue, reflects a broader attitude to women's participation in the literary process in the fifteenth century.

The inquisitive knight's response to her story, however, leads me to consider that perhaps the anonymity of the poet is deliberate. The inquisitive knight's indifference to the narrator's story is certainly not the kind of response any poet would want for his or her work, and the narrator implies that the fundamental reason for his response is her gender. It seems logical to suggest, therefore, that the poet of *The Assembly of Ladies*, whether male or female, would not want to disclose his or her gender. Since the poem's fundamental issue is with the participation of women in literature, it is entirely necessary and appropriate for the poet to remain anonymous in order to make this issue clear to the reader. Were the poet known to be a man, this would have the effect of undermining the plausibility of female participation in literature, when it is ultimately mediated by a man. Were the poet known to be a woman, the poem would risk being dismissed as frivolous and inconsequential, as the inquisitive knight responds to it. Thus the anonymity of the poet appears to be a deliberate act in order to elevate the issue of female participation in literature.

As stated above, feminist critical theory relies on knowledge of the author's gender, yet here in *The Assembly of Ladies* it seems far more important that the poet's gender remain unknown. To attempt a feminist analysis of *The Assembly of Ladies* in light of this would be a complicated exercise. Indeed it would be possible to consider the authority of the narrator, in place of an author, but it seems to me that this will miss the point of the poem. Accepting the anonymous status of the author will be a much more fruitful way to acknowledge that ultimately this poem can be identified as an example of female participation in literature.

The writing process and the authority of the author

Together with the assumptions feminist theory makes about the gender of the authors of texts, the theory also makes an assumption about the writing process itself, which creates further difficulties when applied to medieval literature. Just as feminist theory assumes that the gender of an author can always be known, it is also assumes that an author is the sole intellect involved in the creation of a text. Medieval texts, however, cannot always be regarded as having had a single intellectual creator. There are two particular issues involved.

The first is that literature from the medieval period comes down to us in forms in which it is not always possible to discern a single authorial figure. Incomplete texts, copies, translations, and recensions, all ensure that, on occasions, texts do not exist in a stable form, often they exist in several versions, each slightly different from the other.[13] In such instances it can be impossible to discern the precise degree to which each contributor has impacted upon a text. In the case of *The Assembly of Ladies* there are three manuscript copies extant, all dating from the late fifteenth century. Although this matter will be examined in greater detail in Chapter Six, it is pertinent to state at this stage that in each of the three manuscripts, no author is identified for *The Assembly of Ladies*. In BL Additional 34360 it may be possible that the compiler regarded the poem as one of John Lydgate's as many of the other poems in this manuscript have been attributed to him, but there is no other sense of an implied authorial attribution in the other two manuscripts. All three of the manuscripts appear to have been carefully copied, yet all vary from each other in small but significant ways. It is much more common in manuscript studies today to acknowledge such variants with the expression the "manuscript matrix," coined by Stephen G. Nichols, which allows for a broader interpretation of what constitutes a text. It seems logical to assume that if one draws together all of the manuscript copies of a text and describes that as a unified body constituting the "manuscript matrix" of that text, it is equally logical to accept that in the process one draws together all of the people who were involved in the manuscripts' production as part of that unified concept. As such, when regarding pre-print and manuscript culture, to assert a single authorial intellect for a text is simply not possible nor desirable, as it results in omitting significant factors in the interpretation of a text.

The second issue of concern here is that literature in the medieval period reflects a concept of textual ownership quite different from its modern equivalent. The concept of the text being valued for its purported "originality"–a feature of modern writing–was not a relevant concept in medieval writing. A medieval author may not necessarily have regarded him-or-herself as the sole creative intellect behind the production of a text; rather, the medieval author would more likely have valued being part of a continuous literary tradition, in which the writing process would involve a continuing and developing of themes and ideas expressed by other authors; the modern sense of an individual intellect's creating new and original ideas has little bearing. It may be for this reason that many of the texts that survive from the medieval period are anonymous, since the need for an author to identify him-or-herself was not necessarily as great as it might be today.

These two issues impact directly on this study of *The Assembly of Ladies* insofar as the three manuscripts in which the text is extant are sufficiently different from each other that they each suggest a different interpretation and use of the poem, and, as an anonymous poem that relies heavily on fifteenth-century poetic conventions, the poem constructs a deliberate deferral of authority, away from the author and on to the poetic conventions. This would suggest, then, that attempting a feminist interpretation of *The Assembly of Ladies* would be of limited benefit, as it would necessarily reduce the possible meanings that the poem might generate. It is necessary to consider medieval writing (and reading) as much more of a fluid process than the modern understanding of writing, and it is an act that one participates in not so much to highlight an individual concern, but more to contribute to and participate in a wider understanding and body of knowledge. Clearly this understanding relates to the prevalence of anonymous literature from the medieval period, demonstrating the lack of need to identify the individual contributor to a text as opposed to highlighting the contribution to the subject itself.

Following this introductory chapter, the book proceeds by examining five critical indicators in *The Assembly of Ladies*. Each critical indicator points towards the different ways in which gender is brought to the fore in the poem. *The Assembly of Ladies* refers to specific social conventions that are then correlated with literary conventions in order to elevate gender as a defining issue in the poem. The critical indicators identified here examine the social and literary conventions and how they overtly locate the female voice outside of the literary conventions used in the poem.

Chapter Two considers conventional architectural structures. Within the poem a garden maze is structurally used to represent the social and literary obstacles faced by women. The maze refers to both literary and pictorial mazes and gardens in order to direct attention to literary forms and conventions and how they either exclude the female voice entirely or restrict it severely. The maze, I will argue, acts as a point of intersection between the female voice and the literary text. The maze signifies the masculine world that attempts to contain the female world. The maze directs attention towards the restriction of the female voice in literature.

Chapter Three investigates female social etiquette as a masculine-imposed form of behaviour. The women in the poem imitate literary conventions with the only socially acceptable means available to them, sewing and needlework. The interior of the castle of Pleasaunt Regarde can be seen to signify the way masculine expectations in both social and literary terms are internalised by women and then reproduced as apparently feminine desires and needs, from which the narrator, embodying the female voice, is, indeed, isolated and in which she is unable to participate.

Chapter Four draws a comparison between legal and literary language. The presentation of bills of complaint highlights the way women are not encouraged to use written forms of communication. The female voice here is relegated specifically to oral forms of communication. This portion of the poem emphasises the instability of language; written and spoken language are contrasted and the precarious and varied interpretations of the written word are considered. This instability is revealed in written language, which signals a reference to the participation of women within poetic literature of the fifteenth-century. The contrast between written and spoken language is directly correlated with the contrast between the masculine and feminine voices in literature.

Chapter Five draws on two forms of visual theory, the medieval scientific theory of optics, known as *Perspectiva*, and linear perspective, which are used in the poem to represent conventional ways of obtaining knowledge. In this poem they signify the marginalisation of women from the literary process and are replicated in the structuring narrative frames in *The Assembly of Ladies*. Within the poem there are certain key episodes which, I will argue, suggest the presence of several narrative frames that draw the reader's attention to the gendering of the text. The *Assembly of Ladies* is able to emphasise the narrative frames by drawing significantly on *Perspectiva*, and linear perspective, as employed by painters in the production of visual images. I will argue here that several important features of each theory are used in the *Assembly of Ladies* to create the impression that the female voice is located outside of the narrative frames of the poem.

In Chapter Six I will examine the contents of the three manuscripts in which *The Assembly of Ladies* appears. The manuscripts show us the way in which this poem was regarded during the fifteenth century, and most importantly, show us that the poem was clearly interpreted in a number of different ways, reflecting the way the poem draws on several different social and literary conventions. This examination demonstrates for us the uses of literature in the fifteenth century, and shows that literary interpretation was perhaps a much more flexible and fluid concept than it is today. *The Assembly of Ladies,* I will argue, conveys different meanings in different contexts, as each of the manuscripts demonstrates.

By drawing on contemporary (and clearly influential) texts from the fifteenth century as a comparison, I will show how *The Assembly of Ladies* has integrated social conventions into its themes and structure, elevating for the reader the ways that social and literary conventions impact on women in the production of literature. This book will argue that the purpose behind the advancement of gender as a fundamental issue in *The Assembly of Ladies* is to assert that, in the attempt to inscribe the female voice into literature, the female voice is always marginalised and excluded from the literary process.[14] The book argues that the literary conventions available for use by women in fifteenth-century England succeeded in marginalising those women from the literary process.

CHAPTER TWO

MAZES AND GARDENS: ARCHITECTURAL CONSTRAINTS ON THE FEMALE BODY

The maze of *The Assembly of Ladies* is no ordinary maze, it changes shape and size as the women attempt to negotiate it, thwarting their movements, and signalling a correlation between architectural spatial constraints and the literary constraints imposed upon the women in the poem. Mazes and gardens are relatively conventional settings for medieval love poetry, but here in *The Assembly of Ladies*, the narrator of the poem positions herself and her female companions within the maze as deliberate representations of femininity. The women face obstacles throughout the maze, and their difficulty signifies the maze as a masculine construction that has already determined that the feminine must only operate within its bounds, subordinate to the macro-structure of the maze.

The maze gives the reader the initial impression of being a type of garden hedge maze. Although it is possible that these types of mazes did exist in the fifteenth century, the maze in *The Assembly of Ladies* seems to be drawn from a combination of literary mazes, architectural spatial theory, and historic structures with a view to directing the readers' attention to the convergence between architecture as a social convention and the literary conventions of the poem.[1] While the maze can be seen to signify the physical constraints of social conventions on femininity, it also signifies literary constraints on the female voice. The maze, therefore, acts as a signal to the structure of the poem. By drawing on literary and architectural spatial conventions, the poet demands that the reader correlate the physicality of the maze with the literary conventions used in the poem.

In their analysis of *The Assembly of Ladies*, Ruth Evans and Lesley Johnson clearly reject an association between the maze and a possible "psychological/libidinal significance"; they consider the significance of the maze to be purely social.[2] I, too, would not assert a sexualised interpretation of the maze, but I would suggest that the existence of the female narrator is a deliberate attempt to elevate gender as a salient issue in the poem. I will show in this chapter that the maze is a theoretical architectural structure that symbolises the social constraints imposed on women, which in turn symbolises the literary constraints imposed on the narrator of the poem.

In this chapter I will consider how four particularly pertinent elements of architectural spatial theory, which were prevalent in the fifteenth century, pervade the structure of the maze in *The Assembly of Ladies*.[3] The first is the relationship between the human body and its components. The proportions of the body, each part related geometrically to the others, were viewed as the perfect construction, and thus structures often reflected and attempted to replicate that geometrical perfection.[4] The second element is an expansion on the first, in which structures are regarded solely as functional constructions. A structure will only be situated in a particular location because it is advantageous for the people who live in it to have it situated there. The third element is that of time. A surprising feature of architectural design in the Middle Ages was the awareness that architectural concepts are always time-bound and situated specifically within the context within which they are created. The structure always refers to and reflects the society for which it is built, and also reflects the geometrical similarity between time and space. The final element to be considered here is the literary quality of architecture. Architecture as we know it today concerns the transferral of concepts into concrete structures, yet the elements of architecture that I have outlined above refer to the literary and theoretical understanding of architecture in the Middle Ages; they do not always translate into actual structures.[5] This theoretical literary quality is emphasised by the maze in *The Assembly of Ladies* as the maze is clearly created from other literary sources. These elements are derived from material that would have been readily available and would have been recognisable to a fifteenth-century readership. The poet draws on this recognisable external evidence in order to challenge the reader to correlate the architectural constraints of the maze with the literary constraints on the narrator.

Proportion: The Changing Shape of the Maze

The narrator of *The Assembly of Ladies* introduces the maze to us incrementally, with a deliberate view to directing the reader's eye to consider the maze in relation and in proportion to the other characters and features of the scene. Although this is a feature that will be examined in greater detail in Chapter Five, it is relevant to touch on it here to show its effect on the structure of the maze. The maze is noticeably indistinct in the early part of the poem. The narrator describes the season, the surroundings, and the people in the setting before revealing the existence of the maze, in which her story is located. The maze is the focal crux in a more broadly problematic episode of the poem, and it is introduced gradually to emphasise that the maze must be considered in relation to the setting and the characters. The poem begins:

> In Septembre, at the falling of the leef,
> The fressh season was al to-gydre done
> And of the corn was gadred in the sheef;
> In a gardyn, abowte tweyne after none,
> There were ladyes walkyng as was ther wone,
> Foure in nombre, as to my mynde doth falle,
> And I the fift, symplest of alle.   (1-7)

The narrator introduces the season, the garden, the time of day, the women walking through the garden, and then finally herself. I would suggest here that the first stanza of the poem has a dual purpose. First, the narrator precisely describes the setting in which the events of the poem are to take place, relying on the reader's recognition of the setting, which is very conventional of medieval courtly love poetry. This is particularly important because, as we shall see, the narrator takes the well-balanced and proportional setting and disrupts it. Second, the narrator announces herself to the reader which, I will argue, indicates that she is asserting her gender as a significant factor in her narration. The later disruption in the proportions of the maze and its setting are paralleled by the way the narrator disrupts the narrative of the poem to assert her gender as a feature of the poem.

The autumnal setting of the poem is, in itself, unusual although not unheard of. It is used in Thomas Hoccleve's "Complaint" (c. 1419-20) and in George Ashby's "Reflections of a Prisoner" (1463), and in both instances the seasonal setting is used to convey a sombre tone to the poem and gives the sense that a transition is taking place.[6] Hoccleve's "Complaint" begins:

> Aftir þat heruest inned had his sheeues,
> And þat the broun sesoun of Mighelmesse
> Was come / and gan / the trees robbe of hir leeues
> Þat greene had been / and in lusty fresshnesse,
> And hem into colour / of yelownesse
> Had died / and doun throwen vndir foote,
> Þat chaunge sank / into myn herte roote.   (1-7)[7]

Hoccleve's beginning to his "Complaint" is similar in construction to the opening of *The Assembly of Ladies*; the description contains images of the harvest gathered, trees robbed of their leaves, and the "fresshnesse" of the previous season. Moreover, Hoccleve uses the same periodic sentence structure that is used in *The Assembly of Ladies*, and does so to direct attention to the focal point of the stanza, which is the final line. Here, Hoccleve explains that it was during the season of autumn "Þat chaunge sank / into myn herte roote." The first stanza of *The Assembly of Ladies* also directs the reader's attention to the final line in which the narrator reveals her gender. The reader is urged to reconsider the autumnal setting of *The Assembly of Ladies* in light of the narrator's revelation of her gender.

As a point of comparison, poems such as Chaucer's *The House of the Fame*, Dunbar's "In Wyntir," and Henryson's *The Testament of Cresseid* are set in winter, but none of these poems contains a suggestion of transition in their themes.[8] This would indicate that an autumnal setting of *The Assembly of Ladies* is intended to convey a very specific set of meanings and associations, in particular ideas of change and transition. It is an allusion to the fact that the conventional setting we observe at the start of the poem will change dramatically before too long, a change we see in the maze itself.

In the second stanza the narrator describes the activity of the women:

Of gentil wymmen four ether were also,
Disportyng hem everiche after theyr guyse,
In crosse aleys walking be two and two.   (8-10)

This is first indication of a maze-like structure existing within the garden, but it is brief and not specific. The "crosse alleys" certainly refer to some sort of artificial construction but this is not necessarily suggestive of a maze. The "crosse alleys" seem to bear more relationship to meandering pathways through a garden with perhaps a type of low fence defining the pathways, such as those found in manuscript images of enclosed gardens and as referred to in Chaucer's *The Merchant's Tale*, when January wanders through the garden with May: "So longe aboute the aleyes is he goon," (2324) and *The Franklin's Tale*, in which the friends of Dorigen "in the aleyes romeden up and doun" (1013).

It is only in stanza three, when the narrator tells the inquisitive knight that she is walking about "the mase," that we can be certain that the garden contains a maze. The narrator explains the knight's question: "Whereof I serve? on of hem asked me," (15) and she replies:

To walke aboute the mase, in certeynte,
As a womman that nothyng rought. (17-18)

The ambiguity of the knight's question and the narrator's answer serves to
demonstrate a layered meaning in the speech of the narrator. One level of
her response suggests she has understood the knight's question to mean
"What are you doing?" to which she says she is simply walking through
the maze. On another level, however, her choice of words indicates a
subtext in which the knight's question can be understood to mean "What is
your purpose in life?", and her response can be seen to suggest that her
social circumstances will allow her to do no more than wander aimlessly
within a masculine social system in which she will have no personal
autonomy. The layered meaning of the narrator's response is conveyed
through the pun on the word "maze," in which it is used to refer to the
garden maze in which she is walking, and to suggest "amazement" and
confusion. The dialogue between the narrator and the inquisitive knight is
a verbal representation of the image of the narrator walking through the
maze. The maze signifies a social system that is designed to confuse and
control the narrator.

The choice of the word "maze" on which to pun has a significant
intertextual precedent. Chaucer uses the word "maze" in the sense of
"amaze" in *The Merchant's Tale* when January suddenly regains his sight.
January sees May up the tree with Damian and he cries out "Out! Help!
Allas! Harrow!" (2366), to which May replies: "'Ye maze, maze, goode
sire,' quod she; / 'This thank have I for I have maad yow see.'" (2387-88).
May attempts to convince January that he is bewildered or dazed by his
new-found sight, causing him to see things that are not there, although he
has, in fact, seen perfectly clearly. As May tries to convince January that
she is responsible for the restoration of his sight she uses her words to
overpower his sight. She says he is "mazed" in his mind but uses the word
to hide her own deceit, imbuing the word "mazed" with a duplicitous,
ambiguous quality.

As will be discussed shortly, the women entering into the maze have
the effect of defining it; their movement essentially gives the maze its
structural shape. This apparently removes the impression of ambiguity we
sensed earlier that was attributed to the maze, but the maze is quick to
respond to this. Remarkably, the women entering into the maze then have
the additional effect of changing the shape of the maze. As the narrator
wends her way towards the centre of the maze, it appears to grow larger
and larger. She says:

And as they sought hem self thus to and fro
I gate my self a litel avauntage;
Al for-weryed, I myght no further go,
Though I had wonne right grete for my viage;
So com I forth in to a streyte passage,
Whiche brought me to an herber feyre and grene
Made with benchis ful craftily and clene;

That, as me thought, myght no creature
Devise a bettir by proporcioun.
Save it was closed wele, I yow ensure,
With masonry of compas environ
Ful secretly, with steyres goyng down
In myddes the place, a tornyng whele, sertayne,
And upon that a pot of margoleyne.   (43-56)

The maze initially appeared to be bounded by a series of low railings, yet here, in the centre of the maze, the structures suddenly seem to have become greatly enlarged. The narrator encounters a "streyte passage" but does so in a way that suggests it had not been visible from any other part of the maze, as if suddenly the railings of the maze have grown higher. The "streyte passage" leads to an arbour, a common feature of medieval gardens, and the narrator is careful to notice that it is well enclosed "ful secretly." She describes the arbour as well designed with benches and masonry and with stairs and a "tournyng whele." The description she gives seems quite incongruous with the initial description of the maze. What began as a maze constructed of low rails situated in a garden, seems to have grown into an enormous structure in its centre, with a passage-way, arbour, masonry, and stairs. This simply does not seem physically feasible, even though the narrator's description is quite detailed. She states that "myght no creature / devise a bettir by proporcioun" (50-1). This is a conspicuous remark from the narrator, in which she states that the maze could not have been constructed with any better proportions, that is, she is explaining that the change in shape and size of the maze is exactly as it should be. If we consider that architectural proportions indicate that each element should relate appropriately to the other elements, this leads us to speculate as to why the narrator regards the maze as structurally appropriate and well proportioned. By increasing in size, the maze becomes even more of an obstacle for the women negotiating it, and it is difficult to understand how this could be considered a perfectly proportioned structure.

Yet it is pertinent to recall that as a maze, its purpose is to confuse, thus by altering in shape, it is conforming to its correct structural state.

This also indicates that the women are intended to be in a state of confusion within the maze. As was noted earlier, the maze is described in relation to the other characters and elements in the scene, and as a result it emphasises the relationship between these elements by responding to them and changing in size.

The change in shape of the maze, as a response to the other characters in the scene, also draws our attention back to the narrator. Just as the opening of the poem directed our attention to the narrator and her gender, so, too, does the changing shape of the maze. The maze becomes, through its altering proportions, a masculinised obstacle to the narrator, highlighting her gender by way of contrast to her.

Functionality: The Women's Movement in the Maze

The Assembly of Ladies presents the maze as a symbolic device to draw attention to the way women are marginalised from participating in the production of literature. As such, the women's physical movement in the maze is thwarted by the structure's confining shape. As a structure, then, the maze conforms to the architectural spatial theory that a structure ought to be functional, because the maze is doing the job for which it was designed: it is hindering the progress of the women. The poet highlights the restrictions imposed on the women in the poem by using the physical structure of the maze, and in doing so emphasises that the social structures that impinge on the women, signified by the maze, are accepted social conventions, they are not aberrations from the norm. The restricting nature of the maze is also reflected in the narrative structure of the poem. The narrator shifts between narrative frames frequently, as if in an attempt to circumvent the literary restrictions of the narrative frames in which she in confined.

The maze in *The Assembly of Ladies* reflects masculine-imposed social conventions through which the women must negotiate their lives. As the description of the maze becomes more defined, the impact this has on the women becomes more severe. The women are introduced into the text sequentially and their social positions are determined from the outset of the poem. As the women are defined by their social roles, the maze becomes the location for their social lives; it is the place where their social roles are played out and judged. The narrator describes that the women enter into the maze: "Disportyng hem everiche after theyr guyse," (9) which suggests that their behaviour has a pre-determined quality to it, the women move through the maze according to the social roles to which they have been assigned. It has been noted that the maze in *The Assembly of*

Ladies is described in vague and indistinct terms, but the women entering into the maze have the effect of defining it, their presence gives the maze form and shape.

The narrator says of the women: "Som went inward and went they had gon oute" (34), suggesting the women think they have entered and exited successfully, having no realisation that they are still trapped within the maze. The obstacles encountered by the women are in relation to their position and location in the maze. Here the women can be seen to investigate the boundaries of the maze and their own relation with those boundaries. The maze is a stable object in which the women move; their position is determined in comparison to the stability of the maze.[9] Pearsall also notes a pun in the language on the word "went."[10] The spelling of the second use of "went" in this phrase is unusual, it is more commonly spelled "wende(n)", to mean "thought." This unusual spelling would support a suggestion that the narrator is attempting to draw attention to words of motion, and to suggest that the women in their attempt to take the measure of their surroundings are unsuccessful in doing so.

Another group of women "stode amyddis and loked al aboute," (35) that is, they remained motionless and surveyed the maze as if seeking a vantage point. These women seem to be attempting to measure the landscape and to inter-relate the objects they see within that landscape. The act of these women surveying is similar to the way the narrator initially populated the scene at the beginning of the poem, by gradually adding people so that the reader may understand the relationships between those people. Yet here in the maze the women attempting to survey the land are not succeeding because the maze does not allow them a wide viewpoint. All they will see are a confusing series of twists and turns of which they cannot take the measure.

The narrator describes some of the women in the maze as "ful fer behynde" but no worse off than the rest, indicating their measurable position in relation to the other women. These women who are "behynde" do not learn anything about their surroundings, they learn only about their relationship with the other women.

Notably some of the women are described as "mased in theyr mynde" so that any direction is acceptable to them, "both est and west." (39) Despite being "mased," the women continue to struggle without result. Only a few of the women were so enraged with their lack of success that they "stept over the rayle." These women abandon any attempt to gain knowledge of their world through measuring it; they break the rules and therefore will not succeed. These women point to the likelihood that the women do not seek the centre of the maze, as those who step over the boundaries will surely reach the centre first. These women seek to understand their world, which involves surveying and measuring it, but whatever they do their success is always limited.

In seeking to understand their world, the women also seek to understand themselves in relation to the world. This is even suggested by the narrator when she says of them: "they sought hem self thus to and fro."(43) This statement can of course be understood to mean that the women sought a route through the maze, but it is also possible to understand the statement to suggest that the women really do seek themselves in the maze. The maze can be seen as a metaphor for the world and the movement of the women in the maze is an attempt to determine and judge their place in it by examining and observing its features. Essentially, then, the maze that the women become entangled in can be seen to construct the female body. The maze determines how these women relate to their surroundings.

The behaviour of the women in their effort to negotiate the maze does, however, help to clarify further the structure of the maze. We can note from the women's actions that the maze must be multi-cursal, causing the women to become lost and confused.[11] The walls of the maze, however, must be low to the ground, low enough to step over, and for this reason I would suggest the maze is a purely literary construct. A multi-cursal maze is effective only if its walls (or hedges) are too high to see over. Since these "rayles" are obviously low to the ground, one wonders why the women become lost and confused, surely they would be able to see the correct route to take. Such an illogical point must surely suggest a figurative rather than an actual reference to the maze and to the women's confusion. Moreover, we have seen that the maze appears to increase in size as the women enter further into the maze.

From the narrator's demeanour in the centre of the maze, it is apparent that her subsequent dream is a reflection of her melancholy state of mind while sitting in the centre of her beautiful maze-prison.[12] She says:

> So must me nede abide as for a space,
> Remembryng of many dyvers cace
> Of tyme past, musyng with sighes depe,
> I set me downe and there fil in slepe.   (74-77)

We do not know of what "dyvers cace" the narrator is thinking, but it surely causes her melancholy "sighes depe" and results in her subsequent dream. The narrator, conspicuously, does not become lost in the maze, but reaches the centre before her companions. For her, the maze has a different functional requirement from the way it functions for the other women. For the narrator, the maze is the necessary spatial location for her dream and thus it is essential that she reach the centre unhindered. The dream itself, as is discussed in Chapter Three, is the focal point for the poem, and one would think the location of the dreamer to be irrelevant here. Yet in *The Assembly of Ladies* it is clear that the narrator is located in the centre of the maze for a reason. It is because she has reached the centre of the maze that she is able to reflect and dream, thus the interior and secluded nature of the location is an important feature in triggering her dream.

A feature that has not been noted by scholars previously is that the women's journey into the maze, and their subsequent dream-journey to Pleasaunt Regarde both embody an exterior-to-interior movement. It is difficult to determine a reason for this if we consider only the women's journey into the maze, but if we also consider the dream-journey, then it becomes possible to suggest that both journeys have at their centre the possibility of texts. This is an overt feature of the castle at Pleasaunt Regarde, in which the narrator describes the interior of the castle, and at the inner-most sanctum, there appear stories of famous women engraved on to the walls of the castle. This is clearly an instance of the poet drawing the reader's attention to the fact that, ultimately, this is a poem about literature and how it impacts upon women. It is possible, then, to suggest that the movement of the women in the maze replicates the movement into the castle, and therefore when the narrator reaches the centre of the maze it is possible to interpret her words: "Remembryng of many dyvers cace / Of tyme past," to suggest that the reader is now about to be offered further texts, and more specifically, a dream-text.

The way that the women move in the maze, in relation to it and to each other, highlights for us the nature of its structure. The women's movement defines the maze as signifying the social constraints imposed upon the women, and that those constraints are an acceptable part of society. As the maze conforms to the functionality of architecture, it limits the way the women are able to move and encounter their surroundings. The centre of the maze signifies for us a focus on literature and how women participate in literature. The maze ensures that most of the women do not reach the literature at the centre, and although the narrator does, the story she tells must be resented in the form of a dream to be credible to the inquisitive knight.

Time and the Two Mazes

Although one may not expect the maze in *The Assembly of Ladies* to be tied to time in any way, in fact time is presented as a particularly important

element that impacts on the maze. Although this issue will be taken up
again in Chapter Five in relation to perspective, here it is relevant to note
the uses of time in relation to the maze, in order to show that the maze is a
location for abrupt and significant shifts in time. In this instance the shifts
in time are made to draw the reader's attention to the genre of the poem;
the reader expects certain time-references in a courtly love poem, and the
narrator appears to provide these, but then subtly subverts the time
references. Her reason seems to be that she is highlighting her role as the
teller of the story, in another attempt to remind us of the literary
conventions employed in the poem.

A brief mention has already been made of the autumnal setting, but it is
pertinent to consider this further as it signifies an important reference to
time in the poem and the maze. As the narrator announces clearly to us,
the opening of the poem occurs in September, which is an unconventional
time in which to set a courtly love poem, April or May are more
traditional, in which the spring season is associated with love. Yet the
autumn season does not simply suggest a period without love, rather,
autumn is specifically associated with a sense of transition. As has been
mentioned, poems such as Chaucer's *The House of the Fame*, Dunbar's
"In Wyntir," and Henryson's *The Testament of Cresseid* are set in winter,
but none of these poems contains a suggestion of transition in their themes.
This would indicate that an autumnal setting of *The Assembly of Ladies* is
intended to convey a very specific set of meanings and associations, in
particular ideas of change and transition.

In his article Walter Scheps suggests the winter setting of *The
Testament of Cresseid* positions the poem as the concluding part of the
narrative that began with Chaucer's *Troilus and Criseyde*,[13] suggesting
that the cycle of seasons imitates the narrative of the poem. In light of this,
one could suggest that *The Assembly of Ladies* begins part of the way
through the narrative. The autumnal setting invites the reader to supply the
previous spring and summer, and to consider the possible events that could
have led to its setting.[14] The autumnal setting also suggests that the events
in the poem will show some sort of decline from the spring and summer;
the events of the poem may reflect a sense of loss in some manner.

Thus the poem opens with a sense of transition, a transition that has
already taken place in the previous spring and summer and has led to the
current state of affairs in the poem, and a transition that suggests more
change is to come. This is the dynamic that introduces us to the maze and
establishes a sense of flux and uncertainty in the poem. Very quickly, a
dramatic change does occur. Other scholars have noted that in the centre of
the maze the narrator spends a great deal of time describing the spring

flowers in the arbour, and that this is a sudden jump from the autumnal setting at the start of the poem.[15] Indeed the setting has shifted, but what many scholars have failed to notice is that the autumnal setting is where the narrator is retelling her tale to the knight, whereas the description of the arbour occurs within the framework of the retold story, which, it appears, is set in the springtime. There is no mention of this prior to the description of the flowers and there is a verbal echo that allows one to mistake the setting of the retold story, as the narrator begins her tale by describing the women entering the maze "whan al oure other busynesse was done" (31). The past tense of this phrase recalls the earlier description of "whan the corn was gadred in the sheef" (3). Both expressions create a similar effect of the maze being used for amusement only after other work has been completed and blur the fact that seasonally there need not be any relationship between the two settings at all.

The narrator, then, seems to have deliberately attempted to confuse the reader by blurring the distinction between the time settings in the maze. The maze at the beginning of the poem is experienced in September, during which the ladies, gentlewomen, and knights amuse themselves by walking through the maze, and when the narrator is accosted by the inquisitive knight, who demands to know why she is looking rather serious. The maze in which the narrator describes herself and her companions becoming lost is the same maze, but on an earlier occasion, during springtime. It is in the spring maze that the narrator sits down to await the arrival of her companions, and where she carries the melancholy air that also pervades her later in the autumn setting. Thus when the narrator tells us that she sat down to remember "diverse case," a particular event is already weighing heavily on her mind, which will be voiced later in her dream.

The flowers mentioned by the narrator when she is in the arbour of the maze are "margoleyne," "margerites," "ne m'oublie-mies," "sovenez," and "penses." Pearsall notes that all of the flowers are similar in their emblematic association with constancy in love.[16] The very specific mention of particular flowers is not uncommon in medieval literature, the emblematic function of flowers as well as the spiritual and curative properties of plants ensures that they feature in quite a dominant way in literature.[17] The mid-fifteenth-century poem *The Floure and the Leafe* is a good example of this, in which the narrator lists the plants the female members of the Leafe wear as garlands:

> Some of laurer, and some ful pleasantly
> Had chapelets of woodbind, and sadly
> Some of Agnus castus were also
> Chapelets fresh.[18]

Each of the plants in this example signify a different relationship to love for each of the women, they are not arbitrary choices.[19] Similarly, in *The Assembly of Ladies,* the choice of flowers is not insignificant.

The significance of the "pot of margoleyne"(56) set upon the "touryng whele"(55) in the centre of the arbour in *The Assembly of Ladies* remains unknown, but some suggestions have been made by scholars. Fisher considers the wheel to be something similar to the decorative circular wheels used for training plants around,[20] and Seaton suggests an association between potted marjoram and the secret meeting of lovers.[21] Seaton suggests that the bringing in of pots of marjoram out of the cold in the evenings was used by lovers for meeting in secret, although in this particular instance it seems difficult to believe a pot of marjoram would be placed in the centre of a maze if it had to be retrieved each evening. Pearsall indicates marjoram is "…a flower closely associated with the rites of love…and a symbol of virtue and honour, supposed to preserve true love from the attempts of seducers."[22] Virtue and honour are issues that are discussed in Chapter Three, and truth in love features in Chapter Four of this book; they are clearly issues that are important to the meanings of the poem. I would further offer that the pot of marjoram is intended to allude to one of its common names, knotted marjoram. The name refers to the shape of the buds on the plant, arranged like a tight knot, but it recalls the shape of the maze itself. Robert Fabyan's description of Rosamond's Bower reiterates this: "wrought like vnto a knotte in a garden called a mase."[23] It is possible to consider the pot of marjoram as signifying virtue, honour, and truth in love, but I would also suggest that the marjoram is a reminder of the complexity and confusion that the maze represents.

R. Allen Shoaf considers the importance of the knot symbol in Thomas Usk's late-fourteenth-century text *The Testament of Love*, highlighting the frequency with which this image is used to signify confusion and, further, that the image of the knot can be correlated with meaning. Shoaf says of *The Testament* that:

> …the knot and meaning are felt in the human imagination as correlative. Meaning is a knot, it is knotty, and so when Usk comes in Book 2 to speak of the highest meaning, he calls it a knot, the substantive form of what has been knitted.[24]

I would argue that a similar correlation can be drawn here in *The Assembly of Ladies,* between the maze and literary meaning. The confusion experienced by the women in the maze symbolically draws attention to the textual confusion experienced by the narrator of the poem.

The use of two mazes in *The Assembly of Ladies*, one in autumn and one in spring, allows the narrator to blur the distinction between the two time periods. As a component of architectural spatial theory, time is significant for indicating the contextual environment in which a structure is situated. Here in *The Assembly of Ladies* the setting for the maze changes between two time periods, thus giving the impression that the maze somehow supersedes time, or is timeless in its applicability. If we regard the maze as a symbol of the social conventions that restrict women, then we may regard these social structures as also being timeless, they are applicable to all women, all of the time.

Literary mazes

The final element to be considered here is the literary quality of architecture. Architecture as we know it today concerns the transferral of concepts into concrete structures, yet the elements of architecture that I have outlined above refer to the literary and theoretical understanding of architecture in the Middle Ages; they do not always translate into actual structures. This theoretical literary quality is emphasised by the maze in *The Assembly of Ladies* as the maze is clearly created from other literary sources.

As has been noted, the introduction of the idea of the maze into the text of *The Assembly of Ladies* occurs incrementally and seems to be a concerted attempt to instil an impression of instability, vagueness, and even obfuscation into the poem. This vagueness is mirrored in the autumn setting of the poem, a season conveying ideas of transition. These features of the maze find their precedence not in actual structures, but rather in literary constructions of mazes. For this reason it is useful to consider some examples of literary mazes, as they will help to offer a contextual basis for considering the maze in *The Assembly of Ladies* as an architectural symbol of how women's participation in literature is often restricted.

The vagueness with which the maze is described in *The Assembly of Ladies* is not unlike Chaucer's description of the House of Rumour in *The House of Fame* (ll. 1920-85). I would not suggest that Chaucer's poem is necessarily a direct source for *The Assembly of Ladies*; it is simply not possible to know this with any certainty. It is, however, a useful comparison as Chaucer's maze is one of few found in medieval English literature and appears to promote the idea of the maze as a symbol of instability. As soon as the narrator of *The House of Fame* discovers the House of Rumour, he compares it with a classical maze, describing it as a

"Domus Dedaly, / That Laboryntes cleped ys."[25] The association with its classical source is an important feature and, in particular, the fact that it is first described as a "Domus Dedaly."[26] The maze in *The Assembly of Ladies* is clearly a symbol of social constraints placed upon women, through its twists and turns the maze represents the obstacles the women must overcome, but the name, "Domus Dedaly," also draws our awareness to the mythical creator of the maze, Daedalus.[27] This is a particularly important feature as it seems that the difficulty with which the women in *The Assembly of Ladies* negotiate the maze draws attention to the male creator of the maze, the one responsible for imposing the obstacles in the women's path.

As the classical story of Daedalus and the creation of the maze at Knossos indicates, Daedalus is the architect behind the events that take place. The significance is that Daedalus represents a patriarchal controlling authority that dictates the subordination of women. Piero Boitani identifies Daedalus as the "supreme artificer;"[28] for this book, he signifies the creator of the architectural system that obstructs the women in the maze. But Daedalus also signifies the "artist's activities,"[29] and here Chaucer equates Daedalus' creative power with his own as a poet, linking the mythological associations of the labyrinth with the poetic, literary process. As Penelope Doob notes, the House of Rumour is woven from multicoloured twigs: "it is literally *textus*, like literature…it is interwoven of textual twigs…it is an intellectual or epistemological maze."[30] The maze in *The Assembly of Ladies* can be seen to signify not only an architectural contrivance in which the women are trapped, but the maze also directly refers to the poem as an architectural contrivance in which the narrator is trapped.

Nicholas Havely further emphasises the connection between the depiction of the labyrinth and the poetic text of *The House of Fame* when he notes that lines 1961-76 of the poem all begin with the letter "o." This, he says, "could be mimetic of the holes in the House of Rumour (through which the tidings emerge), thus making the passage a kind of concrete poem."[31] Visually, the list of "tydynges" appear to jump out of the page towards the reader, linking the contents of the House of Rumour with the contents of the poem, perhaps as a warning to the reader.

The maze is also understood by scholars to signify the complexity of the world. Boitani indicates this as one of the meanings of the House of Rumour in Chaucer's *The House of Fame*: "the labyrinth is an all-encompassing image–life, the world, art–dominated by confusion and error."[32] I would like to take this meaning further and relate it to the visual depiction of medieval *mappae mundi*. Doob draws attention to manuscript images of mazes that seem to her to signify a spherical representation of the House of Rumour, a world with multiple doors, but she stops short of making the association of the maze as a microcosm of the world that can be seen in medieval maps.[33] The thirteenth-century Hereford *mappa mundi*, Doob notes, contains a depiction of the labyrinth on the island of Knossos where it is labelled *Laborintus id est domus dedali*, yet it seems to me that the map as a whole can be compared to the maze insofar as both the map and the maze are representations of the world. The map is a geographical representation of the world and the maze can be seen as a figurative representation of the world. The Hereford *mappa mundi* is a significant example of this because it so clearly attempts to encompass the geographical, historical, and mythological features of the world, that it seems appropriate to suggest further a figurative element to its meaning.[34]

A further example of a maze that signifies the world occurs in the story of Rosamond's Bower, a folk tale about Henry II and his lover that has been told in many variations. Scholars such as Doob have actively sought to dismiss the story of Rosamond's Bower, citing a lack of historical evidence to support the story, yet here, too, I would assert that the story contains perhaps more of a figurative than an historic meaning. Robert Fabyan cites a verse that supposedly adorned the tomb of Rosamond:

Hic iacet in tumba, Rosa mundi, sed non rosa munda
Non redolet sed olet, que redolere solet.
The whiche verses to our vnderstandinge maye thus as foloweth be Englished and expounded.
The Rose of the worlde, but not the cleane floure,
Is here now grauen: to whome bewtie was lente.
   In this grave full darke now is her bowre.
   That by her life was swete and redolent.
But now that she is from this lyfe blente.
Though she were swete, now fowly doth she stynke,
A myrroure good for al that on her thynke.[35]

Fabyan's English translation states clearly that "Rosamond" signifies "The Rose of the worlde" and that her life is a moral lesson for others: "Though she were swete, now fowly doth she stynke, / A myrroure good for al that on her thynke." It seems likely that Fabyan's interpretation of Rosamond's Bower is intended to signify deceit in the world rather than to refer to an historical place or event.

The examples of *The House of Fame*, the Hereford *mappa mundi*, and the verse on Rosamond's death all indicate an association between the maze and the world, in which the maze is a miniature figurative representation of the world. In *The House of Fame*, the narrator cannot

enter the maze unaided, he must be flown in by the eagle, and once there
he is overwhelmed by the cacophony within. Ovid describes Rumour as an
all-powerful figure:

> Ipsa, quid in caelo rerum pelagoque geratur et tellure, videt totumque
> inquirit in orbem.

> [Rumour beholds all that is done in heaven, on sea and land, and searches
> throughout the world for news.][36]

The Hereford *mappa mundi* is a textual representation of power in which
the map attempts to display all forms of knowledge–geographical,
historical, mythological, and figurative–as a means of indicating the
power of knowledge. The verses on the death of Rosamond also indicate
the maze as a location of power. The maze that previously protected
Rosamond is eventually the location of her downfall, her position is
subordinate to the maze. All three examples of the maze/world motif can
be considered as intertextual references for the maze in *The Assembly of
Ladies*, in which the maze is an overt symbol of social restrictions
imposed on women. No matter which route through the maze the women
take, whether they "went inward and went they had gon oute" (34) or
whether they went "both est and west" (39), they are thwarted by it. The
maze is an all-encompassing spatial structure that is designed to
overpower the women.

The intertextual references indicate more than the maze/world motif,
however; texts such as *The House of Fame*, the Hereford *mappa mundi*,
and the verses on the death of Rosamond also indicate a correlation
between the maze/world motif and the text. The maze in *The Assembly of
Ladies* can be regarded as drawing on intertextual references to convey the
textuality of the maze and to locate the maze/world motif specifically in
the text of the poem.

The correlation between the maze and the text is a feature of Pierre
Bersuire's fourteenth-century treatment of the classical Cretan labyrinth
story. Here, the maze is frequently described as the *ambages labyrinti*, that
is, circuitous labyrinth, yet it is not coincidental that *ambages* can also be
interpreted in a literary context to refer to a digression or circumlocution in
speech.[37] Bersuire interprets Ovid as a useful exemplary and allegorical
guide for moral conduct, yet his version of the Cretan myth is, according
to Doob, noticeably inconsistent in the many characteristics he attributes to
the characters of the story. Bersuire indicates that Minos can be regarded
as Christ or the devil, Theseus as ungrateful wretch or as Christ, and
Daedalus as envious craftsman or a true contemplative. According to

Doob, "it is as if the *ambages* of the labyrinth had become ambiguities in the text, or as if Bersuire had taken every interpretive path presented in Ovid's multicursal textual maze."[38] Doob draws an association between the twists and turns of the labyrinth, and the twists and turns that Bersuire takes in his interpretation of the Cretan myth. This association between the labyrinth and the text is drawn on in *The Assembly of Ladies* where the poem itself signifies the ambiguities and complexities of the maze in relation to the women subjected to it.

A well-known Chaucerian text that contains the symbol of the maze is *The Legend of Good Women*. In the tale concerning Ariadne, Carolyn Dinshaw associates the maze with Ariadne's body; the ball of thread Ariadne gives to Theseus to assist him negotiating the maze is described as an invitation to her body, it is a "clewe" of twine and a "clue" to sexual knowledge.[39] The female body, described as the site of truth and knowledge, is represented visually by the maze. The twists and turns of the maze are seen to signify the quest to attain knowledge about the female body and establishes the female body as an entity that is inherently enigmatic and, therefore, desirable. Dinshaw emphasises the image in terms of its sexual potency, where the entrance of Theseus into the maze is considered a violation of the female body. Also emphasised are the monstrous qualities of the maze, which Dinshaw compares with the medieval anti-feminist tradition that constructs the female body as monstrous.

Dinshaw also makes an association between the maze and the female body, and the maze and the text, in terms of the text's being a male creation, a body (textual and human) that is reined in and controlled by masculine forces. This is a view that Susan Gubar examines, in which she says: "When the metaphors of literary creativity are filtered through a sexual lens, female sexuality is often identified with textuality."[40] There are numerous instances of this theme in literature, such as Ovid's story of Pygmalion, in which the artist creates his ideal woman, emphasising the female as a male creation. Dinshaw extends this concept further when she considers allegory:

> Woman's body is associated with the truth of the text here–an association also suggested by the image of the allegorical text as veiled female body in Macrobius, Jerome, Richard of Bury.[41]

Chaucer's story of Ariadne, Dinshaw infers, interrelates the maze (as masculine knowledge) and the text (as masculine constraints), both of which signify the female body. Dinshaw's sexual interpretation of the tale of Ariadne is not of primary concern to this book, but the association she makes between the maze and the text is, I would argue, significant for *The Assembly of Ladies*.[42] The notion of the text as a masculine creation does seem to be reflected in the way the maze in *The Assembly of Ladies* is presented. Dinshaw's analysis of Chaucer's story of Ariadne allows us to see that the maze, as well as being an obstacle imposed on the women, is also a convention that draws attention to the disturbance the women create in the maze. Although the narrator manages to negotiate her way to the centre of the maze easily, her emotional state impacts on the text as a textual disturbance. Throughout the poem the narrator's behaviour is erratic and disruptive, as though the role of narrator is fraught with obstacles just as the maze is. The other women must find their way through the maze; the narrator must find her way through the text. As objects, both the maze and the text can be seen as imbued with female qualities, but only insofar as they are masculine creations, they are ultimately controlled by masculine conventions and are thus not available for the use of women on their own terms.[43]

Perhaps the most important text for comparison with *The Assembly of Ladies* is Giovanni Boccaccio's *Il Corbaccio*, a mid-fourteenth-century text that, in many manuscripts, is given the additional title of "Il laberinto d'amore."[44] Some detailed attention will given to this text here as I will argue that it can be considered as the antithesis of *The Assembly of Ladies* in terms of its portrayal of women. The narrator of this text, a love-sick man, dreams that: "subitamente parve entrare in un dilettevole e bel sentiero" [suddenly I seemed to enter upon a delightful and beautiful path], but as he travels along the path, it transforms:

> dove erbe verdi e vari fiori nell'entrata m'erano paruti vedere, ora tassi, ortiche e triboli e cardi e simili cose mi pareva trovare.[45]

> [where I had seemed to see green grass and various flowers at the entrance, I now found such plants as nettles, brambles, thistles, and yews.][46]

The image of the beautiful path through green grass and flowers is a literary convention (not unlike the garden-maze of *The Assembly of Ladies*), but, unlike *The Assembly of Ladies*, the beauty soon transforms into a desolate space, strongly reminiscent of the beginning of Dante's *Inferno*. In addition to the desolate setting, the narrator becomes surrounded by fog and is confused and disoriented. The fog clears with the approach of a guide, who informs the narrator that:

> Questo luogo è da vari variamente chiamato, e ciascuno il chiama bene: alcuni il chiamano "il laberinto d'Amore" e altri "la valle incantata" e assai "il pocile di Venere."[47]

[This place is given different names by various people, and each one is correct. Some call it the "Labyrinth of Love," and others the "Enchanted Valley," and a good number the "Pigsty of Venus."][48]

The labyrinth in which the narrator finds himself is a visual and physical representation of his psychological state of mind. The labyrinth signifies the pain experienced by the narrator when he is spurned in love, but its epithet of the "Pigsty of Venus" indicates that the labyrinth is also associated negatively with the female body. As the narrator's guide explains:

Questa misera valle è quella corte che tu chiami "d'Amore" e quelle bestie che tu di' che udite hai e odi mugghiare sono I miseri, de' quali tu se' uno, dal fallace amore inretiti.[49]

[This wretched valley is what you call "the Court of Love"; and these beasts, which you say you heard and hear growling, are the wretches–of whom you are one–who have been caught in the net of false love.][50]

While the narrator weeps at his frailty, the guide proceeds to lay the blame for the narrator's condition clearly on the behaviour of women. Cassell indicates that the guide's long tirade listing the physical and moral faults of women conforms closely to that found in the *Lamentations de Matheolus*;[51] the details need not be repeated here, but the guide's concluding descriptions are significant. The guide describes the act of sexual intercourse in a thinly-veiled allegory in which the woman's sexual organs are described as:

Del golfo di Setalia, nella valle d'Acheronte riposto, sotto gli oscuri boschi di quella, spesse volte rugginosi e d'una gromma spumosi e spiacevoli e d'animali di nuova qualità ripieni…fiumi sanguinei e de' crocei che di quella a vicenda discendono, di bianca muffa faldellati…Che it dirò adunque più avanti del borgo di Malpertuggio?[52]

[The Gulf of Setalia, hidden in the Valley of the Acheron beneath its dark woods, often russet in color and foaming with foul grime and full of creatures of unusual species…[with] sanguine and yellow rivers that descend from it in turn, streaked with white mould…What shall I say further to you therefore about the village of Evilhole?][53]

By associating female sexual organs with a desolate geographical landscape, the guide makes a clear link with the labyrinth of the story. As the labyrinth is designated as the location of the self-deception of the male narrator, it is also designated as specifically female in nature. This designation can be contrasted clearly with the maze in *The Assembly of*

Ladies in which those subject to the control of the maze are female, and the maze itself can be seen as a masculine construct. Where *Il Corbaccio* is intended to confirm other anti-feminist texts, *The Assembly of Ladies* seeks to counter these attitudes towards women. This comparison points out a significant feature of *The Assembly of Ladies*, that the poem acts in response to already established social attitudes and expectations towards women.

Conclusions

The presentation of the maze and garden in *The Assembly of Ladies* responds clearly to several architectural spatial theories. By doing so *The Assembly of Ladies* focuses attention on the literary conventions utilised throughout the poem and this emphasises the gendered nature of those conventions. This allows one to see that the poetic conventions used throughout the poem actively exclude female participation and emphasise the lack of a legitimate means of expression for women. In *The Assembly of Ladies* the only means of expression available to the women is to present a complaint, a form that is simultaneously shown to be inadequate for their purposes.[54] When Pearsall describes the bills of complaint as tedious, whether knowingly or not, his comment identifies the difficulties faced by the women in the poem.[55] What other means do they have for self-expression? The narrator, too, is unhappy presenting a complaint; her erratic behaviour seems to suggest a frustration at her inability to find a legitimate means for expressing herself. The maze, then, can be seen to signify frustration because it is not designed to assist the women but rather to thwart them. Just as the women cannot adequately express themselves in the poetic conventions available to them, so too the structure of the maze and the difficulty with which the women negotiate it signifies its inappropriateness for them, it becomes a structure imposed upon them but from which they are also excluded because it does not allow them an opportunity to control their own fates.

The presentation of the garden and the maze in *The Assembly of Ladies* can be regarded as an eclectic collection of images and concepts. Yet ultimately the ideas presented appear to be derived from architectural theoretical sources, not historic sources. Both the garden and the maze appear to be symbols associated with the confinement and restriction of the female body, but by drawing these symbols from literary sources *The Assembly of Ladies* also situates that confinement within a literary context. Not only are the women in the poem restricted by a maze that signifies social conventions; the maze can also be seen to signify literary conventions, and thus the construction of literature.

CHAPTER THREE

INTERIOR, EXTERIORS, AND THE VEILING
OF CUPID'S MARTYRS:
SOCIAL ETIQUETTE AND WOMEN'S WORK

The arrival at Pleasaunt Regarde of the narrator and her companions occurs as a series increasingly restricting and confining episodes. Partly modelled on Christine de Pizan's *Le Livre de la Cite de Dames* and on the structure of a monastic household, the female-only castle of Pleasaunt Regarde becomes cumulatively oppressive to the narrator, culminating in the literal veiling of images of Cupid's martyrs in the inner-most sanctum of the castle, so that the women "shuld nat hurt theyr sight." Here, literary conventions of the portrayal of women are shown to have been appropriated by the women of the castle, in which the *integumentum* process is actualised visually by the covering of images with fabric of the women's own handiwork. The women imitate literary conventions with the only socially acceptable means available to them, sewing and needlework.

Female self-confinement and anxiety at transgressing social boundaries is a significant feature of the episode in *The Assembly of Ladies* during which the narrator and her companions arrive at the castle of Pleasaunt Regarde. Five significant features of this episode in the poem cumulatively create the effect of the narrator's increasing isolation from her companions and from the castle's surroundings. The women who inhabit the castle demonstrate female self-confinement, in which they have internalised masculine-imposed boundaries which results in their restrictive lives. The narrator is contrasted with the inhabitants of Pleasaunt Regarde and, increasingly, from her companions, who readily adopt the restrictive regulations of the castle. The episode in the castle becomes progressively restrictive, and the narrator's behaviour becomes progressively erratic as she attempts to create a female space that is not impacted upon by masculine regulations, yet to do this the narrator must overcome her own anxiety of transgression.

The five significant features in this episode of the poem that will be considered here are: the approach of the narrator to Pleasaunt Regarde, the household as the location of female honour, the clothing of the women, the images of Cupid's martyrs located on an interior wall in Pleasaunt Regarde, and the umple covering the images of Cupid's martyrs. The five features to be discussed in this chapter indicate a cumulative progression towards the actual centre of the location, Pleasaunt Regarde, and also a progression towards the literary centre of the poem.

Jane Chance suggests that the narrator of *The Assembly of Ladies* "lacks being, autonomy, individuality."[1] Chance's idea can be seen as a variation of Barratt's suggestion that the narrator of the poem is isolated and emotionally removed from her companions, that is, she does not share in the sense of belonging to the company of women.[2] In this chapter I will argue that the narrator of *The Assembly of Ladies* not only lacks a sense of individuality and is isolated from her companions as suggested by Chance and Barratt, but that her character in fact can be seen as signifying the female voice. The five significant features of this episode in the poem indicate the narrator's attempt to react against the masculine imposed regulations of Pleasaunt Regarde. In doing so, however, she finds herself isolated from the other women in the poem. The narrator's companions and the women who inhabit Pleasaunt Regarde all conform to the masculine regulations of the castle, but because the narrator refuses to do so, she is effectively stifled. The parameters for discourse are masculine, and so, by transgressing them, she loses all means of articulation.

This portion of *The Assembly of Ladies* has been commented on by Lewis and Pearsall,[3] but, where they have considered only the courtly behaviour of the characters, I am concerned to argue that the household of Pleasaunt Regarde is regulated by masculine authority that has been internalised by the women inhabitants. As a masculine-controlled domain, the household of Pleasaunt Regarde is presented as the location of feminine honour.[4] The narrator's rejection of masculine authority ensures that, even when in the innermost part of the castle, she remains an outsider to the events that take place there. By considering the narrator in relation to the castle surroundings and in relation to the other women in the castle, it is possible to view the narrator as embodying the female voice. The narrator refuses to conform to the masculine regulations of Pleasaunt Regarde, which leaves her without a means of articulation in that space. The narrator's lack of articulation is then reflected in the stories of Cupid's martyrs that are depicted on the innermost walls of Pleasaunt Regarde. While the stories appear in the interior of the castle, the stories are, themselves, stifled under a veil of umple.

The Approach to Pleasaunt Regarde

The reader's first encounter with Pleasaunt Regarde occurs in the description given by Perseveraunce to the narrator. Perseveraunce says the castle is fairer than all others, devised well, with high towers and "fanes fresh tournyng with every wynde" (160). Inside, the castle contains chambers and parlours "with bay wyndowes goodely as can be thought" (162)[5] and Perseveraunce assures the narrator that "Ye wold it think a veray paradise"(168).

Perseveraunce's description of the castle is of interest here as it is the first indication for the reader of the importance of the spatial relationships that will become more evident as the narrator enters Pleasaunt Regarde and the way that these relationships impact on the narrator's ability to communicate. Moreover, Perseveraunce's description is notable for its shift from an external, pictorial view of the castle, with "toures high ful plesaunt" (159), to an internal view in which she proposes the narrator's emotional response to the castle, "yef ye were thider brought…Ye wold it think a veray paradise" (166-68). The movement from external to internal that occurs in Perseveraunce's description of Pleasaunt Regarde suggests a spatial relationship between the castle and the narrator. Perseveraunce describes the exterior of the castle as one would if viewing it from afar, with "toures high ful plesaunt" (160) and "fanes fresh tournyng with every wynde" (161). The castle is attractive to look at, "ful plesaunt," but this is not an inviting description. Her description demands that one remain distant from the sight so that one may view the towers and the flags blowing in the wind. This is preceded by the suggestion that it could well be "fore a kyng" (158), which impresses a sense of distance and remove even further. This is a grand castle that is not for the common person to enter, it is accessible only to those of high birth. In addition, we have already learned from Perseveraunce that it is also a castle that is accessible only to women, further emphasising its exclusivity. The distant, initial, view of Pleasaunt Regarde reflects the exclusivity of the castle and prefigures the way the narrator will continue to feel emotionally excluded from the castle even when she is inside it.[6] From the outset of Perseveraunce's description, Pleasaunt Regarde emphasises exclusion rather than inclusion. As the poem progresses, the narrator discovers that entering the castle requires a series of boundary transgressions, and her willingness to transgress causes her to be isolated from the inhabitants of the castle and from her companions.

Perseveraunce's description then shifts to bring us into the interior of the castle, first with a description of the architecture, the "chambers and parlours both of oo sort" (162) and the "bay wyndowes goodely as can be thought" (163). This is followed by a verbal shift further into the interior when she describes the activities that take place in the castle. This progression from exterior to interior clearly situates the women in an enclosed space that is not accessible to the outside world.[7] The women who inhabit Pleasaunt Regarde are not described until Perseveraunce has shifted her narrative sufficiently into the interior of the castle, suggesting a further, interior, psychological space has been entered into. Furthermore, the presence of the women in the interior space of Pleasaunt Regarde specifically equates spatial interiority with femininity. The location of the women in the interior of the Pleasaunt Regarde, as well as the journey made by the narrator and her companions from an external location to an internal one, situates femininity within an enclosed space.[8]

Perseveraunce's description then concludes by suggesting to the narrator how she (the narrator) would feel if she were in that internal space:

> ...wele I wote, yef ye were thider brought
> And toke good hede therof in every wise,
> Ye wold it think a veray paradise. (166-68)

The comparison with paradise is a poetic convention found frequently in medieval literature, yet in this instance there is a slight suggestion that Perseveraunce is not offering the narrator a choice about this description. Perseveraunce's insistence is quite forceful and perhaps even coercive; she uses a literary convention to convey to the narrator that Pleasaunt Regarde is also governed by conventions that must be adhered to. Perseveraunce presents an image that changes from a distant view of the exterior of the castle to the interior view of the architecture of the castle, and then finally to the interior emotional response the narrator could expect to feel when inside the castle.

Perseveraunce's final comparison with Paradise, however, has the effect of placing Pleasaunt Regarde, both its interior and its exterior, within the tradition of the post-lapsarian Eden. This has been signalled previously when the narrator asks Perseveraunce "If we shal any men unto us calle?" (146), to which the reply is "Nat one may come among yow alle" (147). The exclusion of men from Pleasaunt Regarde establishes the castle as post-lapsarian, it is a site of both inclusion and exclusion. Those included are solely high-born women, while all other women and men are excluded. This suggests the castle shows the desire for the paradisal state, its exclusivity exhibits an attempt to return to a state of purity.[9]

The shift from exterior to interior is, of course, a literary device in which the reader is gradually drawn into the psychological space of Pleasaunt Regarde. Yet traversing the space from exterior to interior also has the effect of immediately equating female space with an interior space.[10] Moreover, Perseveraunce's description of Pleasaunt Regarde demonstrates the way the reader's gaze is carefully directed into the interior of the castle. In Chapter Five of this book an examination will be made of the pictorial space of the poem and the use that is made of perspective to direct and control the reader's point of view, but it is appropriate to note here the way that the description of Pleasaunt Regarde invites a kind of voyeurism from the reader. Both the reader and the narrator together see the image of Pleasaunt Regarde from afar as Perseveraunce describes it, and the reader joins the narrator in the approach to Pleasaunt Regarde and is, therefore, able to feel an emotional attachment to the narrator. This is a particularly significant point in a poem in which the narrator is a constant social outsider. Empathising with the narrator allows the reader's point of view to be controlled and determined by the narrator. We experience Pleasaunt Regarde with the same anxiety as the narrator.

The description of Pleasaunt Regarde as a walled castle for the exclusive use of women is clearly reminiscent of Christine de Pizan's *Le Livre de la Cité des Dames* (1405),[11] but, as a comparison with *The Assembly of Ladies* will show, the inhabitants of Christine's city can be seen to have internalised masculine convention concerning feminine behaviour, whereas the narrator of *The Assembly of Ladies* actually rejects masculine convention altogether for herself. The inhabitants of Pleasaunt Regarde are in many ways similar to those of Christine's city, and the narrator's presence underscores the difference between herself, signifying the female voice, and the other women, who have internalised masculine conventions. The anxiety experienced by the narrator occurs as a result of her inability to express herself fully within the boundaries allowed by masculine conventions, which forces her to transgress those boundaries.

Christine's city is a defensive city, built in an attempt to correct the wrongs that already exist in society. Lady Reason announces to Christine that due to the dishonourable treatment that women of great virtue have received, Christine must build a city in which to house virtuous women to protect them from slander and defamation. The city of ladies is created as a response to the existence of anti-feminist literature that, as the three Virtues point out to Christine, defames women. Lady Reason says that women have "suffered the great attacks which, both in the spoken and the written word, have been wrongfully and sinfully perpetrated against women by men."[12] But Lady Reason does not refute the claims made by anti-feminist texts, rather she divides the female community into those who are and are not virtuous. Lady Reason continues:

> We three ladies...have come to you to announce a particular edifice built like a city wall...where no one will reside except all ladies of fame and women worthy of praise, for the walls of the city will be closed to those women who lack virtue.[13]

Only the virtuous women may reside in the city where they will be protected from slander; and as will be argued shortly, Christine's walled city, like Pleasaunt Regarde, is the location of feminine virtue. The objection raised by Lady Reason, then, is not against the claims made in the anti-feminist texts but against the fact that they are directed at *all* women. The inhabitants of the city, while protected from slander, do not seek to reject the claims made by anti-feminist literature.[14] The act of removing virtuous women from society has the effect of reinforcing the accusations.[15]

Christine clearly situates the slander and defamation against women within literary conventions. From the example given above, Lady Reason specifically states that women are attacked "both in the spoken and the written word,"[16] and the impetus for the appearance of the three Virtues is to reassure Christine after she has been so affronted by the work of Mathéolus, *Liber Lamentationum Matheoluli*.[17] In both instances the slander and defamation of women specifically occurs in literature, suggesting that the walled city of ladies is erected as a barrier against literature.[18] The city, then, becomes a site of exclusion from the literary tradition, implying that literature is something that women cannot participate in without risking their virtue. To counter this, Christine populates the city of ladies with numerous mythological women in an apparent attempt to establish a female literary tradition that will give women a standpoint and resource from which to argue against anti-feminist criticism.[19] Yet at all times the mythological women who are described are considered as appropriate role models for women either because they are upheld as examples of virtuous women because they conform to the masculine precepts of a virtuous woman, or because they take on a masculine role in order to achieve a particular goal–they effectively become men. An example of the latter instance can be found in the description of the Amazons of Scythia. Although Christine describes the Amazons as women who "maintain their dominion by themselves without being subject to men,"[20] this independence is coloured by the fact that they are forced into a state of self-rule when "this land lost all the important men living there through war."[21] The Amazons took on self-rule only through necessity not by choice. As Christine points out, the Amazons are also known as "the breastless ones,"[22] but where she considers the removal of a breast as an aid to bearing weapons, implicit in this act of mutilation is the fact that the Amazons must remove part of what defines them as female, they must effectively become more like men.

It is significant that Christine compares the slanderous abuse that virtuous women have endured with the image of a city under siege:

> From now on ladies and all valiant women may have a refuge and defence against the various assailants, those ladies who have been abandoned for so long, exposed like a field without a surrounding hedge...It is no wonder then that their jealous enemies, those outrageous villains who have assailed them with various weapons, have been victorious in a war in which women have had no defence. Where is there a city so strong which could not be taken immediately if no resistance were forthcoming?[23]

Christine's suggestion here is that women require protection against slander, and the best way for women to protect themselves is to lock themselves up behind walls. But such action is merely a response to existing circumstances; it does not attempt to change the conventions that brought about those circumstances. The effect, then, of concealing virtuous women from the outside world simply reinforces the conventions that allow slanderous comments to be made, and perhaps even invites such comment if a woman does not conform to concealment. The narrator of *The Assembly of Ladies* can be seen to invite just such comment by her behaviour within Pleasaunt Regarde.

Elizabeth Grosz, in her article "Bodies-Cities,"[24] indicates that the city is a product of the individual: it is created by individuals, but it quickly becomes an unwieldy entity in which individuals lose their identities and soon wish to leave in order to regain their individuality.[25] Both Christine's city and Pleasaunt Regarde can be seen as examples of different stages in the development of the city. Christine's city is signified by the former part of Grosz's paradigm, each of the women who populate the city are notable for individual behaviour and creativity that set them apart from other women. Pleasaunt Regarde, however, is signified by the latter part of Grosz's paradigm. The castle represents an oppressive space for the narrator in which she feels confined and trapped and unable to express herself. As will be discussed shortly, the narrator does not wear a motto as the other women do, and in this context it is possible to see this as her attempt to retain her individuality within a conventional and conforming environment.

Le Livre de la Cité des Dames is similar to *The Assembly of Ladies* in the way that Christine's city and the castle of Pleasaunt Regarde have been constructed. Pleasaunt Regarde, like Christine's city, is created as a female-only space designed to maintain the honour of its inhabitants by excluding men. Yet the narrator of *The Assembly of Ladies* encounters some difficulty in the castle and stridently objects to some of its regulations. This, I will argue, signifies the narrator's rejection of the environment as a masculine construction. For the narrator, Pleasaunt Regarde is not a place of protection but a place of anxiety and restriction.[26]

The Household as the Location of Female Honour

As the narrator arrives at Pleasaunt Regarde with Diligence as her guide, one of the castle's residents enters the narrative. Discrecioun, the "chief purviour," greets them and the narrator asks Discrecioun a series of questions concerning the etiquette of the castle and her questioning signals the point at which the poem becomes strongly focused on household etiquette. The narrator's entrance into the interior of Pleasaunt Regarde coincides with a display of the functioning of the household.[27] Perseveraunce's description of Pleasaunt Regarde, initially from afar and then becoming progressively more interiorised, has prepared the reader to enter into an enclosed female space, and the reality of the female space is that it is governed by strict rules and regulations that the narrator feels bound to transgress.

The narrator questions Discrecioun about very practical matters: what is Discrecioun's job in the household, who is the herberger (to whom she knows she will need to apply for lodging), have any of the other women in her company arrived yet? Once inside the castle, the narrator's questioning continues as she asks many questions concerning the appropriate people to know and whom to seek assistance from in the presentations of their bills of complaint. Perhaps there is some similarity between the narrator's questioning and the questioning of *Perceval*.[28] On the one hand, the narrator is persistent like Perceval but, on the other hand, her questions do not convey the ignorance or innocence that Perceval shows, the narrator's questions indicate the fact that she must know the appropriate etiquette for this place. Rather than questioning like Perceval, I would suggest the narrator's questioning shows that she does not know the rules that are specific to this household, but is generally familiar with household etiquette.

The functioning of the household of Pleasaunt Regarde plays a large role in *The Assembly of Ladies* and it is helpful to consider here the reasons for this. A mid-fourteenth-century poem known in modern editions as *What the Good Wife Taught her Daughter* is a particularly pertinent comparison for *The Assembly of Ladies* as it is useful for indicating the type of activities that were performed by women in the household, it suggests how girls were instructed in these acts, and it even occurs in one of the manuscripts that contains *The Assembly of Ladies*.[29] The poem conveys instructions to a girl on personal behaviour and on the management of the household, via the persona of the mother. The rules of behaviour that she suggests are not unlike the qualities embodied by the inhabitants of Pleasaunt Regarde. The mother says:

> Be fayre of semblant, my dere douhter,
> Change not þi countenans with grete lauhter;
> And wyse of maneres loke þou be gode,
> Ne for no tayle change þi mode.   (45-48)

The instructions are for the daughter to be reserved and modest in her manner, to show the qualities of discretion and to be pleasant at all times. This behaviour is advised in order that the daughter not publicly lose her honour:

> For and þou any chider be,
> Thy neyhbors wylle speke þee vylony.
> Be þou not to enuyos,
> For drede thi neyhbors wyll þee curse.   (105-108)

Thus the instructions are designed to protect the daughter from public slander and defamation, which is regarded as the most damaging accusation for women. Other poems reiterate this idea, as in *The Floure and the Leafe* when the departing member of the company of the Leafe wishes the narrator well and protection against "the wicked remembraunce / Of Male Bouch, and all his crueltie."[30] Of course, Christine's city of ladies is built solely to protect women from slander and defamation.

As well as her personal behaviour, the mother of the poem also advises her daughter on how to manage her household servants:

> And if thy lord be fro home,
> Lat not thy menehe Idell gone;
> And loke þou wele who do hys dede,
> Quyte hym þer-after to his mede;
> And þei þat wylle bot lytell do,

Ther-after þou quite is mede also.   (133-38)

The sense here is that the daughter must oversee the tasks that must be performed in the household but, as is mentioned later in the poem, if necessary she must perform the work herself if there is no alternative. The household must be ordered at all costs. There is an association implied here that the well-ordered household is an honourable household, thus the woman's honour lies in both her personal behaviour and in her managerial skills in the household. The association is, of course, that the household is a female domain and if the woman does not excel as a housewife she is, indeed, dishonourable.

Felicity Riddy dismisses the likelihood of this poem being authored by a woman and the possibility that a mother would have used such a poem for the instruction of her daughter, noting that a mother would be more likely to teach from experience.[31] Earlier versions of *What the Good Wife Taught her Daughter* appear in manuscripts of religious instruction, and Riddy suggests the poem was more likely used in instances where there was no mother-figure.[32] In the case of the religious manuscripts, she suggests that this poem was probably used as part of a general education for girls,[33] and the example in the Trinity manuscript may have been used by noble women for instructing servants.[34] This is particularly significant for *The Assembly of Ladies*, as the impression given by *What the Good Wife taught her Daughter* is that these are a set of idealised masculine rules imposed upon girls, but presented under the guise of feminine instruction. The Good Wife is a device used to encourage girls to internalise masculine social conventions so that they will ultimately conform in their behaviour. The household of Pleasaunt Regarde is filled with women who have done just that. The names of the women who inhabit Pleasaunt Regarde reveal this quite clearly, they are named Discrecioun, Diligence, Contenaunce, Aviseness, Bealchiere, and Remembraunce, names that are not unlike the list of qualities the Good Wife recommends for her daughter.

In another similar poem, *The Good Wyfe Wold a Pylgremage* (c.1450),[35] the Good Wyfe narrating this poem is more concerned with her daughter's behaviour than in how well she may run the household in her mother's absence:

Dohttur, seyde þe good wife,
Hyde thy legys whyte,
And schew not forth thy stret hossyn
To make men have delytt;
Thow hit plese hem for a tym,

Hit schall be thy despytt.
And men wyll sey
"Of þi body þou carst but lytt."   (49-56)

I present this example here, in which the Good Wyfe warns her daughter not to show her legs in public, for the purpose of comparison with another text. The *Formula Nouiciorum* (c. 1475-80), originally written for the instruction of novice friars but later translated into English and used for the instruction of religious women, contains advice surprisingly similar to that of the Good Wyfe:

> Lete þi goynge be soburli...Nor be not wandrynge with þin ijs, nor shake not þi armys wantonly...When þou sitteste, ley not þiself like a sloveyne in þi one syde nor strecche not oute þi leggis afarre, namly in presens of oþer, for þe owteward ostentacion of þi body is a shewynge of what disposicion is inwardly alwey.[36]

The instruction for sober physical behaviour in the two examples cited is significantly similar whether for lay people or religious. Just as the Good Wyfe urges her daughter not to show her legs in public lest men regard her as caring little for her honour; similarly, in the above text, religious women are urged not to allow their eyes to wander, to wave their arms around, or stretch their legs out, the reason being that their outward misbehaviour will indicate a similar spiritual state of mind. It is also notable that the *Formula Nouiciorum* is a text originally written by and for the instruction of men but which, in this version, was emended for the instruction of women. In a similar manner to the poem *What the Good Wife taught her Daughter*, the *Formula Nouiciorum* is a series of masculine regulations to be imposed upon women in which rules of external behaviour are prescribed to impact upon the internal state of mind. The inhabitants of Pleasaunt Regarde can be seen as the result of this type of instruction. The women have internalised the masculine rules of conduct which impress upon women the understanding that to transgress the rules is undesirable.

It is helpful here to consider briefly some historical evidence concerning the organisation of households, both lay and religious, for, as will be shown, the similarity and overlap between the two bears some influence on *The Assembly of Ladies* in the way the household of Pleasaunt Regarde is ordered. Moreover, the similarity between the ordering of the lay and religious households suggests that female spaces, whether lay or religious, are both subject to the same masculine authoritative conventions.

Both lay and religious households were hierarchical and to varying degrees communal. Positions of responsibility in both communities were specifically appointed and they are not unlike the professions seen in *The Assembly of Ladies*, with a porter, herberger, and secretary. The religious house would be governed by an abbess or prioress, under which was a sub-prioress, a cellarer, a *thesaurissa* (bursar), a *precentrix* and *succentrix* (leaders and teachers of the choir), a *cameraria* (in charge of wardrobe), an *infirmaria* (responsible for the infirmary), an *elemosinaria* (distributor of alms), and a *magistra noviciarum* (teacher of novices).[37] Of note here is the hierarchy of the positions and the manner in which each title indicates the job to be performed.[38] In the lay household, the lady would hold the highest position of authority; under her was the steward, the chamberlain, chaplains, clerks, squires and valets.[39] The lady of the house would also have her personal retinue of gentlewomen and servants.[40] The hierarchy, job descriptions, and communal nature of both lay and religious households are without doubt very similar.[41] Two significant differences, however, are particularly important for this book. First, unlike the lay household, the religious household is entirely composed of women. Eckenstein notes that there were even several instances of women serving as chaplains within religious houses in the late medieval period.[42] Second, the lay household, particularly a large one, was composed of an "inner" household and an "outer" household. The "inner" household was generally the main residence and was run by the lady, and the "outer" household was a more itinerant household that generally travelled with the lord.[43] These two differences between lay and religious households both appear to impact on *The Assembly of Ladies*, insofar as the castle of Pleasaunt Regarde is entirely inhabited by women, and, although there is no overt "outer" household here, the concept of an "inner" household being an exclusive domain of women is particularly pertinent.

Another example from Christine de Pizan would further support such a comparison. In *Le Livre des Trois Vertus* (1405) Christine gives detailed advice on appropriate behaviour and conduct for women, in the household, in public, and in the religious house.[44] In the latter establishment, Christine says women religious should show obedience, humility, sobriety, patience, diligence, chastity, and benevolence.[45] These virtues are mirrored in the advice given for lay women. In the advice suggested by Prudence, a princess should show sobriety, chastity, honour, and wisdom.[46] When giving advice to religious women, Christine notes that "while of course we address our words to you, religious women, all women might lend an ear to hear whatever might be to their profit,"[47] thus reinforcing that the virtuous behaviour espoused is appropriate to all women. These examples indicate the similarity between behaviour and etiquette in the lay household and the religious household, which is useful to consider with regard to the way Pleasaunt Regarde is structured and maintained.

It is significant that many guides for the instruction of nuns and female novices have been thought to be of potential use to the lay woman. The text referred to earlier, the *Formula Nouiciorum*, occurs in another English translation which specifically states that, while it is primarily intended for the use of religious, it is also of use to "all other that desireth to be seruantes of god."[48] In another significant text, *Hali Meiðhad* (c.1190-1230), Millet and Wogan-Browne note that the text "may well be directed toward sustaining those who have already chosen the virgin life, but is equally suitable for young girls facing the choice of marrying or of consecrating themselves to Christ."[49] The significance of mentioning both literary and historical evidence for an overlap between religious and lay worlds is to emphasise that, for women in the medieval period, the two worlds were very similar in terms of their structuring and regulations. The enclosed nature of the religious houses, even more strongly enforced in the later medieval period, shows little difference to the walled city of Christine or the castle of Pleasaunt Regarde. It would seem, then, that the household of Pleasant Regarde is deliberately structured in a manner that is similar to historical records of both religious and lay households, emphasising the similar social circumstances for women whether they exist in religious or lay environments. The structure of Pleasaunt Regarde exposes the effect of masculine authority on female environments.

A poem that identifies many of these issues is of particular significance here. Existing in only a single manuscript, *Why I Can't Be a Nun* is a satiric look at the decline of convents and spiritual values in the early-fifteenth-century.[50] Dean describes the poem as a *chanson de nonne*, although I would question this categorisation.[51] Eileen Power discusses both this poem and the genre of *chanson de nonne* in some detail, and it is clear that the poem does not conform to the content of a *chanson de nonne*.[52] The poem concerns a girl named Katherine who wishes to become a nun. Her father sends out scouts to several English nunneries, who report back on the corruption within the convents. Subsequently, the father denies Katherine her wish. Unable to understand, Katherine, sitting in a garden, laments her situation, falls asleep, and dreams. In the dream she is approached by Lady Experience who takes her to visit a nunnery. The nunnery is peopled with personifications of vices, Dame Sclowthe, Dame Veyne Glory, Dame Lust, and Dame Wantowne, among others. The few virtuous members of the household, Dame Chastyte, Dame Pacience, and Dame Charyte, are confined to a chamber outside of the convent.

Upon seeing this, Katherine accepts it is not appropriate for her to become a nun in such circumstances and decides to live a virtuous life outside of the convent.

According to Power, the *chanson de nonne*, such as is found in French and German, is essentially the lament of a nun who is forced into the religious life unwillingly.[53] If one were to compare *Why I Can't Be a Nun* with the European *chanson de nonne*, I would suggest it strikes one as more of an anti-*chanson de nonne*, in which a willing girl is denied the opportunity to become a nun. The *chanson de nonne* generally presents the speaker of the poem as desiring of the fulfilment of worldly lust rather than spiritual fulfilment, whereas *Why I Can't Be a Nun* depicts Katherine desiring spiritual betterment. The satiric element of the poem is found in the location of spiritual instruction. It should be located in the convent, but Katherine discovers this is not the case in reality.

Why I Can't Be a Nun is a particularly useful comparison for *The Assembly of Ladies*. Although it is likely to have been written as much as fifty years earlier than *The Assembly of Ladies*, both poems point up particularly pertinent social conditions for women in fifteenth-century England, and both convey a desire for an honourable female space. The poet of *The Assembly of Ladies* finds it necessary to create an all-female space in which to house female honour, while the poet of *Why I Can't Be a Nun* asserts that female honour must be housed within the soul. In both instances, however, the structure of a household is used either to support or to reject the location of female honour. This is particularly relevant for this book because the location of female honour in the household, as it is within *The Assembly of Ladies*, indicates the masculine authority that controls female honour. In *Why I Can't Be a Nun*, female honour is located within the soul where it is controlled by the woman herself. Interestingly, the woman who instructs Katherine is named Lady Experience, who is quite a counterpoint to the Good Wife. Riddy suggests that a girl is more likely to learn household rules and regulations through experiential learning rather than through a poem such as *What the Good Wife taught her Daughter*, and the two poems can be seen as contrasting feminine and masculine methods of instruction.[54]

The dominance of the household and its regulations in *The Assembly of Ladies* would seem to suggest that this interior space ought to be the location of female honour, and that the well-organised nature of Pleasaunt Regarde would indicate the castle is, indeed, honourable. Yet it is clear from the examples mentioned here that the rules and regulations governing female behaviour, even those written by women like Christine, articulate female honour according to masculine precepts. The narrator and her

companions in *The Assembly of Ladies* must journey to the location of
female honour, emphasising honour as an imposed quality, rather than
honour being a quality found within themselves, as Katherine would
assert. The narrator's erratic behaviour in Pleasaunt Regarde may suggest
her anxiety at accepting the castle as a place that preserves female honour
when by doing so Pleasaunt Regarde reveals itself as a construction
created in response to masculine authority.

The Clothing of the Women

On arrival at Pleasaunt Regarde the narrator is taken to the chamber of
Contenaunce to wait for her companions. Contenaunce notes that the
narrator, while wearing the required blue dress, does not wear a motto:
"'Yowre worde,' quod she, 'fayne wold I that I knewe'"(310). The
narrator responds in a manner that has been regarded by scholars as both
rude and reticent.[55] She says:

> "Forsoth," quod I, "ye shal wele know and se:
> And for my word, I have none, this is trewe;
> It is inough that my clothyng be blew
> As here before I had comaundement,
> And so to do I am right wele content."   (311-315)

Rather than either rude or reticent, the narrator's response, I would
suggest, has the air of a proclamation about it. She does not appear to be
withholding her motto from Contenaunce, rather, she states quite
forcefully that, just as she had not had a motto "before I had
comaundement" (314) to attend the assembly at Pleasaunt Regarde, she
will not now have a motto either. There is no attempt to withhold this
information either, she is very direct in her speech when she says: "ye shal
wele know and se" (311). The narrator's lack of a personal motto may well
signify her lack of individual identity, as suggested by Chance and Barratt,
but I would suggest that the narrator's refusal to wear a motto is an act of
transgression of the boundaries of Pleasaunt Regarde, which causes some
disquiet and tension between the narrator and the other women. To
investigate this further, however, it is necessary to examine the manner of
dress of the characters of the poem in greater detail.

The narrator is careful to note and describe the dress of the other
characters. On first meeting with Perseveraunce, the narrator says she was:

> Atired wele, nat hye but bi mesure,
> Hir contenaunce ful sad and ful demure,

Hir colours blewe, al that she had upon
Theyr com no mo but hir silf alon.
Hir gowne was wele enbrowdid, certainly,
With sovenez aftir hir owne devise;
On the purfil hir word, by and by,
Bien loialment, as I cowed me avise.   (81-88)

The attention to the detail of Perseveraunce's clothing is repeated in her
description of all of the women of Pleasaunt Regarde. All of the women
are dressed appropriately, "bi mesure," not too ostentatiously but as
befitting their status. All of the women wear blue dresses, with a personal
device embroidered on to the dress, and a personal motto sewn on to the
sleeve. Her companions, too, when they arrive at Pleasaunt Regarde,
change into blue dresses that display their own devices and mottoes. The
devices and mottoes are referred to by the narrator in a way that indicates
they are identifying features, they contain information about status and
class, but they also display the wearer's virtue. At the encounter with
Diligence, the narrator asks Diligence to come nearer so that she may see
her attire clearly. Diligence is, of course, dressed in blue and bears her
device and motto, *Taunt que je puis* [As much as I can], but the narrator's
response is significant. She says: "I was wele apayed, / For than wist I
without any more / It was ful triew that I had herd afore" (208-10).
Diligence's device and motto confirm her virtue in the narrator's eyes.[56]
   The narrator pays close attention to the dress of Contenaunce, which,
in addition to being blue, displaying the device, and the motto, was "Of
goode facion and furred wele with gray" (305). But the narrator's close
inspection causes Contenaunce to question the narrator of her own motto,
"'Yowre worde,' quod she, 'fayne wold I that I knewe'"(310). Clearly it is
a source of disquiet for Contenaunce that the narrator bears no motto, for
without it not only is her status and class unknown, but also her virtue.
Without a motto, the narrator is without identity. Yet the narrator's
protestations are equally disquieting. She has never had a motto before,
she says, and so it is appropriate that she have none now: "it is inough that
my clothyng be blew" (313). Not only is the narrator identity-less within
Pleasaunt Regarde, she has always been so, and, in a sort of reverse logic,
this is where she belongs, "I am right wele content," (315) she says. The
contrast between her appearance without a motto and device and that of
the other women is striking. The narrator takes great pains to learn the
mottoes and devices of the women of Pleasaunt Regarde, and later during
the presentation of the bills of complaints, she introduces each of her
companions by their mottoes. This suggests that she, herself, places great

importance in the mottoes, they are not insignificant to her and she has not carelessly forgotten her own.[57]

While I agree with Chance's suggestion that the narrator, without a motto, is, therefore, identity-less, I would like to suggest further that the narrator, without a motto, signifies the female voice that is unable to communicate. This can be discerned from the importance in the poem that is placed in the physical objects created by women. Lewis negatively criticises the narrator's emphasis on the clothing and décor in *The Assembly of Ladies*, yet clearly the emphasis indicates that these elements convey meaning in the poem.[58] The dresses of the women must be described in detail because they are a means of communication for the women; the dresses display the women's identities in a language that the women understand. Rozsika Parker describes the activities of embroidery, tapestry, and weaving as enabling "women to negotiate the constraints of femininity,"[59] by which she means that women were able to use these skills to exclude the masculine world. I do not entirely agree with this as the activities are instigated by masculine authority in the first instance. Parker's suggestion, however, is of interest here because the narrator's own struggle is not unlike that of a woman negotiating the "constraints of femininity." The narrator's frustration lies in the fact that, as a woman, femininity should not be a constraint.

Pleasaunt Regarde contains other such examples of objects created by women in the presence of tapestries and in the umple that is hung on the walls to cover the engravings of Cupid's martyrs, both of which can be considered similarly to the embroidery on the dresses insofar as the creation of all of these activities is sanctioned by masculine authority but all convey meanings beyond masculine expectation or understanding.

Yet the narrator, without a motto, is excluded from this means of communication and, as her emphatic statement to Contenaunce indicates, she has no wish for it either. It seems unusual that the narrator desires to be distanced from a means of communication that is almost exclusive to women, and which she is happy to use for the identification of others. The narrator's objection to wearing a motto, I would suggest, signifies an objection to the internalisation by women of masculine values. The means of communication used by these women, embroidery and tapestry, are activities sanctioned by masculine authority and the women's practice of these activities reinforces that masculine precept. Masculine authority deems embroidery and tapestry to be female activities, thus by practising such activities the women condone masculine authority. I would suggest that the narrator's rejection to wearing a motto indicates her objection to internalising and recapitulating masculine authority. She states that she does not have a motto, which I would suggest indicates that to wear an embroidered motto is to condone masculine authority and this would negate her identity as a woman. Without a motto the narrator is only identity-less in regard to masculine authority because she does not acknowledge the activities that are deemed appropriate by men for women to perform. The narrator overcomes her anxiety about transgressing the masculine imposed regulations of Pleasaunt Regarde by refusing to wear a motto. To represent herself as a woman, it is, indeed, as she says, "inough that my clothyng be blew" (313).

Susan Crane draws attention to the use of mottoes on clothing, a feature that appears in late medieval French customs.[60] An illustration of Charles d'Orleans exemplifies this, in which his motto is depicted as embroidered across his traditionally black attire. Joan Evans notes embroidered mottoes as a uniquely French custom that was not practiced in England.[61] Perhaps this would support the argument for a French influence in the composition of *The Assembly of Ladies*, an argument that would conjoin with Ruth Marie Fisher's argument for the poem having been authored by a woman from the courts of William de la Pole, the Duke of Suffolk, who had considerable French connections.[62] *The Assembly of Ladies*, however, is not the only instance in English literature of embroidered mottoes: John Lydgate's *The Temple of Glas* also features a character with a motto on her dress.[63] Perhaps a more supportable argument is that literary and social trends in France were known in England, and vice versa. This is not at all surprising given the political events in England and France in the fifteenth century.

Another particularly dramatic example of writing appearing on clothing occurs in *The Flowing Light of the Godhead*, a mystical text by Mechthild of Magdeburg (c.1210-1282). There is surely no direct influence on the composition of *The Assembly of Ladies*, but a comparison may provide some additional meaning to our poem. Mechthild, a beguine, wrote what in many ways was a conventional mystical dream vision. I suggest it was conventional because the text, both in its Latin and German versions, uses well-established secular literary conventions. The centre of the text focuses on a dream experienced by Mechthild that I will argue draws our attention to the literary authority Mechthild garners in her text, which may well be applied to the narrator of *The Assembly of Ladies*. In her dream, Mechthild is invited to join a company of saints and the holy family. Her concern is that she is inappropriately dressed to be part of such company, at which the Virgin Mary transforms Mechthild's clothes into grander attire. As she looks closely, Mechthild notices that her new clothes are covered with embroidered words, and the words are those of her own narrative. She does not make further mention of this, but surely the reader is struck by the slippage between narrative frames this image creates. We are, with this image, made aware of three Mechthilds: Mechthild the author, the ultimately authority behind the words on the clothing, Mechthild the narrator, who describes these events to us, and Mechthild the dreamer who experiences the clothing first hand. This is a narrative slippage that occurs in *The Assembly of Ladies* and which is considered in some detail in Chapter Three. In addition to the narrative slippage, the presence of writing on clothing draws our attention to the way women can initiate their own authority to write. Here, in Mechthild's case, the dreamer experiences her literary clothing with great reverence, enacting respect for an author and acknowledging the authority of the author. Perhaps we can regard this as another strategy available to women to participate in literature. Where Christine de Pisan attempted to create a lineage for women writers by peopling her city with such authoritative women, Mechthild demonstrates authority for women writers by creating a scene in which her words are considered worthy of the company of saints.

Such an interpretation, however, does not satisfactorily explain why Mechthild's writing should appear on clothing, of all places. This, I would argue, reflects the same intention as the appearance of mottoes on the women's clothing in *The Assembly of Ladies*. The purpose of mottoes, historically and with *The Assembly of Ladies*, was to identify and define the wearer. There is, of course, a close correlation between coats of arms symbolising a family or a lineage, but the appearance of mottoes reflects a much more personal identification. Thus Mechthild the dreamer, wearing the words of Mechthild the author, as narrated to us by Mechthild the narrator, embodies the specific identity of Mechthild, emphasising a self-sufficient autonomy. One could consider the religious and political implications of such an assertion of complete authority. Alexandra Barratt certainly identifies that one method by which women were able to be heard in a literary environment was to claim instruction from God to behave in such a manner.[64] Indeed, this is a feature of the writings of many women mystics, who, by circumventing the censorship of the church, risked accusations of heresy. No doubt a disclaimer that God requested these women write down their visions protected many from these accusations, although for others it did not.

Mechthild's clothing highlights for us that the women's mottoes and devises in *The Assembly of Ladies* are not insignificant features, they contribute to the meanings generated by the poem. It emphsises, too, the significance of the narrator refusing to wear a motto.

The Images of Cupid's Martyrs

As the narrator and her companions are led through the castle to the assembly room to present their bills of complaint to Lady Loiaulte, the narrator describes the décor:

> But wite ye wele, there was a paved floore,
> The goodelicst that any wight myght see;
> And furthermore aboute than loked we
> On eche a corner and upon every wal,
> The whiche is made of berel and cristal;
> Wheron was graven of storyes many oon. (451-56)

The floor of Pleasaunt Regarde is, like the floor of the garden arbour, well paved, but of greater significance are the walls. Made from beryl and crystal, two precious stones regarded as having magical properties, the walls are covered in engravings of the stories of famous women wronged in love. Joan Evans discusses the popularity of lapidaries in the later medieval period, in which the curative and magical qualities of precious stones were of greater importance than their beauty or rarity.[65] Beryl is one of the twelve precious stones used in the foundations of the New Jerusalem, as described in Revelations 21.19-20, but in this instance the two stones are more likely included here for the way they signify clarity and brightness. In the lapidary of Oxford, Bodleian Library, MS Douce 291 (c. 1325-50), beryl is described as:

> A stone þat is a colour like to water when þe sonne shyneth, &...norissheth loue between man and woman...who-so berith berill nere his flesche ayeins þe sonne, þt þe fire þat cometh oute cacheth þe flesche; þat signifieth thoo þat arne assembled & speken with holy men þt ben fired with charite & bren of himself.[66]

In the same manuscript, crystal is described as:

> frost harde as thise olde Auncestres seyne...This stone conceiueth wele the fire atte the sonne-beem, & catcheth & brennyth.[67]

Both stones are attributed with the ability to capture the sun which, in the case of beryl, is likened to the burning of the soul with Christian fervour. The brightness of the two stones on the walls of Pleasaunt Regarde, however, is regarded in a more practical than spiritual manner. The brilliance apparently causes the walls to be draped in a "fyne umple" so that "folk shuld nat hurt theyr sight" (472).

It would certainly be possible to identify many medieval poems that
contain lists of Cupid's martyrs, but for this book I would like to compare
briefly the wall engravings of Cupid's martyrs in *The Assembly of Ladies*
with the painted images on the external walls in *Le Roman de la Rose*.[68]
All of the images in both poems are depicted as females, but in *Le Roman
de la Rose* the images of women are personifications of undesirable
qualities, such as poverty, old age, and greed, whereas in *The Assembly of
Ladies* the images are famous narratives of women. Yet this comparison is
appropriate given the similar method used to present the images. Engraved
and painted on to stone walls, the images are given the quality of
permanence about them which creates the impression that in both cases
neither is open to interpretation or alteration, in both cases they are
presented as constant universals that contribute to the governing of the
world, whether they be the undesirable qualities of poverty and greed, or
the martyrdom of Thisbe and Phyllis.[69]

In *Le Roman de la Rose* the images occur on the external walls as a
warning to those who enter that these ill-favoured qualities must be left
outside the garden of Deduit. Of course, we know that the interior of
Deduit is not as pure as this rule would suggest, but the pictures establish
the social conventions that are acknowledged in the poem. In contrast, the
images of Cupid's martyrs in *The Assembly of Ladies* appear on the
internal walls of Pleasaunt Regarde, as the company of women make their
way to Lady Loiaulte's chamber. Despite Pleasaunt Regarde being
presented as a women-only environment, the images on the walls serve to
remind that the influence of the masculine world has not been left behind.
As such it is appropriate the images appear in the interior of a women's
space, rather than on the exterior as in *Le Roman de la Rose*, the point
being that the images are themselves masculine interpretations of women
posited directly into the centre of a female space. Through their physical,
spatial, location within Pleasaunt Regarde, the images are a masculine act
to coerce women to internalise the ideas that these images represent,
instilling anxiety at the prospect of transgression.

The stories engraved upon the walls of beryl and crystal are
particularly significant here, as they are the well-known collection of
classical stories concerning women wronged in love, many of which are
based loosely on the stories within Ovid's *Heroides* and *Metamorphoses*,
or on later interpretations of Ovid. This is not the place to consider the
specific source texts used by the poet of *The Assembly of Ladies*, it is more
useful to consider the meanings generated by these stories in their spatial
position within Pleasaunt Regarde. The stories described concern Phyllis,
Thisbe, Cleopatra, Mélusine, and Anelida, although the narrator does also

state that there were "many mo than I reherce yow here – / It were to long to telle yow al in feere" (468-69).

The narrator describes Phyllis as having died from "wommanly pite" for the love of Demophoön, in a story found within Ovid's *Heroides*. Her story is interesting in the context of *The Assembly of Ladies* as although Demophoön is responsible for her fate by having abandoned her, she also comes to the realisation that her own behaviour is partially responsible as well. She says:

> Oft have I been false to myself in my defence of you...
> Tell me, what have I done, except not wisely love?
> And by the very fault I might well have won you for my own.
> The one crime which may be charged to me
> Is that I took you, O faithless, to myself.[70]

As this extract suggests, Phyllis is well aware she was willingly deceived by Demophoön. According to Harold Isbell, Phyllis "has not merely loved unwisely, she has in fact contrived her own downfall. The predictable treachery of Demophoön has been matched by her own foolish generosity."[71] Chaucer's retelling of the story in the *Legend of Good Women* is apparently based largely on Ovid, but it is noticeable that he places a great deal of emphasis on the lineage of Demophoön. Demophoön is the son of Theseus, and Chaucer states on several occasions words to the effect of "like father, like son": "wiked fruit cometh of a wiked tre" (2395); "And lyk his fader of face and of stature, / And fals of love; it come hym of nature." (2446-47); "ryght so Demophon / The same wey, the same path hath gon, / That dide his false fader Theseus." (2462-64).[72] In the *Legend of Good Women* Chaucer impresses upon the reader that Demophoön is fated to betray Phyllis, although it is not clear whether or not this exonerates Phyllis. Phyllis, herself, is aware of Demophoön's lineage, and perhaps Chaucer's interpretation suggests that Phyllis should have known better.

Percival describes Chaucer's attitude in the tale of Phyllis as indicating a kind of camaraderie between Chaucer and Demophoön, that Chaucer's retelling of the Ovidian story is a literary equivalent of Demophoön's behaviour.[73] In his translation of Ovid, Chaucer chooses "only the best bits, he deflowers Phillis' letter and, like Demephon, 'piked of hire al the good he myght.'"[74] The association is relevant to this book because it directly relates masculine conventions with literary conventions. Unlike the Ovidian story that describes Phyllis' suffering, Chaucer's interpretation focuses more on Demophoön's falsity, which is then appropriated by Chaucer in the final lines of the tale:

Be war, ye wemen, of your subtyl fo,
Syn yit this day men may ensaumple se;
And trusteth, as in love, no man but me. (2559-61)

Percival describes the final line as "an artful and slightly ribald invitation
[to women] to submit themselves to the poet's seductions."[75] While it is
impossible to know if the poet of *The Assembly of Ladies* had Chaucer's
version of the story of Phyllis in mind, it is certainly appropriate to
consider in light of the focus of this book. Chaucer directly emphasises the
masculine nature of the literary act, to which women will always be
subject. In *The Assembly of Ladies*, the story of Phyllis signifies the
impossibility of women being able to control their own fates without
transgressing the boundaries imposed by masculine convention. The death
of Phyllis acts as a warning of the consequences of transgression. Despite
the castle of Pleasaunt Regarde being a female-only domain, it is still
impacted upon by masculine conventions and the women are still subject
to masculine restraints.

Although drawn from Ovid's *Metamorphoses* or a later interpretation
of Ovid, the mention of the story of Thisbe on the internal walls of
Pleasaunt Regarde is, nevertheless, unusual.[76] Thisbe is not an example of
a woman betrayed in love like Ariadne or Phyllis, rather her death occurs
after a series of unfortunate and coincidental events. Yet the deaths of both
Pyramus and Thisbe are worth comparing for the differences they show
between the suicide of a woman and the suicide of a man. In Chaucer's
version, Pyramus' late arrival at the well to meet Thisbe results in his
finding Thisbe's head-scarf covered in blood from the lioness.[77] His
assumption is, of course, that Thisbe has been killed by the lioness, yet, as
Elaine Tuttle Hansen has pointed out, Pyramus does not commit suicide
because of Thisbe's presumed death. She says: "Pyramus is less concerned
with the loss of Thisbe than with his own failure as a man to protect her."[78]
As Hansen suggests, it seems Pyramus' discovery of the bloody head-scarf
has the effect of emasculating him. His desire for Thisbe has caused his
unmanly behaviour and the fact that Thisbe is not, in fact, dead further
emphasises this. It is because of his own behaviour that he must die, not
because of Thisbe's supposed death. Thisbe's actual death, however,
attempts to change this. Once Thisbe sees the bloody head-scarf and
Pyramus' sword, she realises the events that have occurred. She says: "I
wol thee folwe ded, and I wol be / Felawe and cause ek of thy deth" (894-
95), Thisbe decides to commit suicide to justify Pyramus' death. Her
suicide shifts the focus of the narrative away from Pyramus and on to
herself, but this can occur only with her own death. The inclusion of
Thisbe's story on the walls of Pleasaunt Regarde is an overt instance of

literary and social transgression. Thisbe's suicide is a deliberate attempt to appropriate both the meaning of Pyramus' death and the meaning of the text.

Cleopatra's death is not unlike that of Thisbe, insofar as neither is abandoned by unfaithful lovers, but they join their lovers in death. Cleopatra's presence here on the walls of Pleasaunt Regrade is slightly unusual if the engravings are intended as examples of good women, or even if they are intended as cautionary tales. Cleopatra's story does not come from an Ovidian source, but is found in Boccaccio, Chaucer, and Gower.[79] In Chaucer's version it is notable that her failings are glossed over or elided completely and that, like many of the tales in the *Legend of Good Women*, the focus is more on the man than the woman. While Cleopatra's death is similar to Thisbe's in the way she follows Antony's suicide with her own, it is hard to view her death in any way that is noble. Indeed, it is significant that Christine de Pizan does not include Cleopatra in her city of ladies.[80]

With the three stories mentioned so far it is clear there is some difficulty with establishing them simply as women betrayed in love. Phyllis, according to Ovid's version, must bear some responsibility for her fate, Thisbe commits suicide in order to control the meaning of Pyramus' death, and Cleopatra actually prompts Antony's suicide by abandoning him in battle. These stories concern women whose lives and loves are far more complicated than is often credited when they are compiled among a list of Cupid's martyrs, and both Percival and Dinshaw remark on the way Chaucer must resort to reducing and eliding events from his sources in order to have the women's lives fit into the paradigm of secular saints.[81]

A particularly unusual inclusion in the list of women's stories depicted on the walls of Pleasaunt Regarde is the story of Mélusine.[82] Principally based on the late fourteenth-century *Roman de Mélusine* by Jean d'Arras, the story appears in two fifteenth-century English translations, one in prose and one in verse.[83] Mélusine was a half-human and half-fairy who married a man on the condition that he promised never to see her on Saturdays, when she would transform into a serpent from the waist down. The promise was eventually broken, condemning her eternally. In light of the women's stories discussed so far, the story of Mélusine brings together an overriding theme of women who are not as simple as social convention would wish. The *Roman de Mélusine* is noted by critics for its linguistic complexity and ambiguities, a feature that is also present in the principle character.[84] Mélusine signifies, of course, the masculine fear that all women are demons underneath a veneer good behaviour, yet her character is more complicated than this. Her ultimate crime is that of the transgression of social boundaries. Gabrielle M. Spiegel points out that, as a twin, Mélusine's very existence transgresses social boundaries, she is monstrous from birth, which is then physically embodied when her mother condemns her to transform into a serpent every Saturday.[85] Mélusine also transgresses the boundaries of male and female domains when she magically builds castles and cities.[86] As a mother she dutifully produces ten sons, but they are all disfigured with monstrous deformities. Her disappearance every Saturday leads to social speculation she must be having an illicit love affair, causing her husband to spy on her. He is relieved to see she has not transgressed the sanctity of marriage, but horrified to discover her serpentine body. Everything about Mélusine embodies transgression, but what is of even greater significance to this study is the turn of events when her true nature is discovered. Her husband, spying on her, sees her body transformed, but he says nothing to her and hopes she is not aware that he has broken his promise to her. In fact she does know, but says nothing because he does not make his knowledge public. This is particularly significant because it indicates that she will determine whether or not his promise is broken, and, therefore, whether or not she will be condemned. Moreover, it appears that what is at issue is not her serpentine body but her public defamation. She may be half-human and half-fairy, but her fate is no different from that of any other woman, she will lose her honour only if her secret is revealed publicly. The public defamation does eventually occur, but not for many years and only after one of her sons has brutally murdered one of his brothers, causing her husband to denounce her as monstrous and as having borne monstrous offspring.

The story of Mélusine, however, offers one further important piece of information for this book, and helps to suggest why she is included in the stories on the walls of Pleasaunt Regarde. Kevin Brownlee identifies a correlation between the hybrid nature of Mélusine's body and the hybrid nature of the text.[87] The mere fact that the story is entitled *Mélusine* draws the comparison between her body and the text, suggesting a deliberate blurring between the two. Brownlee says: "Both Mélusine the female subject in Jean d'Arras' romance and the romance as a whole are constructed from radically divergent generic, rhetorical, and narrative components."[88] The comparison between Mélusine's body and *Mélusine*, the text, can be seen in the way that the character is not condemned until her physical deformity is actually articulated. The merging of the body of Mélusine and the text *Mélusine* suggests that the story is positioned on the walls of Pleasaunt Regarde to correlate social and literary transgressions.

The final story of a woman wronged in love that is mentioned in *The Assembly of Ladies* is of Chaucer's Anelida. The narrator says: "Ther was also Anelada the quene / Upon Arcite how sore she did complayne" (465-66). There is little in the poem of *Anelida and Arcite* to suggest Anelida is particularly unusual in the way that the other women discussed so far have been, but the feature that the narrator of *The Assembly of Ladies* draws our attention to is not the entire poem, but only the written complaint of Anelida. We have seen the way the story of Mélusine drew attention to the power of the public defamation, and the complaint of Anelida can be seen as an extension of this. Anelida's complaint must exist in a written format, that is, a format that is publicly accessible, in order for her voice to be heard. This does, of course, foreshadow the events to take place in Pleasaunt Regarde, in which the narrator and her companions will publicly present their bills of complaint.

The narrator concludes her description of the stories on the walls of Pleasaunt Regarde by saying: "Al these storyes wer graven ther certayne / And many mo than I reherce yow here- / It were to long to telle yow al in feere"(467-69). From this is it possible to see that the narrator is suggesting the five women's stories already mentioned do form a homogeneous group, along with the numerous other stories she has not the time to describe. It would be simple to suggest that these are stories of women who have been wronged only in love but, as has been shown, the women's lives and circumstances in these stories are not quite that simple. I would suggest that the women's stories that have been described here and the many more that are alluded to indicate the limited means of expression available to women. In the stories concerning Phyllis and Cleopatra, Chaucer glosses over their faults so that they may fit into the convention of good women. This act of textual excision has the effect of defeminising the women; they lose their identities as individuals when they are textualised. Thisbe attempts to take control of her narrative when she sees Pyramus dead, yet the price she must pay for that control is her own death. Mélusine's fate is directly controlled by public articulation, if her story, the truth of her, is made known she will die. And finally Anelida can be seen to exist solely within her written complaint; she laments and falls into a swoon at Arcite's abandonment:

> But when she saw that her ne gat no geyn,
> Upon a day, ful sorowfully wepinge,
> She caste her for to make a compleynynge,
> And of her owne hond she gan hit write.   (206-09)

The stories that appear on the walls of Pleasaunt Regarde, then, are not chance selections. The women in the stories are significant for the way their stories conjoin masculine authority with textual authority and indicate the way women are excluded from self-expression.

Umple as *Integumentum*

Perhaps the most unusual feature of the engraved images on the walls of Pleasaunt Regarde, however, is that they are covered with fine gauze. The narrator describes this:

> And bicause the wallis shone so bright
> With fyne umple they were al over-spredde
> To that entente folk shuld nat hurt theyr sight,
> And thurgh that the storyes myght be redde.   (470-73)

Umple is a type of fine linen and this example is one of the earliest uses of the word.[89] Furthermore, I am not aware of any other medieval example of umple used in this manner. The practical use of the umple is not surprising as the narrator has already informed us the walls are made of beryl and crystal, two stones known for their brilliance. Yet the image of the engraved stories on the walls partially shielded from view is a dramatic one that requires further examination.

I would assert that the umple is in fact a failed feminine attempt at articulation. The veiling of the engraved images on the walls of the Pleasaunt Regarde is the physical embodiment of the literary device of *integumentum*. The stories of Cupid's martyrs are reduced in meaning by an act of female self-confinement as the women who inhabit Pleasaunt Regarde attempt to imitate the literary convention of *integumentum*. Alastair Minnis describes the "process of integumental interpretation whereby the veils or garments of allegory [are] judged to clothe profound truths relating to physics or ethics."[90] *Integumentum* is a means of interpretation, in which a text is judged to contain certain underlying truths which are hidden beneath a veneer of narrative. This is made clear by Macrobius, who says of Nature:

> ...her sacred rites are veiled in mysterious representations so that she may not have to show herself naked even to initiates. Only eminent men of superior intelligence gain a revelation of her truths.[91]

The implication of the integumental process, then, is one of exclusion. *Integumentum* acts as a key to knowledge of the truth, a key that only very few possess, only "men of superior intelligence." The necessarily restricted nature of *integumentum* is emphasised by other writers as well. William of Conches claims that "only the wise should know the secrets of the gods, [arrived at] through the interpretation of integumenta,"[92] and Alan of Lille makes the distinction between "the sweetness of the literal sense, meant to soothe the ears of boys," and "the sharper subtlety of the allegory, which is designed to whet the advanced intellect."[93]

Integumentum, it would seem, is a double-edged sword. It is used as a means of clarifying and understanding a concept, it is a way of bringing to light a truth. Yet at the same time access to the concept or truth is limited and selective. It is the latter, exclusive, aspect of *integumentum* that is of particular interest here. In *The Assembly of Ladies*, the umple covering the images engraved on the walls acts as veil beneath which the stories of the women are partially hidden from view. The narrator explicitly states that the umple is there "[to] that entente folk shuld nat hurt theyr sight" (472), that is, to reveal the truth of the pictures to the uninitiated would hurt their sight, they would not be able to comprehend the images if they were displayed in full view, and to do so would be a transgression of both social and literary boundaries.

The presence of the umple covering the pictures can be likened to the process of *integumentum*; it is a feminised version of *integumentum*. It has been noted earlier in this chapter that use is made in the poem of traditional female skills and activities, such as tapestry and embroidery, and the umple is another such example. As a fabric, its signification is located completely within the female domain, yet its placement, covering over the narratives on the walls of Pleasaunt Regarde, imitates that of *integumentum*.

The use of the umple to cover the engravings on the walls of Pleasaunt Regarde signifies the literary limitations imposed on women. *Integumentum* is the preserve of those of "superior intelligence" and learning, who, it is implied, are not women. The umple is, then, the only recourse the women have to participating in the integumental process, but their participation is not complete, it is only an imitation of *integumentum*. The veil of umple demonstrates an awareness of the veil of allegory, but it is not the same thing as *integumentum*. The purpose of *integumentum* is to discover the truth of a text, it is a means of interpretation that allows one to reveal what lies underneath the narrative. Yet the umple veil does the exact opposite. It is, in every way possible, a feminine version of *integumentum*, except in its resulting effect. The umple conceals the stories beneath it, it does not reveal them.

The concealing of the stories engraved on the walls reduces their possible meanings and simplifies the women depicted in them to mere stereotypes, and this, I would suggest, is the intended impression. The particular women mentioned by the narrator are, as has been shown, not in any way conventional but represent the way the women are excluded from the literary process because their stories demonstrate an association between masculine authority and literary authority. The veil of umple further reduces their existence as individuals because it conceals from view their individually distinguishable features and reduces them to stereotypes. I would suggest this is intentional because the presence of the umple emphasises the way the women are excluded from the literary process; the umple, their only means for imitating *integumentum*, does not reveal any truths about the women's stories, but conceals them further. The question that is left unanswered by the poem is whether the integumental process is any more able to reveal the truth of the text than the umple can.

Conclusions

The stories depicted on the walls of Pleasaunt Regarde do not reveal any truths while under the cover of the umple. The umple represents a failed feminine attempt at articulation where the only means for female expression, through the use of fabric, can, at best, only imitate the integumental process but will not reveal anything. This stifling of the stories of women, using the masculine-sanctioned activity of weaving fabric, can be seen as evidence of the women of Pleasaunt Regarde participating in their own silencing. By accepting and internalising masculine-sanctioned activities, the inhabitants of Pleasaunt Regarde are honourable according to masculine precepts, but they are also unable to express themselves in any manner outside of this structure.

The narrator of *The Assembly of Ladies* observes the interior of Pleasaunt Regarde, she is familiar with its rules and regulations, but she does not comply with the rules that would silence her means of expression. By refusing to wear a motto and device she excludes herself from fully participating in the conventions of Pleasaunt Regarde, but she retains her honour, like Katherine in *Why I Can't be a Nun*, within herself.

CHAPTER FOUR

LEGAL AND LITERARY LANGUAGE: WRITING AND SPEAKING IN THE BILLS OF COMPLAINT

The nine bills of complaint presented by the narrator and her companions to Lady Loiaulte have received the most negative of all scholarly criticism for the supposedly pedantic and detailed manner in which these bills are described. I suggest, however, that there are very important reasons for this manner of presentation, reasons that demonstrate the poet's awareness of legal forms of trothplight and the legal value of aural and visual tokens. These features of medieval law allow the poet to highlight a rupture in the continuity of the poem. The written text is equated with masculine language, but the interruption of specifically oral forms of legal language signal a rupture in the written text. The female voice is specifically located within the oral forms of legal language. The poet exploits the manner in which much poetry of the medieval period uses expressions and phrases common in legal contexts, particularly complaint and debate poetry, but here the poet of *The Assembly of Ladies* uses legal language to exploit the distinction between written and spoken language. The nine bills of complaint presented by the narrator and her companions to Lady Loiaulte can be seen to signify overtly the correlation between social and linguistic representations of gender in the poem. The bills of complaint in *The Assembly of Ladies* indicate a division between written and spoken forms of language, which are then equated with masculine and feminine forms of language.[1]

It is possible to consider in the bills of complaint the instability of language, in which written and spoken language are contrasted and the precarious and varied interpretations of the written word are considered.[2] Within the poem written language is posited as the standardised means of communication in a patriarchal society, but its flaws and weaknesses are demonstrated throughout and are seen to be remedied by the use of spoken language, which is associated with the feminine voice. The use of the language of contract law within the poetic language of the poem allows the emphasis of the contrast between written and spoken language because the language of the law in the setting of this poem has recourse to utilise both modes of communication.[3] This highlights the poem's position situated in an historical period in which written and oral legal agreements co-existed, and in which written agreements were not seen to supersede oral agreements. Where a comparison between legal and poetic language might be thought to suggest a contrast between empirical and emotional methods of communication, the poet demonstrates that both legal and poetic language have cause to utilise empirical and emotional forms of communication in different circumstances, and in particular the poet implies that empirical communication is equated with the written document, which is innately masculine in nature. This portion of the poem acts as a warning against reliance on such methods of communication, and the poets highlight several examples of ruptures within the text signalling where empirical communication is insufficient for conveying the "entente" of a matter.

This chapter will examine each of the bills of complaint in turn in the light of other literary texts that use legal situations and records of historical legal cases from the medieval period to show the position in which the poet has situated the poem. This comparison will suggest that the poet has created a deliberate ambiguity in the meaning of the complaints, emphasising the indistinct characteristics of the female speakers, and show that this ambiguity is then replicated in the narrator's unusual behaviour at the assembly.

The presentation of the bills of complaint by the narrator and her eight companions to Lady Loiaulte occurs at the centre of the poem and is arguably the structural focus of the poem. Prior to the presentation of the bills, the reader is given no indication as to the subject matter of the complaints, Perseveraunce simply announces to the narrator that the women are to attend the court of Lady Loiaulte, where they may make any request they wish:

And be nat ye abasshed in no wise,
As many as bien in suche an high presence;
Make youre request as ye can best devise
And she gladly wil yeve yow audience.
There is no grief nor no maner offence
Wherin ye fele your hert is displeased
But with hir help right sone ye shul bien eased.   (120-26)

Perseveraunce does not indicate what issues the women should raise with Lady Loiaulte, only that Lady Loiaulte will do her best to help them.

This act of concealing the content of the bills until later in the poem is arguably quite deliberate. The narrator attempts to pressure Perseveraunce into revealing more about the events to take place at the assembly but Perseveraunce refuses to explain further. The only hint given is that Perseveraunce insists that no men may accompany the women to Pleasaunt Regarde. As a result, when the moment arrives for the presentation of their bills, the reader apparently does not know what will be discussed, or that all the women will raise the same issues. In fact I would suggest that the emphatic manner in which Perseveraunce refuses to reveal more details creates a specific set of expectations in the reader, expectations that later will be undercut when the bills are actually presented. By avoiding an explanation the poet encourages the reader not to allow the women to express themselves adequately. The women's bills are shown to be repetitive and unoriginal within the bounds of the literary conventions, but the narrator's bill and her behaviour at the assembly signify the female voice, that does not fit into the boundaries of masculine literary convention.

It is useful at this point to consider some examples of the medieval love complaint poem and the debate poem as a comparison for *The Assembly of Ladies*. Lydgate's *Temple of Glas* (c. 1400-03) and Sir Richard Roos' translation of *La Belle Dame Sans Merci* (c. 1450) are two particularly appropriate examples of the love complaint poem.[4] The *Temple of Glas* appears to have had a great deal of influence on the poet of *The Assembly of Ladies* and *La Belle Dame Sans Merci* is a contemporary poem of similar length to *The Assembly of Ladies*. For examples of debate poems in English, the *Owl and the Nightingale* (c.1189-1216) and the debate portion of Chaucer's *Parliament of Fowls* are obvious examples.[5]

As examples of the love complaint poem, the focus here on the *Temple of Glas* and *La Belle Dame Sans Merci* will be solely on the manner in which these poems present their complaints, so that a comparison may be made with *The Assembly of Ladies* in respect of this particular matter. Lydgate's *Temple of Glas* introduces the complaints of the two lovers after the narrator has entered into Venus' temple and observed the images of Cupid's martyrs on the walls. The narrator notes the various groups of people in the temple, each with bills of complaint written out, waiting for an audience with Venus. The narrator listens to the complaint of a woman whom he introduces as bearing the embroidered motto *De mieulx en mieulx* [better and better]. The woman's complaint focuses on her lack of freedom in love; she says "For I am bounde to þing þat I nold, / Freli to chese þere lak I liberte" (335-36). Later, she says:

> For he þat haþ myn herte feiþfulli,
> And hole my luf in al honesti,
> With oute chaunge, al be it secreli,
> I haue no space wiþ him forto be.   (363-66)

Her request of Venus, then, is to ask that she may be able to be with the man whom she secretly loves. Venus immediately replies, assuring the woman that, due to the sincerity of her request, it will be granted, but she must remain forever faithful to him. The narrator leaves the crowd of people surrounding Venus and notices, a little way off, a handsome man lamenting his lack of fortune in love. He is the man whom the woman secretly loves, but he does not approach Venus in the same formal manner as the woman had done with a written complaint. The narrator says "For by himself, as he walk vp & doune, / I herd him make a lamentacioun," (565-6); it appears the man is speaking aloud to no one in particular. His complaint focuses on the fact that he loves the woman but is unable to confess this to her for fear she will reject him. Eventually he directs his request to Venus herself, asking for her assistance in the matter. Venus agrees to remedy his situation provided he be patient. Subsequently, the man makes his plea to the woman, she accepts, and the matter is resolved.

Lydgate's poem is of interest to this book for several reasons. The complaints of the man and the woman are preceded by the narrator's description of the temple of Venus, including the depictions of Cupid's martyrs, and the large number of people in the temple all awaiting an audience with Venus.[6] From the outset, the indication is that Venus' temple is the venue in which one would make a love complaint, and thus when we actually hear the two complaints, their contents is in no way surprising.[7] The narrator of *The Assembly of Ladies* also prefaces the bills of complaint with a description of the interior of Pleasaunt Regarde, including a description of the engraved images of Cupid's martyrs on the walls. The similarity between these series of events leads one to assume the bills in *The Assembly of Ladies* will be conventional love complaints as they are in the *Temple of Glas*. Yet the differences between the two texts are quite remarkable. On the one hand, the requests made by the lovers in the *Temple of Glas* concern very practical issues, the social circumstances of the woman prevent her approaching the man, and the man fears rejection. On the other hand, *The Assembly of Ladies*, the nine bills of complaint are concerned with a dissatisfaction about existing relationships, but the redress sought by the women is moral not practical. Moreover, the focus of *The Assembly of Ladies* is entirely female, whereas a much more balanced view is presented in the *Temple of Glas*. The female narrator in the *Assembly* is also one of the complainants, whereas the narrator of the

Temple of Glas is merely an observer, and so the point of view of the two texts is different–the female narrator has a vested interest in the outcome of the complaints, whereas there is apparently no particular issue at hand for the narrator of the *Temple of Glas* and thus his impact on the text is less conspicuous.[8] This feature will be discussed in greater detail later, but here it is pertinent to observe that at this point the narrator of *The Assembly of Ladies* is a more dramatically active character than the narrator of the *Temple of Glas*, and the performance of her own bill of complaint becomes the central focus of the assembly.[9] The effect, then, of the way the bills of complaint are introduced into *The Assembly of Ladies* seems to serve as an intertextual reference point in which the conventions of the love complaint are evoked in order that they may then be identified as insufficient for the female voice.

La Belle Dame Sans Merci is, in many ways, similar to the *Temple of Glas* for the manner in which the bills of complaint are presented. The bills here are also presented by a woman and a man, and the narrator keeps conspicuously in the background.[10] Yet a significant difference is that these bills are not presented to Venus in order for her to act as an intermediary. In this instance, the man presents his case directly to the woman, and after the ensuing debate she eventually rejects his offer. Of course, the title of the poem indicates that this will be the outcome, but it is still a useful poem to consider for the assumptions raised about the love complaint genre. The man's complaint is very similar in content to that of the man in the *Temple of Glas*–he asks the lady for the right to woo her and that she show him mercy. The significant difference in this poem, however, is that woman herself clearly does not desire the man's attentions. Her rejection clearly points up the illogic in the disputation, in which he clearly makes her responsible for his well-being. A conventional feature of a man's love complaint is that unless the woman shows mercy to him and accepts his love, he will surely die of a broken heart.[11] *La Belle* does not undercut the convention of the love complaint, however, unlike *The Assembly of Ladies*. Having been rejected in love, the man does, indeed, die and the poem is thus named after the woman who, apparently, caused his death. A notable feature of both *La Belle Dame Sans Merci* and the *Temple of Glas* is the conclusive resolution that each poem reaches. The *Assembly of Ladies*, in some respects, finishes inconclusively with Lady Loiaulte deferring judgment on the bills until a later date. Although this is unlike the *Temple of Glas* and *La Belle Dans Sans Merci*, it is a common occurrence in debate poetry, to which we will now turn.

The models for the medieval debate poem were, according to Thomas L. Reed, academic and legal disputes and while the subject matter of a poem like the *Owl and the Nightingale* may not have been entirely appropriate for an academic debate, its use of rhetoric is, according to Reed, the "most untrammelled employment of Aristotle's tools of argument."[12] The *Owl and the Nightingale* is, admittedly, dated much earlier than *The Assembly of Ladies*, but it is relevant to this discussion for its clear demonstration of the debate genre, and provides a useful comparison between the debate poem and the love complaint, both of which, I would suggest, *The Assembly of Ladies* draws on. The *Owl and the Nightingale* is a poem that self-consciously draws on the debate tradition; while the focus of the debate is on whether the bird-song of the owl or the nightingale is better, a seemingly trivial issue, it is dealt with by the two birds in the most serious of manners. The genre is conspicuous by the way in which the reader is able, at times, to gain a psychological insight into the birds formulating their arguments. Here the nightingale tries desperately to think of a strong response to the owl:

> An hire of þuhte þat ho hade
> Þe speche so for uorþ iladde,
> An was offered þat hire answare
> Ne wrþe noht ariht ifare.
> Ac noþeles he spac boldeliche;
> Vor he is wis þat hardeliche
> Wiþ is uo berþ grete ilete,
> Þat he uor arehþe hit ne forlete:
> Vor suich worhþ bold hif þu flihst
> Þat wle flo hif þu nisvicst;
> Hif he isiþ þat þu nart areh
> He wile of bore wrechen bareh.   (397-408)

By providing this internal view of the construction of an argument, the poet highlights the structure of the argument. Moreover, this example also shows the performative quality of the debate, insofar as the nightingale must steel herself to confront the owl and not show her fear of being unable to give a suitable response.

Perhaps the most conspicuous feature of the poem for this discussion is its lack of resolution. The debate between the owl and the nightingale becomes increasingly illogical as the poem progresses, with both birds attempting to score points against each other using whatever means possible, even going so far as to reverse their original arguments. Where the nightingale initially seems to support a kind of libertarianism and the owl ascetic conservatism, we find later in the poem that the nightingale suggests her song is a remedy for lust: "Ich teache heom bi mine songe /

Þat swucch luue ne lest noht longe" (1449-50), and the owl sympathises
with women "driven" to commit adultery by their oppressive husbands:

> He hire biluþ mid keie & loke:
> Þarþurh is spusing ofte tobroke,
> For hef heo is þarto ibroht
> He deþ þat heo nadde ear iþoht.   (1557-560)

This example and many others like it make the logic of the poem
laughable and point towards the impossibility of a resolution to the poem.
As Kathryn Hume suggests, the point of the poem seems to be more in the
spectacle of the debate rather than in logical content.[13] The lack of
resolution, however, is a feature of many debate poems and love
complaints, and the lack of resolution in *The Assembly of Ladies* seems to
be drawing on this feature in the debate and complaint poem tradition.

Chaucer's *Parliament of Fowls* is another debate poem noted for its
lack of resolution, and in particular, for the deferral of a final judgment.
The final portion of the poem in which the parliament takes place is
presented as a debate between three tercels who are vying for the love of
the formel. Each of the tercels presents his argument, yet despite their best
efforts, the debate over love is not really in question. As the birds listening
to the debate pick up the story, they are concerned not with the question of
which tercel loves the formel the most, but with the question of social
status and position.[14] Their discussion turns quickly to a verbal brawl and
the poem concludes with the formel apparently deferring her choice of
suitor until the following year. Yet the deferral is not made because the
formel cannot decide between the tercels. The formel clearly blushes after
the speech of the first tercel, indicating her preference, and Nature had
previously indicated that the first tercel was the appropriate choice because
his social standing was higher than the other tercels.[15] Thus it is fairly clear
that the following year the formel will, indeed, choose the first tercel as a
mate. The effect of the formel's deferral then acts as a delay of the
inevitable, rather than as a period in which a decision must be made, so
while the poem finishes apparently inconclusively, in reality the decision
of the formel has been made.

As a comparison for *The Assembly of Ladies*, then, the deferral of
judgment by Lady Loiaulte is similarly a delay in the inevitable judgment
in favour of the women. She says:

> In al this wherein ye fynde yow greved
> There shal ye fynde an open remedy,
> In suche wise as ye shul be releved

Of al that ye reherce here triewly.   (722-25)

Clearly Lady Loiaulte will judge in favour of the women and offer remedy
to them at a later date, thus the women leave the assembly content with the
outcome.

This brief examination of some debate and complaint poems illustrates
the manner in which *The Assembly of Ladies* uses both genres in the
presentation of the bills of complaint, but also signals the areas in which
the poem departs from the conventions of those genres, specifically where
the complaint and debate genres do not sufficiently allow the expression of
the female voice. The one significant point that has been raised only
briefly in this section, but which affects the comparison with all of the
poems mentioned here, is the fact that the complaints in *The Assembly of
Ladies* are completely one-sided. In the *Temple of Glas* and *La Belle Dame
Sans Merci* we hear both sides of the love complaints, irrespective of
whether the complaints are resolved happily or not. In the *Owl and the
Nightingale* and the *Parliament of Fowls*, however, their very nature as
debate poems requires that they present several points of view in the
disputes. Yet *The Assembly of Ladies* significantly does not present the
masculine argument. This may appear as a failure on the part of the poet,
yet, as I will show, this stems from the fact that the poet is not attempting
to present empirical evidence to be weighed up dispassionately. In their
complaints the women seek to have their honour restored to them, not to
have their complaints judged as either true or fair.

The presentation of the bills is performed in a notably ceremonial
manner. The nine women, dressed in blue and wearing their personal
mottoes (except for the narrator who refuses to do so) are ushered through
the crowd of women into the assembly room, where Lady Loiaulte
commands the chamberlain to "take these billes unto the secretarye" (553).
This is the first mention that the bills are in a written format and it seems a
significant point for a poem that is focused on women and their
participation in literature. Perseveraunce had previously suggested to the
narrator that they each simply present a complaint concerning whatever
"ye fele your hert is displeased" (125), but there is no suggestion that the
women stopped to write down their complaints prior to the assembly. It
could be argued this is a slip on the part of the poet, as has been argued for
the similar apparent confusion at the end of the poem where the narrator
seems to have already written down her poem,[16] but it seems more likely
that there is a very important ceremonial and visual component to this act
of presenting the bills in a written form, which the poet is drawing
attention to by shifting the bills from an oral to a written format.[17]

All this is seemingly undercut by the following event in the poem, where the bills, solemnly placed upon a tapestry by the secretary, are then read aloud by her.[18] This seems an unusual series of events, in which the complaints began as oral, are miraculously transformed into written documents, but are then presented in an oral fashion after all. It is clear that the events are intended to have a symbolic significance, yet the assumption is that this would be for the purpose of referring to the allegorical genre. There is, however, no obvious reference to be found to the genre of the poem. If there was once an allegorical significance to these events, it appears now to have been lost.[19] I would suggest, however, that this is not the best interpretation of these events. When viewed in terms of legal forms of trothplight, the symbolic meaning of the shift from oral to written and back to oral becomes clearer.

Richard Firth Green uses a particularly helpful example to demonstrate the symbolic significance of oral trothplight in the medieval period, and it is useful to repeat it here.[20] The example is from *Le Livre des Serfs de Marmoutiers* and concerns an event that occurred in the eleventh century in which a man named Baldonet entered the church of the local monastery of St Martin with a set of bell ropes around his neck and four pennies carried on top of his head.[21] He walked to the high altar and made an offering of the ropes and pennies, and the event was witnessed by at least twelve people in the church. This seemingly odd event is an instance of a man plighting his troth to perpetual servitude of the church. The elaborate, performative, manner in which this was done with the carrying of tokens is, according to Green, "part of the practical machinery of daily life in a society that had yet to learn to trust written records."[22] It is easy to see that in a predominantly pre-literate society one would have used other methods for proclaiming a legal arrangement, rather than the signing of an agreement. It is not obviously so easy to see how this may impact on a fifteenth-century text such as *The Assembly of Ladies*, which is a poetic, not a legal document, and which was written at a time when literacy was far more widespread than in eleventh-century France.

The example cited above, however, demonstrates the way in which contract law operated within the medieval period and actually shows that oral agreements were in no way encumbered by the fact that they were not written down. This is a significant element because it suggests that written agreements did not automatically supersede oral agreements, both might be used in different circumstances by a particular social group and I would assert that this is what is occurring within *The Assembly of Ladies*. It is easy for us to see the value of a written document as it records empirical data in an accurate way, although this is not necessarily how a document was viewed in the fifteenth century. A document, once removed from its original context may take on different meanings and the original intent of an agreement may be misinterpreted at a later date.[23]

The value of an oral agreement, however, lay in its direct reference to a particular time, place, and person or group of people. The unusual event recorded at Marmoutiers was able to be recorded at a later date because its unusualness ensured that it remained in the witnesses' memories.[24] Green describes this kind of event and the tokens used in it as containing an essential "thing-ness,"[25] by which he means the tokens and the performance of trothplight turn the agreement into an event that is almost tangible and which is more likely to be remembered in the future by the witnesses. The benefit of an oral agreement over a written agreement is, according to Green, that the oral agreement "remains inextricably enmeshed in the human lifeworld, only recoverable through active human intervention."[26] An agreement centred on a specific group of people can thus be exclusionary unlike a written document that may be read by anyone, and, allowing for faulty memories, an oral agreement is less likely to be misinterpreted than a written document. This shows how an oral agreement can contain a greater sense of certainty and stability than a written document, a feature to be discussed in greater detail later in this chapter.

The bills of complaint in *The Assembly of Ladies*, however, are far more complex than this. These bills shift between oral and written as though it is not clear which form is best for accurately portraying the complaints. I would suggest that the bills in their written format act more as symbolic tokens than as a written form of a legal document. Although it is stated that the complaints are written out–the narrator even states that the bills were "delivered" to Lady Loiaulte–which suggests an understanding of the value of the written document, the fact that they are ceremonially laid out on to a tapestry in a very performative manner indicates the documents carry a more symbolic meaning than a literal meaning.

M. T. Clanchy examines the prevalence of the use of tokens in legal agreements in which physical objects, such as a knife or a turf of soil would be transferred in the view of witnesses to symbolise the legal transaction taking place.[27] Green also details a similar use of tokens in later centuries, and it is significant to note that legal tokens were in use even when written documents were readily available enough to make the use of tokens unnecessary.[28] An interesting example that Clanchy notes is an instance of a written document being used as a legal token, which indicates that value was not found in the words of the document but rather in the document as a physical object to be witnessed in the transferral of property.[29] From these examples it is possible to regard the physical presentation of the bills of complaint in *The Assembly of Ladies* as comparable to legal tokens. The ceremonial manner in which the bills are displayed on the tapestry suggests their physical state is of greater importance than the words they contain.

The complexity of the presentation of the bills of complaint extends further than the transformation between written and oral forms. The first eight bills are apparently read aloud by the secretary–"In oure presence she rede hem everychone" (564), the narrator says–but the voice we hear in the text is that of the narrator reporting from memory the words of the secretary.[30] Yet even then there are many instances that seem confused, where the narrator seems to be recalling the written documents rather than the secretary's spoken reportage. It would seem from line 583 that the narrator is reading aloud when she says of the first ladies' complaint: "thus she wrote in hir bille." Later, the narrator seems to emphasise that she is reading the bills rather than hearing them when she says of the first gentlewoman:

> One of hem wrote *C'est sanz dire*, verily;
> Of hir compleynt also the cause why
> Withyn hir bille she put it in writing,
> And what it saide ye shul have knowlachyng. (627-30)

Were the narrator's concern merely with the reporting of the bills of complaint, there would be no need for her to spend four lines explaining how the bill was written, a description of the contents would be sufficient. Yet it seems that the narrator is emphasising this feature of the bills by self-consciously describing that she will now read out what was written. One effect of this is to remind the reader of the framework of the poem, that the narrator is telling her story to the inquisitive knight accompanying the women into the maze, and therefore the story is, at all times, delivered orally. The issue of the narrative frames of the poem will be discussed in Chapter Five in more detail, but it is appropriate at this point to note that the narrator's intrusion into the bills of complaint adds weight to the idea that oral complaints must be witnessed to become legal, and thus the narrator's act of re-telling the events of her dream is in itself an oral expression–perhaps even a complaint–that is witnessed by the inquisitive knight in the poem. The fact that she is reporting the contents of legal complaints emphasises the legal nature of the complaints, not their concern with love. The effect of the narrator's reportage of the bills to the inquisitive knight is to demand that he be a witness to them, and the nine complaints then become one single complaint of her own.

Another effect of the emphasis on the oral reporting of a written document is that this presentation indicates the performative quality of the entire event; the assembly of women become the legal witnesses to the complaints and the highly formal, ceremonial, manner in which they are presented acts as an aid for the memory. Indeed this will no doubt be of particular importance as Lady Loiaulte defers her judgment to a later date, when she will have to recall these events to mind.

The first bill presented by one of the ladies is a brief complaint about promises made and broken:

> The first lady, beryng in hir devise
> *Sanz que jamais,* thus wrote she in hir bille:
> Compleyneng sore and in ful pitous wise
> Of promesse made with faithful hert and wil
> And so broken ayenst al maner skille,
> Without desert always in hir party,
> In this matier desiring remedy. (582-88)

We do not know the exact nature of the promise that was made and broken and, although the lady is "desiring remedy" (589) for this situation, it does not appear that she wants the offending party to reinstate the promise, or for Lady Loiaulte to hand down a punishment to the offender. The lady's personal motto, *Sanz que jamais* [Without ever (giving occasion)], is an indication that the lady's concern is her own honour and reputation and it is this that she is asking Lady Loiaulte to reinstate. It may seem an unusual concept to consider in a legal sense but it has many precedents in literary works and in historical records, in which a complainant asks not for a logical assessment of the evidence to determine guilt or innocence, but an assessment of the complainant's personal moral worth. An obvious example of this occurs in Chaucer's *The Franklin's Tale*, where the narrator asks "Which was the mooste fre, as thynketh yow?"[31] in the issue of the honour of Averagus, Aurelius, Dorigen, and the philosopher. The question is not intended to create a logical examination of the evidence of the events in the story but to consider their honour as a moral quality.[32]

In a comparable historical example, an incident concerning the honour or "trouth" of a complainant is recorded from a 1386 petition to Parliament, in which the London guild of mercers complain they have been slandered by a former mayor of London, Nicholas Brembre:

And we ben openlich disclaundred, holden vntrewe & traitours to owre Kyng... the which thyng to lyke to yowre worthy lordship by an euen Juge to be proued or disproued, the whether that trowthe may shewe, for trouthe amonges vs of fewe or elles no man many dorst be shewed.[33]

The complaint of the guild members is not a denial of Brembre's accusation of treason against the king, but that their "trouth" has been defiled, and in the petition they are seeking to have their "trouth" reinstated.

The complaint of the second lady begins with her motto, *Une sans chaungier* [One without changing], whose complaint is thus:

Though she had bien gwerdoned for her service,
Yit nothyng, as she takith it, pleyne,
Wherfor she cowde in no wise restreyne
But in this case sue until hir presence,
As reason wold, to have recompence.   (591-95)

This complaint, when compared with the first complaint, shows clearly the manner in which both complaints seek moral redress. Where the first lady's complaint concerned a promise made and broken, a fairly clear issue, it was the moral reinstatement of her honour that she sought. Here, in the second lady's complaint, the concern is that she does not feel she has been rewarded sufficiently for her loyalty. The difference between these two complaints is that the second lady has already passed the empirical judgment on the case herself, she is certain she ought to be rewarded further. Yet ultimately the recompense she is asking is to have her honour verified by Lady Loiaulte, not to receive any tangible reparation. She does not even state the exact nature of the reward she has received in order that it may be judged inadequate because this is not the issue for her. This particular complaint displays the legal difference between "soth" and "trouth."[34] The "soth" of the case is not in question, the lady has judged the case to be valid, but she asks for Lady Loiaulte to judge her "trouth" in the matter, to use legal reasoning to establish the lady's honour and veracity.[35]

The third lady presents her complaint by stating that although she receives "joye, comfort and gladnesse" (604), it is not given consistently, leaving her in constant doubt of her social position:

Hir bille was made compleyneng in her guyse
That of hir joye, comfort and gladnesse
Was no suerte, for in no maner wise
She fonde therin no poynt of stabilnesse,

Now ill nov wele, out of al sikernesse;
Ful humble desiryng of her grace
Som remedy to shewe in this case.   (603-09)

Although she is relatively forthcoming about the exact nature of her
grievance, she does not ask Lady Loiaulte to change her relationship but
seems to be seeking assistance in her emotional state that she may cope
with the inconstancy. Her motto is *Oncques puis lever* [I cannot ever rise],
which indicates the difficulty of her circumstances.

It is significant that the narrator prefaces the third lady's complaint by
saying "As I can remember that matiere / I shal yow telle the processe al in
fere" (601-602). Here the narrator is reminding us of the fact that she is
recalling the events of her dream as a witness might recall the events of
trothplight. It is particularly significant that this should occur in the
complaint primarily concerned with instability in love and I will show that
this indicates a correlation between the instability of relationships for
women and the instability of written texts. In Chapter Five of this book the
narrative frames of *The Assembly of Ladies* will be examined in detail, but
the narrator's intrusion into the story at this point reminds us of the frame
of the poem, and indicates that it, too, is unstable insofar as the narrative
constantly shifts in and out of the dream framework and reminds us of the
way the narrator shifts between oral and written modes of discourse. By
reminding the reader of the textual instability of the poem at precisely the
same moment that the third lady complains about the instability in her
personal relationship suggests that the poet is attempting to draw a
comparison between the relationships women have with people and with
texts. In both instances the relationships are unstable and are controlled by
external masculine regulations, leading the third lady to complain that
while she enjoys the circumstances in which she finds herself, she feels no
certainty of its continuance, and similarly the narrator indicates through
the instability of the text that her participation in the writing process is
regulated by patriarchal literary conventions. The third lady and the
narrator both display similar qualities, the women here experience
difficulty in maintaining stable relationships with either people or texts.

It is useful at this point to consider some other medieval literature that
highlights textual instability because all of these texts utilise legal
language for the purpose of bringing to light the legal differences between
written and oral language. By emphasising the differences between written
and oral language it is possible to see that written language is often
shunned in these texts in favour of oral language. This is a useful
distinction for *The Assembly of Ladies* because there seems to be a clear

preference by the narrator for orality, and a comparison with other texts will allow the reasons for the narrator's preference to become clear.

One text that emphasises the instability of written texts compared with the honesty of the spoken word is the early-fifteenth-century poem *Mum and the Sothsegger*, an alliterative satire heavily influenced by *Piers Plowman*.[36] In this poem the narrator seeks to understand why Mum has usurped the position of the Sothsegger in society, and we learn that the Sothsegger is unable to speak in "termes" (49), will not "glose" (141) a text, and will always "pleynely telleth" (1174) the truth of a matter, whereas Mum will always obfuscate and avoid speaking out. The royal court, which has come under the influence of Mum, is characterised by the "momeling" (595) speech of its members who will not speak the truth. Most significant of all, however, is that the narrator of the poem opens a bag of books that contain "vice and vertue fulle to þe margin" (1346). The books are legal rolls and pamphlets that had allowed courtiers to deceive the king:

> There is a quayer of quittances of quethyn goodes,
> That bisshoppz han begged to binde al newe,
> And a penyworth of papir of penys þat þay fongen
> For lemmans and lotebies in þees late dayes. (1348-1351)

This is just a sample of the extraordinarily long list of falsified documents contained in the bag, and it directly equates written legal documents with untrustworthiness, whereas the simple, oral, speech of the beekeeper, of whom the narrator dreams, is regarded as more genuine and trustworthy. The reason this distinction is made is because of the necessary temporality of the spoken word, its meaning can be much firmer than that of a written document because the context of the utterance is essential for it to have meaning, whereas the written document becomes unstable because it may be interpreted differently on different occasions.[37] In this sense the narrator of *The Assembly of Ladies* emphasises the orality of the complaints; that they are more trustworthy when in a spoken format than a written format in the context of the assembly.

It is even possible to compare the illicit bag of books in *Mum and the Sothsegger* with the bag of idle words collected and written down by the morality play character Titivillus. It is appropriate that a play like *Mankind* (c.1464-71), which is so clearly concerned with knowing the difference between good speech and bad speech should contain a character like Titivillus.[38] In both *Mum and the Sothsegger* and *Mankind* there is the distinction between good words and bad words, and, in the case of the bad words, tend to be in written form, implying their instability. In *The*

Assembly of Ladies the preference for the spoken word over the written word is visibly demonstrated through the transferral of the complaints from a written to an oral format. Although, as we have seen, the narrator blurs the preference for oral presentation by constantly referring back to the complaints in their written format, I would suggest that ultimately she is privileging the oral presentation of the complaints by the fact that she is equating the written word with having the potential for ambiguity and misinterpretation.

In *Piers the Plowman's Crede*, a late-fourteenth-century poem in the alliterative tradition, truth is found in the words of the humble ploughman, not from the supposedly learned friars.[39] All of the four friars encountered by the narrator promise to teach the narrator the Apostles' Creed but only if he agrees to donate money to their orders, and the narrator refuses to participate in such corruption. It is the narrator's introduction that indicates that the concern of the poem is with the difference between good and bad speech. The narrator says:

> A and all myn A-B-C after have I lerned,
> And patred in my Pater Noster iche point after other,
> And after all myn Ave Marie almost to the ende.
> But al my kare is to comen, for I can nohght my Crede. (5-8)

The narrator's concern is that he will be called to give account of himself at the time of his death, at which time he will be unable to recite the Apostles' Creed. While the poem's focus demonstrates a clear Lollard sentiment, one can see within this sentiment the distinction between good speech and bad speech. Good speech is associated with the pure, unsophisticated learning of Piers the ploughman, who is able to teach the narrator the Apostles' Creed, whereas bad speech is associated with the institutionalised learning of the Friars who use their learning for sinful purposes.

Mum and the Sothsegger and *Piers the Plowman's Crede* are both poems heavily influenced by *Piers Plowman* (c. 1370-90), and Langland's poem is perhaps the best medieval example concerning the corruption of social, legal, and religious institutions. I will not discuss *Piers Plowman* in great detail, such an examination is outside the scope of this book, but it is appropriate to consider an example that acknowledges the concept of the instability of the text. The corruption of the legal system in *Piers Plowman* is so entrenched that reasoning is all but impossible. In her defence, Mede gives examples of the way in which money has become important within society; her reasoning is to suggest that the existence of a particular behaviour validates it:

Men that kenne clerkes craven of hem mede.
Preestes that prechen the peple to goode
Asken mede and massepens and hire mete also.
Alle kyn crafty men craven for hir prentices.
Marchaundise and mede mote need go togideres:
No wight, as I wene, withouten Mede may libbe! (222-29)[40]

To contrast this with *The Assembly of Ladies*, the bills of complaint use legal reasoning to indicate the injustice they suffer, whereas in *Piers Plowman*, Mede misuses legal reasoning to validate an injustice. In both instances, however, legal reasoning is the virtue that is upheld, whether it is sought in the case of *The Assembly of Ladies*, or its corruption is ridiculed, as in *Piers Plowman*. As with *Piers the Plowman's Crede* and *Mum and the Sothsegger*, the distinction is made between good speech and bad speech. The language of the law in *Piers Plowman* is not in itself corrupt, but the language is deliberately misused and misinterpreted.[41] The result of this distinction is that language is rendered unstable and dependent on the morals of the speaker.

The motto of the fourth lady, *Entierment vostre* [Entirely yours], causes her some discomfort as she admits that despite her pledge of devotion she is angry that she is unable to see her love when she wishes to. She says:

And upon that she made a grete request,
With hert and wil and al that myght be done,
As until hir that myght redresse it best,
For in hir mynde thus myght she fynde it sone
The remedy of that whiche was hir bone;
Rehersyng that she had seyd before,
Besechyng hir it myght be so no more.   (617-23)

It is not clear if the lady is seeking Lady Loiaulte's assistance to grant her more time with her lover, or to help her control her anger. Yet it might well be that the lady is also seeking Lady Loiaulte's assistance to reconcile her outward persona, exemplified in her motto, with her inner turmoil. Here, as with the previous complaints, the assistance sought may well be more of a moral nature rather than a tangible form of redress.

After the complaints of the four ladies have been presented, the secretary then presents the complaints of the four gentlewomen. The complaint of the first gentlewoman is very similar to that of the second lady, insofar as she also complains of a lack of reward for her loyalty and faithfulness. A significant difference, however, is that the first gentlewoman has clearly experienced this state for much longer than the second lady and she has given up all hope of any redress. And yet she presents this complaint to Lady Loiaulte in the hope that perhaps she may be able to effect a change. She hopes that Lady Loiaulte "for hir wold se a bettir way" (639), although it is not clear what this may be, whether it is a change in the relationship or a change in the gentlewoman to enable her to cope with her circumstances.[42]

The second gentlewoman, whose motto is *En dieu est* [In God is (my trust)], is the first of the women actually to state that it is her "trouth" that has been disregarded. She suggests she is amazed that this could have occurred to her, saying in defence "For trowth somtyme was wont to take availe" (649). This is the only clear instance of any of the characters in the poem using a proverbial statement and it appears in this context as revealing a double standard.[43] The gentlewoman's understanding of "trouth" from the proverb is at odds with the way "trouth" is actually valued in her day to day circumstances. The nature of "trouth" will be considered in greater detail shortly, but in this instance the gentlewoman is clearly certain that the wrongs she has suffered will be remedied either by God or by Lady Loiaulte.[44]

The third gentlewoman is apparently reluctant to put her complaint in writing, yet she has grudgingly done so, and it appears her complaint concerns the fact that her love is in another location and she may not see him when she would like. Her motto is *Sejour ensure* [Rest assured], and seems to imply the security and certainty she would like to have. There is a clear similarity between this complaint and that of the fourth lady. Both women complain that they may not see their love when they would wish, although each of their responses is slightly different. Where the fourth lady was angry that she was unable to see her over, the third gentlewoman seems far more desperate, by being initially unwilling to put her complaint into words. The reluctance of the gentlewoman to write her complaint down may be due to her resignation that such an act will be insufficient to express her concerns fully.

The fourth gentlewoman, rather strangely, has no complaint to make at all. Her motto is *Bien monest* [Well advised] which suggests perhaps she has already been given and put into practice the type of advice that Lady Loiaulte is likely to give. Her only request is to ask Lady Loiaulte for the continuance of her current situation. The participation of the fourth gentlewoman's bill of complaint seems out of place within the context of the other complaints, when she actually is not raising a grievance at all. I can find no other instance of this in literature contemporary with *The Assembly of Ladies*, and thus this demands some further attention to consider exactly why her bill has been included at all. The narrator says of her:

> The fourth surely, me thought, she liked wele,
> As in hir port and in hir havyng,
> And *Bien monest*, as ferre as I cowthe feele,
> That was hir worde, til hir wele belongyng;
> Wherfor til her she prayde above al thyng,
> Ful hertily, to say yow in substaunce,
> That she wold sende hir goode contenuance. (673-679)

The fourth gentlewoman is described in a conventional manner, where her physical appearance, her "port" and her "having," are used as a judgment of her personal character.[45] From her appearance we are to deduce that she is content with her circumstances and thus asks Lady Loiaulte for her situation to continue as it is. Of the eight complaints examined here, the previous seven share similar concerns, and I would even suggest it is possible to see a correlation among the complaints of the ladies and the complaints of the gentlewomen. Both the ladies and the gentlewomen desire their "trouth" to be reinstated or acknowledged, they wish for stability and certainty in their circumstances, and for their loyalty to be rewarded. One of the most significant features of the complaints is the amount of repetition among them. There are essentially only three issues of concern to them and they could easily have been made by a single complaint. I would suggest this indicates that there is some weight attached by the poet to the cumulative effect of several complaints that are all similar.[46] There also seems to be a sense of unity and solidarity among the women–perhaps this is what causes the eighth woman to contribute to the complaints for the sake of loyalty to her companions even though she has no complaint as an individual. It is useful at this point to refer back to the petition brought by the London mercers against the former major of London Nicholas Brembre. In that example the complaint laid by the guild of mercers is a collective complaint that does not identify any of the mercers individually. The complaint states that Brembre said "that xx or xxx of vs were worthy to be drawn & hanged,"[47] yet at no time are any individual names mentioned. The petition begins with "we ben openlich disclaundred, holden vntrewe & traitors to owre Kyng" which widens the scope of the complaint even further. Twenty or thirty men may have been slandered by the Brembre, but the complaint indicates that all of the members of the mercers' guild have been offended by this act and wish to have their "trouth" verified by the court. We do not know how many members there were of the mercers' guild in London in 1386, but the indication from the petition is that there were more than the twenty or thirty suggested by Brembre. The reason for the mercers' complaint including all of its members in the petition is rhetorical, the slander appears far more serious if it is made to appear that all of their members have been harmed by Brembre's accusations. I would suggest that the same effect is employed in *The Assembly of Ladies* so that while each of the women have their complaints presented seemingly as individuals, in fact they are making a collective complaint by repeating and restating each others' concerns, and this extends to the fourth gentlewoman adding her voice to the complaints even though she has no personal complaint to make about her own circumstances. At the beginning of the poem the narrator describes the women as "My felawship and I" (30), which creates the sense that these women form a close group, and although the narrator begins to describe them walking through the garden maze as though they are the only partakers in the activity, she then adds, almost as an afterthought, "And yit in trowth we were nat alone: / Theyr were knyghtis and squyers many one" (13-14). Although the men accompany the women into the maze, this description of them creates a sense of separation that maintains the women's unity as a group on their own. The indication, then, from the complaint of the fourth gentlewoman is that the complaints must be considered collectively and even incrementally; as we will see, the narrator's complaint is the climax of the complaints.

Having noted the social hierarchy among the women as consisting of ladies and gentlewomen, it is appropriate at this point to consider this further. The social position of the lady in medieval literature could range from queen to the head of a household, however humble. The position is one of authority that demands the reverence of others.[48] In *The Assembly of Ladies*, the title of the poem suggests that all of the participants at the assembly are ladies and are thus social equals, and yet clearly Lady Loiaulte is the authority figure to which all of the other participants show reverence. Similarly, the social position of the gentlewomen is slightly blurred in this poem. The position of gentlewomen seems to be that of an aid to a lady, yet the role clearly carries a certain amount of authority in itself.[49] The interesting significance of the role of the gentlewomen in *The Assembly of Ladies*, however, is that there seems to be little distinction made between the ladies and the gentlewomen. Certainly the narrator establishes their social positions from the outset of the poem, but there are few other occasions when the subordination of the gentlewomen is demonstrated. In an entirely unannounced and slightly vague portion of the poem in which the narrator stops to change into her blue clothing before approaching Pleasaunt Regarde, a gentlewoman mysteriously appears to assist the narrator with her clothes. The two women admire the blue clothing in a clearly reciprocal and friendly manner, but the gentlewoman then slips from the narrative as mysteriously as she had appeared. The narrator arrives at Pleasaunt Regarde and nothing more is mentioned of the gentlewoman, until the full company gather at the assembly to present their bills.[50] Aside from this unusual event, the only other suggestion of a hierarchy among the women is the fact the ladies present their bills before the gentlewomen.

An unusual point about this company of women, however, is that they are nine in number. There are five ladies, but only four gentlewomen. Were the number even, it would be possible to speculate that the gentlewomen were servants to each of the ladies, but this suggestion cannot be made with certainty. While there are instances of the women clearly demonstrating their hierarchical social roles, generally the women give the impression of coexisting in an equal manner. All of the women enter into the maze together, it is not stated as though the ladies enter followed or accompanied by their gentlewomen, and all of the women present complaints that are effectively a single collective complaint. It is not certain, then, of the exact nature of the relationship between the ladies and the gentlewomen. It appears to be much more intimate and socially equal than their titles would suggest, and I would assert that this blurring of the social roles of the women is a significant feature of the poem, indicating a collectivity between all women regardless of their social positions and of the narrator's refusal to conform to the regulations of Pleasaunt Regarde.[51]

In addition, it is interesting to note the parallel between the narrator and her company and the images of Cupid's martyrs on the walls of Pleasaunt Regarde. As has been noted in Chapter Three, the stories of the women depicted on the wall of Pleasaunt Regarde are reduced in meaning by the masculine conventions in which they exist. As a result, the women's stories become stereotypes; whatever the individual circumstances of their lives and social positions, beneath the cover of umple they are noted only for their deaths.[52] These figures act as a parallel to the company of women attending the assembly, they all have their own particular social positions, but in the act of presenting their bills of complaint their concerns are reduced by the literary conventions they are forced to use.[53]

The narrator's own complaint is the climax of the assembly and it marks a significant shift in the narrative style of the poem. Although it has already been noted that the women form a collective unit, there is, however, a sense that the narrator is somehow isolated from the group

while still being part of it.[54] She herself draws attention to this from the
outset of the poem where she describes herself among the other ladies as
"I, the fift, symplest of alle" (7), already demarking her position as part of
the company, yet at the same time somehow removed from it. Her
complaint also sets her apart from the other women in the company and is
noted by many scholars for its erratic nature and for the narrator's unusual
behaviour, which will be examined shortly.[55]

It is appropriate first, however, to consider an unusual portion of
dialogue that occurs just prior to the narrator's complaint. In two stanzas
there is a dialogue between (at least) two characters, none of whom is
named. Pearsall suggests the dialogue is between Lady Loiaulte and the
narrator, but Barratt has suggested that the dialogue is between the narrator
and Lady Loiaulte, with some direct references to the inquisitive knight
who is listening to the tale.[56] Certainly the poem is unclear at this point,
and even observation of the manuscripts in which *The Assembly of Ladies*
appears sheds no light on the matter. All of the manuscripts agree in the
presentation of this passage, so whether the ambiguity of the passage is
deliberate or that all of the manuscripts were copied from similarly corrupt
exemplars is cannot be known.[57] The passage is as follows:

> "Ye have rehersed me these billis alle,
> But now late se somwhat of your entente."
> "It may so happe peraventure ye shal."
> "Ye shal, parde, have knowlache what I ment;
> But thus I say in trowth, and make no fable,
> The case it silf is inly lamentable,
>
> And wele I wote that ye wil think the same
> Like as I say whan ye han herd my bil."
> "Now, goode, telle on, I hate yow, be seynt Jame."
> "Abide a while, it is nat yit my wil;
> Yet must ye wite, bi reason and bi skil,
> Sith ye knowe al that hath be done afore."
> And thus it sayde, without any more: (680-93)

The punctuation here is Boffey's; none of the manuscripts contains
punctuation beyond capitalisations, which creates further confusion for
establishing the identities of the speakers. It is certain there are at least two
speakers, and I am inclined to agree with Barratt that there may even be
three speakers in this section–the narrator, Lady Loiaulte and the
inquisitive knight–for the reason that this exchange bears a great deal of
resemblance to the opening exchange between the narrator and the knight.
In that portion of dialogue the knight is impatient to know the story, "Telle

on, late se, and make no taryeng" (23), to which the narrator says "'Abide,' quod I, 'ye be an hasti one; / I lete yow wite it is no little thyng...'" (24-25). Clearly this is very reminiscent of the exchange between the narrator and the anonymous speaker, who says, "Now, goode, telle on, I hate yow, be seynt Jame" (689), to which the narrator replies, "Abide a while, it is nat yit my wil" (690). The similarity between the two episodes is clear, although this does not, of course, prove the identity of the unknown speaker. It is equally plausible that the narrator is speaking to someone entirely within the dream framework and the poet is, by echoing the earlier exchange, emphasising the narrator's desire to be in control of her story, to reveal it when she is ready to do so.

There is one other feature of this episode that deserves some attention. This is the point at which Lady Loiaulte says: "Ye have rehersed me these billis alle, / But now late se somwhat of your entente" (680-81). The significance of the use of the expression "your entente" at this point opens the speech up for further examination. To have used the word "your" admits an ambiguity to the dialogue where it is not clear if the speaker is addressing the narrator, who has not yet presented her bill, or if she is addressing the entire company. Perhaps she is suggesting that, having heard the eight formal presentations of the bills, she now wishes to know what they really mean, the women's "entente." Helen Barr discusses the difference between the written or spoken word and its intent or underlying meaning, and notes that "In its physical manifestation, words, and language more generally, are not identical to the incorporeal intention that precedes it."[58] A good example of this is found in *Mum and the Sothsegger*, in which the narrator asks of the king that the "entente" of his words be understood:

And if ony word write be þat wrothe make myghte
My souereyne, þat suget I shulde to be,
I put me in his power and preie him, of grace,
To take þe entent of my trouþe...   (76-9)

Here a clear distinction is made between the written word and the underlying "entente" of the word, which acknowledges the instability inherent in the written word where its underlying intent is not obvious and requires interpretation. It is appropriate to consider the same feature in *The Assembly of Ladies* since one of the fundamental issues of the poem is its underlying, subconscious element. If regarded in this way, it would appear that the narrator's bill of complaint, which, unlike the others, is delivered in the first person, contains the "entente" of the other bills. If we accept that there is, indeed, a third speaker in this portion of dialogue, the inquisitive knight, then it would appear that that speaker also considers that the narrator's bill will explain the intent of the other eight bills, his impatience to hear her bill would suggest this.

The narrator's bill of complaint is the central focus of the dream-vision and of the entire poem. In contrast to the other bills of complaint already presented, here the narrator's complaint is reported in the first person. She says:

> "Nothyng so lief as death to come to me
> For fynal end of my sorwes and peyne;
> What shuld I more desire, as seme ye-
> And ye knewe al aforne it for certeyne
> I wote ye wold; and for to tell yow pleyne,
> Without hir help that hath al thyng in cure
> I can nat thynk that it may long endure;
>
> And for my trouth, preved it hath bien wele-
> To sey the soth, it can be no more-
> Of ful long tyme, and suffred every dele
> In pacience and kept it al in store;
> Of hir goodenesse besechyng hir therfor
> That I myght have my thank in suche wise
> As my desert deservith of justice."   (694-707)

The meaning of the narrator's bill is difficult to decipher if one is attempting to judge it alongside the other eight bills already presented. But if one regards the narrator's bill as containing the emotional, underlying "entente" of the other women's bills, then its function becomes much easier to understand. In the first stanza the narrator attempts to show the emotional dead-end in which the women feel they are trapped. The narrator indicates that this is the underlying state of mind of the company of women, who each suggest in their bills that they seek redress for their circumstances, yet avoid stating the consequences if that redress is not forthcoming. The narrator states on behalf of the group that "Without hir help that hath al thyng in cure / I can nat thynk that it may long endure" (699-700), that is, death would be a better option for them.[59]

The narrator emphasises the "trouth" of her words in the second stanza of her speech, a word that has been discussed briefly here already, yet further discussion is appropriate at this point because the narrator quickly follows with a reference to "soth," and the significance of the two words used in such proximity is important. Green examines the word "trouth," which he says has always had several meanings, all of which can be implied simultaneously. "Trouth" is certainly a medieval legal term to indicate a contractual agreement, but Green also identifies further ethical, theological, and intellectual meanings for the word, which are supported by the *Middle English Dictionary*. While the expression "to plight one's troth" indicates a legal understanding of the word, the expression also indicates that an ethical sense of "trouth" developed from the legal sense, in which "trouth" "was thought of not as an independent entity to which they individually subscribed, but a combination of their separate consents."[60] The development of this meaning suggests the word "trouth" came to include an understanding of "the quality that makes the agreement workable."[61] Here it is possible to see how "trouth" came to be associated with the word honour, a word found frequently in medieval literature. When the Black Knight in the *Book of the Duchess* demands that the narrator "Swere thy trouthe therto,"[62] the legal sense of swearing an oath is there, but there is also a sense of being seen to do the honourable thing. Similarly, when Criseyde betrays Troilus, he asks of her "Where is youre love? Where is youre trouthe?,"[63] which ambiguously could be referring to her broken promise or to her infidelity. It is not hard to see the development of the ethical sense of "trouth" into a theological sense, in which "a truth" became "the Truth." It is in the theological sense of the word "trouth" that the word "soth" appears. It has been noted by scholars that in Old and Middle English translations from Latin texts, "trouth" was often the desired translation of *justititia*, and "soth" the desired translation of *veritas*, and here the different meanings of the words are quite clear. "Soth" contains the sense of an empirical weighing of evidence, whereas "trouth" contains the understanding of righteousness or being correct in the eyes of God.[64] Yet it is true that in the later middle ages the word "trouth" started to supplant the word "soth," to embody an understanding of empirical truth as it is used today, as well as to continue as a word indicating honour and a legal contract. The intellectual understanding of "trouth," is equated with the empirical weighing of evidence to deduce the truth of a matter.

It is significant, then, to note that the narrator of *The Assembly of Ladies* uses both the word "trouth" and "soth" within her speech to Lady Loiaulte. This raises the question of whether these two words have a different meaning implied in them, or are they synonyms used for emphasis. The narrator says: "And for my trouth, preved it hath bien wele- / To sey the soth, it can be no more-" (701-702). The subject of the stanza appears to be the narrator's "trouth," and here it seems to be loaded with several of the meanings discussed above. There is the definite sense that "trouth" is a contractual agreement or a sworn oath that she and the other women have taken but which has been abused, and they ask Lady Loiaulte to address this issue. Yet they do not ask Lady Loiaulte to punish the criminal in a judicial sense, and this indicates that the narrator is also drawing on the understanding of "trouth" as a form of public honour, and it is this that the women wish to have restored to them. The contractual agreement may have been broken by another party, but the issue for the women is not that this contract be restored but that any blame for the broken contract not be laid against them. From the way the narrator uses both "trouth" and "soth," it seems that "soth" is used to infer empirical truth, particularly because the narrator says "preved it hath bien wele" (701). The proof she talking about is proof of her "trouth," yet it requires that the proof itself be described as "soth"–there is empirical evidence that proves the narrator's honour. This would suggest that the meaning of "trouth" does not encroach on the meaning of "soth" in this instance. I would suggest, therefore, that the narrator uses the word "trouth" to mean honour, and is a means of signalling the instability of the text by drawing attention to the existence of a division between "trouth" and "soth."

Even if the narrator's bill is regarded as containing the emotional "entente" of the other women's bills, there is still the unusual feature of the narrator's behaviour leading up to her presentation. Even if we accept that it is difficult to determine the number and identities of the speakers, the narrator is certainly reluctant to speak when invited to do so. The narrator is addressed (presumably) by Lady Loiaulte who asks her to speak, which suggests that the narrator has not submitted her bill in writing as the other women have. Yet even then she is reluctant to begin and it is not clear why this is the case. Pearsall describes her behaviour at this point as "rude"[65] and Stephens as "downright childish."[66] Barratt regards the narrator's behaviour as "coy reluctance" towards the inquisitive knight.[67] Certainly these suggestions are all possible but I would further suggest that, whether she is being rude, childish, or coy, the episode acts as a performative delaying technique. Just as Baldonet's act of walking into St Martin's church with bell ropes around his neck and pennies on his head was a visual display of his trothplight designed to commit the event to the memory of those witnessing, so in this passage the narrator draws attention to herself for the purpose of memorialising her complaint.[68] There are other features to support this possibility. The women had been instructed that they were required to wear blue clothing and bear their personal motto on their clothing. While the other women do so, the narrator insists she will only wear the blue dress, she refuses to wear a motto. Visually, such a refusal would have been very obvious and thus, along with her unusual behaviour, would have created a dramatic performance in the court, certainly one that would be easily remembered, which, I would suggest, is the objective.

In addition, the narrator's erratic behaviour during this portion of the poem can be seen to signify her inability to express herself fully within the boundaries of the complaint genre. The eight other women have stated their cases according to convention, but the narrator is unable to conform. For the narrator to present her complaint, she must overstep the boundaries and therefore her behaviour appears as incongruous within Lady Loiaulte's assembly.

Significantly, Lady Loiaulte realises the practical difficulty of addressing all of the women individually, and decides it best to address the women together, reinforcing the fact that the women form a collective unit whose complaints may be addressed together. She says:

> We have wele sen youre billis by and by
> And som of hem ful pitous for to here.
> We wil therfor ye knowen this al in feere:
> Withyn short tyme oure court of parlement
> Here shal be holde in oure paleys present,
>
> And in al this wherein ye fynde yow greved
> There shal ye fynde an open remedy,
> In suche wise as ye shul be releved
> Of al that ye reherce heere triewly.
> As of the date ye shal knowe verily,
> Than ye may have a space in your coming,
> For Diligence shall bryng it yow bi writing.   (717-28)

Lengthy though this passage is, it is useful to consider it in its entirety because it contains a great deal about the assumptions made in the bills of complaints. Lady Loiaulte defers her judgment to another date, but in doing so creates the impression that the nine bills of complaint are, indeed, one single complaint. There is no indication in her speech that shows she regards the complaints individually or that the women require individual remedies. Interestingly, the women all accept Lady Loiaulte's deferral: "In suche wise as we hielde us content" (733), which seems unusual as there is the distinct sense in the complaints that these women would not be able to cope much longer without redress. I would suggest that in fact the women are content to have had their complaints voiced in public, where they have been witnessed and thus it is no concern that they may have to wait for a verdict. With their complaints heard and witnessed, there is no doubt that a resolution will come. Lady Loiaulte herself indicates that the verdict will be in favour. There is no doubting of the veracity of their complaints, the "soth"–the empirical evidence–of the women's complaints has proven their honour or "trouth."

Conclusions

The bills of complaint in *The Assembly of Ladies* signal clearly an intertextual relationship with contemporary fifteenth-century texts, both literary and legal, in order to show the instability inherent in the written text. A comparison with medieval debate poetry demonstrates the scholarly mechanics of the bills, heightening awareness of the way the complaints function as literary compositions. Other love complaint poetry indicates the tradition in which *The Assembly of Ladies* is situated and from which it deviates. Poetry that draws on legal forms of language indicates the division between the written and the spoken word, in which the written word is seen to be less stable in its potential meaning than the spoken word. The *Assembly of Ladies* appears to exploit this division, utilising both forms without a clear indication of preference. Although I would suggest that the spoken word is generally privileged over the written word in the narrative of the poem, this is clearly not a simple matter. The poem is, ultimately, a written document despite the fact that the narrator presents herself as retelling the poem orally to the knight. The blurring of the mode of discourse at the end of the poem perhaps best highlights that the poem does not unquestioningly prefer oral speech over the written word, as the narrator, without pause, indicates a change from narrating her tale to writing it down, a shift that also occurs in the presentation of the bills of complaint which shift between oral and written formats. The purpose of this type of presentation, I would suggest, is to destabilise the text, which allows for the possibility of a glimpse of the subconscious layer of narrative. By drawing attention to the subconscious narrative, the poet references the female voice which is subjected to the destabilising effect of the written word. The blurred distinction between the spoken and written word, I would suggest, indicates the manner in which the indistinct quality of the women is subjected to masculine constraints whether orally or in written format. Although the spoken word is presented as more trustworthy, even it is still controlled and determined by masculine forces, as demonstrated by the presence of the listening knight. His presence has the effect of determining the nature of the narrator's story because of his role as an aural audience. As Ong indicates, every telling of a verbal narrative is different according to the demands of the audience, which attributes a great deal of control to the listener.[69]

CHAPTER FIVE

PERSPECTIVA, PERSPECTIVE, AND THE NARRATIVE FRAMES: SCIENCE AND ART IN A LITERARY CONTEXT

The Assembly of Ladies is able to emphasise the presence of its narrative frames by drawing significantly on two particular forms of visual theory, *Perspectiva*, that is, the medieval scientific theory of optics, and linear perspective, as employed by painters in the production of visual images. Neither *Perspectiva* nor perspective is directly referred to by name, suggesting an assumption of the reader's prior knowledge of such contextual topics, but I argue that several important features of each theory are used in *The Assembly of Ladies* to create the narrative frames. In particular, I argue that several features of *Perspectiva* and perspective allow and even demand a moral judgment by the reader/viewer on each narrative frame of the poem.

The focus in this chapter will be on the structuring narrative frames in the poem and the female narrator, who traverses the many frames of the poem, is a constant reminder to the reader that one of the poem's most significant issues is the marginalisation of female participation in literature. The narrator's presence is a constant reminder that within each of the frames of the poem, her impact and participation is limited and our view of her is always partially obscured. A basic analysis of the frames of *The Assembly of Ladies* can be shown as follows:

1. Lines 1-28: 2.00 o'clock on a September afternoon
2. Lines 29-77: an afternoon in the maze, perhaps in springtime
3. Lines 78-735: the dream vision
2. Lines 736-739: awakening in the arbour of the maze
1. Lines 740-755: discourse with the listening knight
4. Line 756: direct address to the audience

There are four clearly defined frames within *The Assembly of Ladies*. The first is the September setting in which the narrator is confronted by the inquisitive knight and the second is the narrator's account of her and her companions' previous attempt to negotiate the maze. The most substantial frame is, of course, the recounting of the dream, indicated as frame three. The poem then reverts back to frame two in which the narrator awakens from her dream but is still, presumably, in the arbour of the maze and thus still recounting the tale to the inquisitive knight. With the inquisitive knight's speech, the poem shifts back to the first frame of the September setting. The final, fourth, frame exists only in the final line of the poem, although its existence at all suggests that perhaps, in retrospect, it encompasses the entire poem. This frame performs perhaps that most important function of all the narrative frames, because this frame directly addresses the reader and requires the events of the poem to be judged by the reader.

The structure of the narrative frames, however, is frequently interrupted and there are numerous moments when, it will be argued, the narrator shifts momentarily from one frame to another. The shifting from one frame to another, I would suggest, is an indication of the narrator's inability to express herself fully within any one single frame. The narrator shifts between frames frequently in an attempt to find an effective means of communication, yet these shifts do not succeed and result, instead, in emphasising her marginalisation within the poem.

Perspectiva, the name given to the works of several natural philosophers concerning theories of light and vision, will be considered here for the way that theories of light and vision promoted an apparently contradictory means of knowing and understanding the visible universe.[1] The study of *Perspectiva* encouraged learning about the universe through experience and experiment, yet the result of such investigations, while the basis for our modern scientific method, simultaneously demonstrated the limitations of such investigations.[2] *Perspectiva* created a means of knowing the world but also revealed how much more there was still to know. It is primarily this contradiction that will be investigated here as the acknowledged limitations of knowledge are paralleled in the framing narratives of *The Assembly of Ladies*.

Theories of linear perspective similarly operate apparently to reveal visual truth in painting, yet here, too, perspective can be shown to conceal and limit sight.[3] Linear perspective is also strongly associated with linear narrative, and here an examination of the relationship between the visual and verbal means of expression will reveal that the limitations of visual perspective are also found in verbal perspective. In both visual and verbal expression, the frame is a device used to signify the limitations of knowledge.

This chapter will show that, while both *Perspectiva* and perspective attempt to advance methods of understanding the world, both methods simultaneously reveal their own limitations. Both *Perspectiva* and perspective offer significantly flawed ways of understanding the world– flawed because each method inherently draws attention to its incompleteness. The flaws of both of these methods of understanding are a signal to the role of the narrator, who is unable to express herself fully within the narrative frames of the poem, indicating that, despite seeking an effective means of communication, the narrative frames are, themselves, a flawed method of understanding.

The Assembly of Ladies draws together the theories of *Perspectiva* and perspective to signify the limitations of knowledge in a poetic context. Through the presence of the narrator, the poem considers these ways of knowing in a gendered context. By using *Perspectiva* and perspective to signify the limitations of knowledge, *The Assembly of Ladies* is able to align the limitations of knowledge with the limitations of female participation in literature. The *Assembly of Ladies* uses the female narrator to suggest that methods of knowing, such as *Perspectiva* and perspective, are inherently masculine. The limitations on such ways of knowing, the poem asserts, signify the limitations on female participation in the literary process. Just as *Perspectiva* describes the limits of physical vision, and perspective describes the limits of painting, *The Assembly of Ladies* asserts the limits of literary participation.

Perspectiva

It is not necessary or appropriate here to examine the many diverse theories of *Perspectiva* and optics in their mathematical detail, which range from the discoveries of Al-Kindi through to Newton's theory of optics. Such detail is beyond the scope of this book. It is, however, useful to consider some of the general principles of *Perspectiva* that circulated in the medieval period to demonstrate the impact such theories had on literature and, more specifically, on *The Assembly of Ladies*. That such theories were widely circulated and known can be determined by references in such texts as, for example, *Le Roman de la Rose*, *The Squire's Tale* and *The House of Fame*, to name a few.[4] It is also significant to note that these three texts all present ideas relating to theories of *Perspectiva* without *Perspectiva* becoming the focus of each text. The inclusion of theories of *Perspectiva* in these texts is a small addition in support of other themes of the texts, suggesting that theories of *Perspectiva* were sufficiently well-known not to require a great deal of attention or explanation.[5] Theories of *Perspectiva* appear to have been disseminated widely enough that they filtered through to a wide range of medieval life. In *The Assembly of Ladies*, theories of *Perspectiva* do not feature in the sense of forming an overt part of the narrative, but rather appear more epistemologically, influencing the psychological state of the characters and in the structure of the narrative frame.[6]

The term *Perspectiva* is used in this study to situate the theory in the medieval period, and to differentiate it from its modern equivalent, the study of optics.[7] *Perspectiva* was a field of study that covered a wide range of topics, including the nature and propagation of light and colour, the eye and vision, the properties of mirrors and refracting surfaces, image formation by reflection and refraction, and meteorological phenomena involving light.[8] Here it will be necessary to consider only the nature of light and vision, but the wide scope of *Perspectiva* is significant to note because it indicates a unified approach to the range of topics. *Perspectiva* investigated and incorporated mathematics, physics, physiology, psychology, and epistemology of light and the visual process.[9] The wide scope of *Perspectiva* is of interest here because it correlates with one of the main aims of *Perspectiva*: to develop a way of knowing and understanding the nature of the universe.

Early-twelfth-century texts from Adelard of Bath determined sight to be the most important of all the senses for its ability to observe light.[10] The fundamental significance of light had been asserted by Augustine, who regarded light as "the most nearly immaterial of physical substances"[11] and, therefore, that it "contained most overflowingly the creative energy of God."[12] With this understanding, light was equated with space, "the irradiation of physical light through the universe, the result of the irradiation of God's creative energy, created the spatial universe of material form."[13] Alexander Neckam (1157-1217) noted, however, that despite the pervasive nature of light, the eye did not necessarily discern the truth. Water, in particular, Neckam realised, could distort the image of an object.[14] Neckam clearly responded to the concept of space surrounding objects, but was yet to understand the implications of perspective in which the eye is unable to see all that the mind knows is there. The limits of such inquiries were remedied by Robert Grosseteste in the early-thirteenth century through Grosseteste's access to texts of Euclid, Aristotle and Al-Kindi. Grosseteste was able to conceive of the world "created by the self-diffusion of a point of light into a spherical form."[15] He considered light as an emanating ray which impacted upon the objects it encountered. It is a significant step as it explains Neckam's concern about objects appearing different under different circumstances and is fundamentally grounded in the Augustinian notion of light being the source of life. Despite such advances, Grosseteste was, himself, hampered by a limited numbers of sources; it was not until Ptolemy's *Optica* and Alhazen's *Perspectiva* were translated and became widely known that theories concerning the nature of light could advance.[16] Indeed, such was the abundance of material available by the late-thirteenth century that later natural philosophers such as Roger Bacon, Witelo and John Pecham significantly advanced the study of *Perspectiva* and increasingly utilised a more complex mathematical basis.

The ability to understand light and space through a mathematic and linguistic vocabulary led to the concept of intelligible light:

> Light, therefore, while not form was the agency for creating form–creating forms or ideas or concepts in the mind precisely as in the physical worlds it created forms, space, and a complex organization of physical things. Light was a mental force as well as a physical one.[17]

The examination of the nature of light was clearly situated within a Christian ethos; light, as Grinnell explains, contained "the creative energy of God."[18] Thus the use of mathematical concepts to define and measure light and space were fundamentally methods of knowing God.

The examination of the nature of light and, therefore, the space it defines, allows for the possibility of the measurement of that light and space. Holley emphasises this feature of *Perspectiva* as measurement is a means of quantifying and judging that relies heavily upon sight: "Perspectivists sought a way of knowing by explaining the way we see."[19] To be able to explain the force of light by measuring it was to reveal the structure of the created universe by experience.

Linear Perspective

The study of perspective and its development are, of course, too large to cover in great depth within this book, but it is appropriate and necessary to consider some of the most significant aspects that will be seen to bear on *The Assembly of Ladies*. A useful starting point is to consider some the fundamental assertions made by Leon Battista Alberti in his *De Pictura* of 1435.[20] Alberti's theories of perspective were certainly not the first to be made, but rather were the result of a development that can easily be traced back through the works of numerous European painters.[21] Nevertheless, Alberti's book considers and furthers many significant ideas about perspective.

Fundamentally, Alberti asserts the use of mathematical measurement in the construction of a painting, and concurs with medieval *Perspectiva* in terms of regarding the eye of the viewer as the apex of a cone or pyramid. The cone is the field of vision of the viewer, and the picture plane, that is, the surface of the painting, intersects the cone of vision. Perhaps the most significant aspect of this definition is that it actually calls the viewer into being; the viewer must now actively engage with the painting, and is the point of comparison for the objects in the painting. As John White explains:

> Alberti points out that all the appearances of things are purely relative, and that it is the human figure [the viewer] which alone provides the measure of whatever else the artist cares to represent.[22]

The emphasis of the position of the viewer is seen clearly in Alberti's assertion that the picture plane is like:

> quidem mihi pro aperta finestra est ex qua historia contueatur, illique quam magnos velim esse in picture homines determine.

> [an open window through which the *historia* is seen, and there I determine how large I want the figures in the painting to be.][23]

A further emphasis in Alberti's definition of perspective is in the acknowledged presence of space. Space had always been an acknowledged component of the painted object, but, according to White, Alberti's theory asserted that: "Space is created first, and then the solid objects of the pictured world are arranged within it in accordance with the rules which it dictates. Space now contains the objects by which formerly it was created."[24]

Perspective, for Alberti, used the idea of the imitation of reality as a starting point, but Alberti appears not to have been aware of the limitations of perspective. Perspective requires an acceptance of geometrical conventions that do not necessarily correlate with the artist's visual experience of the world. According to White: "The theoretical perfection of the system, as a system, takes no cognizance of the aesthetic sensibility, and the fundamental honesty of the eye."[25]

Linear perspective, then, produces images that can be mathematically measured, but do not necessarily conform to what the eye would see. An example of this can be seen in Andrea del Castagno's painting of *The Last Supper*.[26] The painting is a unified whole insofar as it positions the viewer's eye at the height of the table and in the centre of the painting, and all of the objects in the painting are positioned according to the viewer's stationary eye. There is, however, a significant difficulty in the way the people are depicted which demonstrates one of the limitations of linear perspective. In order for the painter to have made all of the people visible from the position of the viewer, he has had to position them, frieze-like, along one side of the table. Mathematically, this representation is perfectly acceptable, but aesthetically it is uncomfortable to view because the viewer's experience indicates the artificiality of the composition.

A particularly significant feature of visual perspective, however, is its relationship with the written text. To refer back to Alberti's statement that the picture plane is like: "...quidem mihi pro aperta finestra est ex qua historia contueatur, illique quam magnos velim esse in picture homines determine,"[27] it is notable that Alberti uses the expression "*historia,*" that is, story. According to Charles Hope, this is an entirely conventional use of the word *historia* and indicates a well-known concept in painting:

> In texts about painting throughout western Europe from late antiquity onwards pictures were regularly divided into two broad categories: stories, or representations of historical events, and images or figures, that is to say non-narrative representations of people.[28]

The association between painting and writing is, of course, significant for this examination of *The Assembly of Ladies* and it is notable that Alberti regards both activities as having the same goal. Alberti was not alone in this interpretation. Cennino Cennini, in his *Il Libro dell'arte* (1437), states that it is necessary for the painter to use imagination in the same way as the poet.[29]

The relationship between the written text and the painting is addressed in the early-fifteenth-century text of *Dives and Pauper*.[30] The issue debated by Dives and Pauper is whether or not the presence of paintings in churches is in contradiction of the First Commandment prohibiting the worshipping of images. Dives begins by stating that they are forbidden to worship anyone other than God: "...noo grauyn þing, noo lyknesse þat is abouyn in heuene ne þat is benethyn in erthe ne of noo thyng þat is in þe water vnder þe erthe."[31] But Pauper's reply insists that some images are exempt, such as when Moses made the image of two angels:

> God defendyht nought meen to makyn ymages, for he bad Moyses maykn ymages of too aungelys þat been clepyd cherubin in þe lyknesse of too hongge meen, as we fynden, Exodi xxxvii.[32]

Pauper's replies to Dives' argument are so persuasive that Dives gives up and asks in desperation: "How shulde I rede in þe book of peynture and of ymagerye?"[33] to which Pauper begins a long analysis of the interpretation

of religious iconography. What is significant about this excerpt is Dives'
reply, in which he asks how to "rede" the paintings. Pauper's response to
present numerous interpretations of paintings further supports Dives'
inference, which is that paintings are narratives.

In her analysis of medieval pictorial composition, Athene Reiss draws
a correlation between textual and visual images in the way both make use
of the narrative frame. In both instances, according to Reiss, the frame is a
significant part of the narrative; it is not an afterthought or merely a
necessary background structure. The frame participates in the narrative. A
visual example of this can be seen in a painting of the Annunciation to the
shepherds, from the Wharncliffe Book of Hours, in which two distinct
scenes are visible.[34] The interior scene depicts the shepherds in the
foreground listening to the angels, while in the background, beyond the
farm, can be seen a series of buildings. The exterior scene is really a
composite of three separate but interrelated scenes of the shepherds. Near
the bottom of the folio are two shepherdesses with their flock; the women
look as if they are playing with a pet dog while the sheep wander out of
the pen, unnoticed. To the left of this is a scene in a wood, in which a pair
of lovers can be seen. Above this is the depiction of a wolf escaping with a
sheep, hotly pursued by a shepherd. While frame that seemingly separates
the interior and exterior scenes indicates the religious qualities of the
interior scene and the secular qualities of the exterior scene, the use of
linear perspective has the effect of joining the scenes together so that the
two narratives interrelate. The three separate pictures that make up the
exterior scene are positioned according to the vanishing point in the
interior scene, which is somewhere near the angels. The island on which
the shepherdesses are sitting clearly draws the eye upwards, through the
frame, and up to the angels. The angle at which the lovers in the wood are
shown similarly draws the eye upward. The picture of the wolf stealing the
sheep is positioned much higher on the page and subsequently the
perspective dictates the near horizontal angle, again which draws the eye
through the frame and towards the angels. In addition to these scenes, the
background of the exterior images is a highly floral chevron motif that also
has the effect of drawing the eye into the interior scene. This example,
then, illustrates the narrative quality of the images, and also the way that
linear perspective has been used to draw the two narratives together
despite the separating frame. The exterior images act as a filter through
which one sees the interior. The eye travels from the exterior to the
interior, and thus the narratives become intertwined.

Another particularly significant example of how a painter may construct
a painting in which the viewer's eye is required to travel around an image

is Dieric Bouts' painting of *The Last Supper*.[35] The initial impression is that Bouts has used a linear perspective construction for the painting; the table and the patterned floor all tend to a single vanishing point directly in the centre of the false fireplace. Yet the positioning of the people and objects in the room does not conform to this vanishing point. The height of the vanishing point places the viewer up above the level of the people depicted, so that the view we see ought to be of the tops of their heads. In reality all of the people appear as though at the viewer's eye level, quite out of proportion to the perspective of the table. David Hockney theorises that this effect is achieved in a collage-like process in which the painter sketches each of the people and objects individually then inserts them on to the pre-prepared background. The result of this process, according to Hockney, "is to bring everything (even distance) close to the picture plane."[36] The apparent distortion of the perspective is not, I would suggest, accidental. It seems more likely that Bouts has deliberately used linear perspective for its ability to give a sense of unity and depth to the entire composition, but has then effectively "shifted" the viewer down to the level of the people. This is particularly noticeable in the representation of Jesus, where he appears much taller and larger than the other people in the painting, and he appears to be looking directly at the viewer. The unity of the room is governed by linear perspective and contains a three-dimensional depth, but Jesus appears to be almost coming right out of the picture, or at least right up to the picture plane. This shows how Bouts is able to manipulate linear perspective to emphasise certain parts of the narrative.

The development of linear perspective in painting can be seen as a visual realisation of the concepts of *Perspectiva*, yet with the added potential for narration. As we can see from the way many painters utilised perspective, it was a significant tool that enabled them to tell stories. The limitations of perspective were well known to painters, but these limitations could be used for effect, to emphasise a feature of the painting's narrative.

To return briefly to Adelard of Bath's contemplations on the workings of the eye, he says:

> Some say that the mind, sitting in the brain as its chief seat, and looking forth upon outer things through open windows, gets knowledge of the shape of things, and when it has got knowledge of them, judges them.[37]

Adelard understands the eye as the point of interaction between the mind and the outside world. Similarly, Alberti describes the picture plane as: "quidem mihi pro aperta finestra est ex qua historia contueatur," [an open

window through which the *historia* is seen.][38] Alberti's picture plane is the
point of interaction between the mind and the *historia*. The similarity
between the statements of Adelard and Alberti raises a feature that is
common to both *Perspectiva* and perspective, which is the ability of both
to pass judgment on the objects under consideration. In fact, both
Perspectiva and perspective demand that a judgment be made: both create
the presence of the viewer, who must then measure or quantify the object.
The act of measuring is a judgment, it asserts a spatial relationship
between objects, and relates objects to an exterior frame.

Athene Reiss notes the judgmental element of the frame in pictorial
representations. The framed object is an ordered, virtuous object because
the frame allows the object to be measured, quantified, and controlled; the
unframed object is uncontrolled and without virtue because there is no way
to measure it. Reiss compares the images of the Mercies and the Sins from
a wall painting at St George's Church in Trotton, Sussex, in which each of
the Mercies is represented within the bounds of an organised circular
frame, whereas the Sins are depicted as protruding from a hideous mouth,
without control and without a frame. Reiss says: "The Trotton painting
strongly suggests that an untidy composition carried negative overtones in
the Middle Ages."[39] The moral dimension conveyed by the pictorial frame
can be associated with the role of the viewer, the one who must pass
judgment on the object depicted. A clearly delineated object that could be
measured and quantified within a frame was a virtuous thing; the erratic,
haphazard, depiction that overstepped the frame, was not.

In *The Assembly of Ladies* the narrator urges the reader to make a
moral judgment on the events that take place in the poem, but, as will be
seen, she does not tell her story simply according to the dictates of either
Perspectiva or perspective. The narrator of *The Assembly of Ladies* takes a
more aesthetic approach, similar to the way painters can be seen to use
some of the features of perspective some of the time. As with Bouts'
painting of *The Last Supper* in which the viewer's eye is moved and
shifted around the pictorial space, the narrator of *The Assembly of Ladies*
constantly shifts her position from one frame to the next and causes the
reader to consider the poem from several different points of view. The
difficulty presented to the reader is how to judge a poem that seems to
defy boundaries and does not conform to the virtuous frame.

The Narrative Frames of *The Assembly of Ladies*

The first frame that the reader knowingly encounters in *The Assembly
of Ladies* is the 2.00 o'clock September afternoon setting in the maze.[40]

This portion of the poem has been mentioned in Chapter Two but it is useful to revisit this episode for the new insights that *Perspectiva* and perspective can offer. The first stanza of the poem offers three significant examples of the literary use of *Perspectiva* and perspective, one that refers specifically to *Perspectiva*, one that refers to perspective, and a third that suggests a literary melding of the two visual theories into a literary form. The stanza is as follows:

> In Septembre, at falling of the leef,
> The fressh season was al to-gydre done
> And of the corn was gadred in the sheef;
> In a gardyn, abowte tweyne after none,
> There were ladyes walkyng, as was ther wone,
> Foure in nombre, as to my mynde doth falle,
> And I the fift, symplest of alle. (1-7)

Specifying the autumnal season is a clear indication of time existing outside the bounds of the poem. As has been mentioned in Chapter Two, an autumnal setting is unusual although not unheard of, and there are several other examples of medieval poetry that specifically use the autumnal setting to convey a sombre tone. At this point, however, it is pertinent to consider the way that the opening of the poem can be likened to a visual image and the way that the reader's eye is specifically directed and controlled by the narratorial voice. It is useful to consider this portion of the poem in relation to Meyer Schapiro's suggestion that the frame or boundary of a text "is like a window frame through which one glimpses only a part of the space behind it."[41] Schapiro's window frame, which is similar to Alberti's "quidem mihi pro aperta finestra est ex qua historia contueatur," [an open window through which the *historia* is seen][42] suggests that what the viewer sees in an image is only a portion of a wider scene, the rest of the action is taking place just outside of our range of sight. Moreover, if we could step closer to the window, even pass through it, we would be able to take in the wider scene and perhaps even engage with the activities that are occurring there. An excellent visual example of this effect can be seen in an illustration from London, British Library MS Harley 4425, which accompanies the text of *Le Roman de la Rose*. In this painting, time is interrupted to present several images from the book as if they are occurring simultaneously; Amans stands at the gate with Oiseuse, we then see him walking through the garden, and we see the God of Love and his entourage. What is significant about the image for this study, however, is the way that the edges of the images are cut off by the frame. On the left of the picture some of the people are only partially visible, and on the right we can see the pathways in the Garden of Deduit continue beyond the edge of the picture frame. In addition, the picture also relies on the reader's knowledge of the story. Thus when we look at this scene, we are able to fill in mentally other details about the garden. Although we cannot see the well of Narcissus, for example, we know it is there. The frame of the picture acts as a window frame on the events taking place. Our view is physically limited to this scene, but mentally we can look around the edges of the frame to see the rest of the garden.

In literary terms, the same could be said to occur in *The Assembly of Ladies*. The September setting in *The Assembly of Ladies* is not unlike the view through the window. Just beyond the sight of the viewer are the other the months and seasons of the year. It is even possible that the narrator invites us to peer around the edges of the frame when she says "The fressh season was al to-gydre done" (2). Just out of view is the "fressh season;" it has now passed but it seems sorely missed by the narrator. The "view," then, of the beginning of *The Assembly of Ladies* is strictly limited to the September setting, but the narrator ensures that we know of, even though we cannot see, the previous summer. The reader's point of view is defined by the limitations imposed by the narrator. Holley utilises this feature of visual perspective in her analysis of several Chaucer texts; she states that the key to understanding visual theory is to note that "perspective asserts limitation."[43] Here in *The Assembly of Ladies* the narrator directs and limits the reader's eye to the September setting.

The narrator, however, is even more specific about the setting beyond establishing the season and month. The poem begins specifically at 2.00 o'clock in the afternoon. Reference to such a specific time of day indicates the importance of time in this poem, and the passage of time. The "fressh season" has passed, the morning, too, has passed, all before the poem has even begun. The importance of the reference to such a specific time of day would indicate that the narrator does not refer to the passing of time in a vague, generalised manner. Time, in *The Assembly of Ladies*, is a quantifiable, measurable concept. The ability to measure, or to take the measure of a subject suggests a means of knowing that subject. As Holley states: "Action gains meaning when it is measurable,"[44] that is, the ability to measure allows one to come to an understanding about a subject. The concept of measurement as it appears in *The Assembly of Ladies*, particularly the measurement of time, can be compared directly to concepts found within medieval *Perspectiva*. Roger Bacon states clearly the correlation between physical measurement, that is, geometry, and knowledge of the natural world:

Nam proculdubio tota rerum sapientia veritas jacet in sensu literali, ut dictum est, et maxime rerum geometricarum, quia nihil est nobis as plenum intelligibile, nisi figuraliter ante oculos mostros disponatur.[45]

[For without a doubt the whole truth of things in the world lies in the literal sense and especially of things relating to geometry, because we understand nothing fully unless its form is presented before our eyes.]

For Bacon, understanding the world, the "tota rerum sapientia veritas," can only be achieved through "geometricarum," that is, through physical observation and measurement.[46] For *The Assembly of Ladies*, then, the specific reference to the time of day, in addition to the reference of the season and the month, indicates the narrator's need to measure and quantify the world that she inhabits, the world of the poem. The reference to the time of day at the outset of the poem allows both the narrator and the reader to measure and, therefore, to understand how the action of the poem is situated in relation to other seasons, months, and times of day.[47]

It seems unusual that the narrator requires a means of measuring and judging her circumstances as this is, after all, her own narrative. This would suggest that the narrator is in a state of some confusion and seeks a means to understand her world. The narrator's apparent confusion has been mentioned by scholars and is considered briefly in Chapter Four in relation to her erratic behaviour at the assembly of Lady Loiaulte.[48] The narrator, in fact, seems to be largely defined by her inability to understand and judge situations, and yet she constantly strives to do so. As has been mentioned in the previous chapter, the narrator emphasises her separation and distance from the other characters in the poem: she does not wear the motto and device and she initially refuses to present her bill of complaint.[49] These episodes emphasise the narrator's lack of ability and desire to understand and conform to the situations presented to her. On arrival at Pleasaunt Regarde the narrator asks numerous questions of the inhabitants; she seeks desperately to know and understand the rules of the castle, yet despite this she remains in a state of confusion. The narrator never achieves sufficient understanding or knowledge to be able to judge her surroundings. The narrator's failings bring to light similar failings in *Perspectiva*. Holley says:

For medieval scientists, theologians, and artists, visual theory offered a mode of knowing. The geometric conceptions of linear perspective offered a model of moral order and human perfection and brought God into the focus of man.[50]

Yet, as has already been noted, one of the primary features of *Perspectiva* is its limitations. A common image in medieval painting is the depiction of God as a master architect;[51] yet because God is the ultimate creator, any attempt by man to imitate this will always fall short: "In spite of the pleasure of discovering ways to measure origins and limits of force, realization of the limitation of finite measurement, compared to God's infinite vision, was humbling."[52] The Perspectivists would never completely understand the world through measurement. Despite seeking to understand the world, *Perspectiva* succeeds only in defining its limits.[53]

The narrator of *The Assembly of Ladies* imitates verbally the concept of space and time found in both *Perspectiva* and perspective in the first stanza of the poem. The narrator uses a construction similar to the periodic sentence used by Chaucer in the opening to the General Prologue to *The Canterbury Tales*.[54] The technique verbally paints a picture of the scene in which she, herself, takes part. Yet it is noticeable from the first stanza of the poem that the order in which the narrator introduces elements to the scene is significant. The first element is the month, September, which is emphasised by the image of the "falling of the leef." Just outside the scene is the "fressh season" mentioned already, then a rural reference is made to the corn "gadred in the sheef." Thus far, the month and its visually recognisable features have been described and contrasted with the previous summer season, but as yet we do not know what is to occur within this scene. The delay is lengthened further with the narrator specifying "In a gardyn, abowte tweyne after none," narrowing both the setting and the time frame, as if directing our line of sight to a particular portion of the wider painting. The verbal echo between the opening line "In Septembre" and line 4 "In a gardyn" is the verbal equivalent of painting from the outside of the frame towards the centre. The background features of the setting are established before any central detail is supplied. It is only after having described this wider view of the scene, then narrowing the view to 2.00 o'clock in a garden, that we learn the garden is peopled: "There were ladyes." And finally, in the fifth line, a verb to indicate action, the ladies are "walking" through the garden. Although only five lines have passed, the sense of delay is remarkable. The scene has been created by the narrator beginning with the outer-most edges of the frame, the month and season, even indicating the space beyond the frame, the "fressh season," then the description gradually moves the reader's eye closer to the centre of the image, a garden, and finally, after the scene has been set, the narrator fills the scene with ladies walking. Yet this is not all. The narrator further specifies there were four ladies, then finishes the stanza by stating "And I the fift, symplest of alle." Even after the narrator has stated the action that is taking place—ladies walking—there is a further refining of the image to specify the exact number of women. The act of gradually bringing the reader's eye to the centre of the image, or of gradually filling the space with people, is a verbal indication of both time and space.[55]

The narrator, of course, continues to populate the scene in the subsequent stanza. We learn there are four gentlewomen, and also many knights and squires. It is useful, however, to consider how the narrator gradually fills the scene with people. Four ladies are mentioned first, and she then includes herself among their number. The ladies are followed by gentlewomen and then finally the knights and squires are introduced to the scene. The methodical order in which the narrator introduces the people in the scene establishes a series of spatial relationships that can be associated with what Holley would describe as a measurable entity; the spatial relations between the characters indicate measurable space, a way of quantifying the people within the environment and in relation to one another.[56] The order in which the people are introduced to the scene suggests a hierarchy and indicates the relationships between the people. The four ladies are introduced first and, although the narrator counts herself as a lady, she is verbally separated from the other ladies by the way she introduces herself after the other women. Moreover, the narrator further attempts to reduce her own status by declaring her relationship with the other women, she says she is the "symplest of alle."

The gentlewomen do not feature in the first stanza; they must wait to be introduced in the second stanza:

Of gentil wymmen foure ther were also,
Disportyng hem everiche after theyr guyse,
In crosse aleys walkyng be two and two,
And som alone after theyr fantasyes.
Thus occupied we were in dyvers wise,
And yit in trowth we were nat alone:
Theyr were knyghtis and squyers many one. (8-14)

They are verbally removed from the presence of the ladies, which suggests a separation between the two groups of women. The women do, however, form a unified group when compared with the men. The knights and squires are introduced in the final line of the second stanza. The narrator uses the rhyme royal structure to emphasise the separation between the men and the women. The women are constructed by the "a-b" portion of the stanza, while the men interrupt with the "c" rhyme. Spatially, there is a sense of separation between the two groups of women, yet with the introduction of the men into the scene, the women become characterised as a single unit. The spatial relations demonstrate the impact of the men on the women.

Stanzas three and four concern the direct speech between the narrator and the inquisitive knight. This is a further narrowing of focus in the poem; having begun with the wide view of the month and season, narrowed to 2.00 o'clock in a garden, the view now is extremely intimate. The intimacy of the conversation between the narrator and the inquisitive knight is emphasised by the wider setting. In a pictorial sense, it is as if the narrator and the inquisitive knight occupy only a very tiny portion of the canvas, they are central to it, and one's eye is specifically directed towards them, but our view of them and their conversation is affected by our awareness of their surroundings. The reader takes the measure of the narrator and the inquisitive knight in comparison to the surrounding garden in an attempt to understand the scene. A visual example is occurs in Jean de Wavrin's *Chronicles of England*, in which a man and woman are depicted in a garden sharing a meal. The garden is enclosed, emphasising the intimacy of the scene, yet to one side it is possible to see far into the countryside, where there are castles, ships, and perhaps a joust about to take place. Thus, in this scene, the intimacy between the man and woman is measured against the scene in the background; the intimacy is quantifiable.

The impression of intimacy between the narrator and the inquisitive knight, created by the way the two characters are spatially related to their surroundings, leads the reader to expect and hope for a personal revelation of some sort.[57] The knight, too, seems to hope for a personal revelation from the narrator. As the inquisitive knight questions the narrator about her pale colour, why she is in the maze, and whom she seeking, the impression is that the knight is, himself, seeking to understand the narrator. His questions indicate that if only he can ask the right question, the narrator will reveal all. The knight's first question, "Wherof I serve?" has been considered in Chapter Two, but it is of some significance to consider here the other two questions he poses to the narrator. The narrator tells us: "He asked me ageyn whom I sought / And of my coloure why I was so pale" (19-20). It has not been apparent to the reader thus far that the narrator is seeking anyone at all, and certainly she had suggested as much to the knight when she described herself as a "womman that nothyng rought" (18). Nevertheless, the knight is quite sure she must be seeking someone, as if this is the purpose for being in the maze. The suggestion that the narrator is seeking someone is a verbal cue to the reader to look about the narrative, as if by doing so we, too, may see whom the narrator seeks and this may allow us to understand her better. The importance of the knight's question seems to be in directing the eye to seek on behalf of the narrator.

The knight also questions the narrator as to why she is so pale. Her physical appearance is registered as an indication of her inner state of mind which is, at the very least, discontented. Returning to Bacon's suggestion that "nisi figuraliter ante oculos mostros disponatur" [we can understand nothing fully unless its form is presented before our eyes,][58] we are reminded of the precedence given to sight as a way of knowing not only external phenomenon, but also internal phenomenon. By visually examining the external state of the narrator, the inquisitive knight is able to know, as if seeing into, her internal state.

The preferencing of sight referred to by Bacon, however, presents the judgmental reader with some difficulties. It is possible for the reader to consider the first frame of *The Assembly of Ladies* as a complete unified entity which the narrator has populated "by measure;" all of the people can be compared and measured against their surroundings and each other. But the difficulty presented by the narrator is that she has alluded to the fact that this is not the complete picture. Just around the edges of the frame there is another world, and the limited view we have through the viewing window indicates that any judgment ought, somehow, to include what is not visible. This is, of course, an impossible task, but the narrator constantly reminds the reader that our view is always limited. In this way the narrator of *The Assembly of Ladies* demonstrates her desire to create a new way of speaking or knowing, but it also demonstrates her inability to do so.

In the second frame of *The Assembly of Ladies* the narrator describes the spring afternoon in which she and her companions walked through the maze and became hopelessly lost. The narrator eventually reaches the centre of the maze but must wait there for her companions, and while waiting, she falls asleep.

The stanza that begins the narrator's tale is full of references back to the first frame of the poem. She says, "my felawship and I" entered "this mase;" she does not need to explain who her companions are, the inquisitive knight already knows as does the reader. Similarly, she refers specifically to "this mase;" the maze in the tale is the same one that she and the inquisitive knight are, presumably, standing in. These are very direct references to the first frame of the poem, but there are other, less obvious, verbal echoes of the first frame as well. As with the first stanza of the poem in which we had "[i]n Septembre" (1) and "[i]n a gardyn" (4), here we have "in an after none" (29). The language is similar and the time is similar. The season, notably, is not mentioned at this point and we

assume (incorrectly) that this, too, is autumn since all the other features of
the setting seem to be the same as the first frame. The similarity of the first
and second frames to each other seems to be a deliberate invitation from
the narrator for the reader to confuse and blur the distinctions between
them, and certainly there is scholarship that has inadvertently confused the
two frames.[59] Visually, this is not unlike a picture that contains two
images. The images are each independent narratives, but they have a
reciprocal relationship with each other. Each picture refers to the other
while still maintaining its own autonomy. A visual example of the
interrelationship between framed images occurs in a painting of the
Annunciation, by Giovanni di Paolo.[60] In this painting, there are two
separate narratives, on the left is the expulsion of Adam and Eve from
Paradise, and on the right is the Annunciation to the Virgin. The two visual
narratives are presented as though occurring within the same location;
Paradise is situated just outside of the pavilion in which the Virgin is
seated. Yet the two scenes are still sufficiently separated for one to
understand them as separate narratives. What is significant about the scene
for this book is that, while maintaining their respective frames as separate
visual narratives, the scenes interact with each other. The Annunciation to
the Virgin can be seen as the rectification of the sins of Adam and Eve,
and so her narrative has a direct impact on the scene of Paradise. Similarly,
the scene of Adam and Eve has a direct impact on the Annunciation scene
insofar as it generates the need for the Annunciation. A further interaction
between the scenes can be seen with the representation of God in the
painting. God is situated in the top left corner of the painting, and from his
position he appears to be watching both scenes simultaneously. In fact, it
is even possible to suggest that the scenes are depicted according to the
sight of God. We may be able to view the scenes, but they are depicted
from God's point of view; there are direct lines of perspective visible that
emanate from God to both of the scenes depicted beneath him.[61] The gaze
of God ensures that both scenes interrelate, even though they are depicted
as separate narratives.

Similarly, in *The Assembly of Ladies*, the two narrative frames
discussed so far interact. The first frame creates the space and necessity for
the second frame, and second frame directly refers back to the first frame.
The effect of the interaction between the frames is to create the sense of
several narratives occurring simultaneously.[62] Just as the first frame refers
to events just out of the reader's view, the second frame requires the reader
to consider both frames together. The impression given is that the
narrator's story is somewhat larger than first appears. Various events are
shown to the reader, but we are made aware that there are still other frames

to consider that contribute to the meaning of the text. The interaction of the narrative frames creates a sense of textual instability and fluidity; the narrator is able to, and does, slip from one narrative to another and as she does so she invites the reader to consider the narrative frames that lie beyond the immediate view. As the narrator mentions to the inquisitive knight, the second frame is set in "this mase," a phrase that indicates she has already verbally jumped from the second frame to the first.

The most dramatic image in the second frame is the maze and this can be seen to function as an example of the measured world. One particularly significant depiction of labyrinths and mazes in history has been to regard them as a metaphor for the world and particularly as the route through the world.[63] In *The Assembly of Ladies* the maze can certainly be regarded as a tortuous route through the social world of the women. As has already been discussed in Chapter Two, the maze in *The Assembly of Ladies* functions to draw a comparison between textual mazes and textual confusion, and here, in this instance, it is possible to supplement that analysis to consider the maze as an obstacle to a quantifiable knowledge of the world.

The maze exists within both the first and second frames of the poems, and in each instance the women walking through it are apparently doing so at random. In the first frame the narrator says:

> Disportyng hem everiche after theyr guyse,
> In crosse alleys walking be two and two,
> And som alone after theyr fantasyes. (9-11)

In the second frame she says:

> To passe oure tyme in to this mase we went
> And toke oure weyes yche aftyr other entente. (32-3)

The two descriptions of the way the women negotiate the maze suggest their movement is random and unplanned. I would suggest, however, that there is a subtle indication of orderliness within these descriptions. In the description from the first narrative frame the initial impression is that the women wander without plan or motivation, "everiche after theyr guyse," sometimes together and sometimes alone. Yet it seems clear that there is a specific sense of predetermination to their movements. The example given, that the women walk "everiche after theyr guyse" can also be seen to suggest that the women walk according to their already established desires. The women do not walk randomly and without thought, they walk according to their wills and needs. Similarly, in the description from the second narrative frame, the women walk "yche aftyr other entente," (33) once again suggesting that they move according to an internal, emotional, controlling force, their "entente."

The pattern of movement of the women within the maze can be seen as a highly structured and organised activity, but their goal is not necessarily to reach the centre of the maze before anyone else. The "entente" of the women in the maze is to take the measure of their surroundings. The women move around the maze so they may come to know it because, according to Bacon, "nisi figuraliter ante oculos mostros disponatur" [we can understand nothing fully unless its form is presented before our eyes.][64]

It has been noted in Chapter Two that the maze functions as an optical illusion; the centre of the maze appears to be much larger than its exterior would initially suggest. We know from theories of *Perspectiva* that early scientists sought "a way of knowing by explaining the way we see,"[65] and in this regard it is possible to consider that the maze in *The Assembly of Ladies* signifies knowledge through observation, but then determines the observation process to be faulty. Since theories of *Perspectiva* preferenced the observations of the eye above any other sense and even above what the mind knew to be true, reliance solely upon visual observation required the eye to be held accountable for the truth; the observer was responsible for seeing the truth.[66] Holley says of the early perspectivists: "To be able to explain the force of light by measuring it was to reveal the structure of the created universe by experience;"[67] experience and visual observation became to be regarded as a means to understand the world. Yet observation was sometimes faulty. As painters knew, one could paint a picture using linear perspective in which only one side of a building was visible, but the picture required the observer to provide mentally the other three sides of the building to create the truth of the picture.[68] In this sense, sight was faulty because it only allowed one to see one side of the building. This was not the truth of the building; the mind had to supply the missing walls. *Perspectiva* determined the concept of knowing the world by observation even though sight alone was insufficient to reveal completely the truth of the world. In *The Assembly of Ladies* the maze represents visual truth as a way of knowing the world. The eye may attempt to determine the best route to take through the maze, but the result will be confusion because the eye cannot see around the twists and turns of the maze. To negotiate the maze successfully one must be open to alternative ways of knowing, which is analogous to suggesting there are other narrative frames in *The Assembly of Ladies* that contribute to the meaning of the poem. Just as the frames of *The Assembly of Ladies* indicate other narratives and other frames just beyond our view, so, too, the maze indicates that sight alone is insufficient for negotiating the maze. Other ways of knowing must be sought.

As the narrator reaches the centre of the maze, she describes her surroundings in the arbour, and she mentions the idea of remembrance several times. Stephens has argued for remembrance to be regarded as the central theme of *The Assembly of Ladies*.[69] While I would not consider remembrance to be the central theme, I would suggest that remembrance is a particularly important feature of this frame of the poetic narrative. Pearsall notes the flowers in the arbour are all known for their associations with serious, constant love.[70] Clearly, however, flowers such as "Ne m'oublie-mies" and "sovenez," from their names, one can also suggest that these flowers are significant for their associations with remembrance. Then, as the narrator sits down to wait for her companions to arrive:

Remembryng of many dyvers cace
Of tyme past, musyng with sighes depe,
I set me downe and ther fil in slepe. (75-77)

The narrator states clearly that she is reminiscing about "tyme past." The second frame, once again, makes references to a world outside the immediate frame, but on this occasion it is not a reference directly back to the first narrative frame. Here the narrator seems to refer to another narrative frame entirely, perhaps even something similar to the "fressh season" mentioned in the first stanza of the poem. While our point of view has been directed to look carefully at the contents of the arbour, the narrator simultaneously suggests the existence of another world entirely. Perhaps the features of the arbour remind her specifically of another time and place, certainly we can see she reminisces with "sighes depe," suggesting it is a world now lost to her. In this instance, the world that is now lost seems to be situated clearly within the narrator's memory, it does not take on the physical properties of the first stanza of the poem, in which we have the impression of the "fressh season" existing just out of view, around the edge of the frame. The arbour, however, clearly reminds the narrator of the world now lost, and causes the reader to look about the arbour to try to reconstruct mentally the lost world from the visible clues. The narrator's reminiscences direct the reader's eye to examine the arbour and to seek some significance in its contents, the "tornyng whele," the fountain, and the pot of marjoram.[71]

The second frame of *The Assembly of Ladies* introduces the reader to a series of allusions to different worlds either existing just outside our field of view, or which formerly existed in the past and are now only memories. There are simultaneous references to the first frame of the poem, to the world as represented by the maze, and to a former world that is memorialised by the narrator in the arbour. As will be shown, when the narrator returns to this frame later in the poem, her immediate concern is that her dream, the third frame of the poem, "shuld nat out of remembraunce" (742). Remembrance is a significant feature in the second frame of *The Assembly of Ladies* that is used as a means of maintaining the existence of other worlds, and other ways of knowing them.

Here in the second frame of *The Assembly of Ladies* remembrance is a significant reference to a world that exists only in the narrator's mind, but which cannot be ignored by the judgmental reader because it clearly impacts on the narrator in the present. Similarly, the maze cannot elicit a positive judgment from the reader because it represents an uncontrolled and disordered world. The women approach the maze in an orderly manner, but this does not allow them to negotiate the maze successfully. The maze is an unruly and disordered world which the women unsuccessfully attempt to measure. For the reader, then, the ability to pass judgment on the second frame of the poem is constantly thwarted because the point of view constantly shifts. The narrator attempts to create a new discourse in which the female voice is located, but is unable to do so within the bounds of the physical limitations of the maze or within the masculine literary limitations. The narrator first refers back to the first frame, itself defying judgment, then presents the maze, which ought to signify order but does not, and finally refers to a world within her memory. As with the first frame of the poem, the reader cannot judge the second frame because there is no stationary vanishing point from which to take the measure of the scene. The narrator attempts to present the reader with a new way of speaking about relationships, but without a stable vantage point the reader is unable to assess the information.

It is not necessary here to re-examine the narrator's dream in great detail as this has been considered in Chapters Three and Four. It is useful, however, to note some particular features of the dream that relate specifically to the theories of the *Perspectiva* and perspective. The narrator's journey to Pleasaunt Regarde is a significant portion of *The Assembly of Ladies* which can be seen as drawing on the theories of both *Perspectiva* and perspective.

Unlike the first frame of the poem, where the month, season, and time of day were carefully specified, in the dream there is only a vague sense of time impacting upon the action. Diligence explains to the narrator that travelling to Pleasaunt Regarde will be "'A dayes journey,' quod she, 'but litel lesse,'" (214) but despite the lack of specificity about the time of day, there is always a sense of urgency that pervades the entire dream. The time of day may not be actually stated as it is in the first frame, nevertheless time must not be wasted. Diligence urges haste when she says:

> Wherfor I rede that we onward dresse,
> For I suppose oure felawship is past
> And for nothyng I wold that we were last.   (215-17)

Diligence does not explain why they must hurry, but fears that the other women in the company have overtaken them, although how this could have occurred is not explained. In the second frame, the narrator clearly arrives at the centre of the maze before the other women, therefore why, suddenly, in the third frame one should suppose the other women are further ahead is unclear.

At a certain point in their journey, the narrator suggests to Diligence that they stop for a moment:

> "Nowe lete us rest," quod I, "a litel space,
> And say we as devoutly as we can
> A Pater Noster for seynt Julyan."   (222-24)

It would seem that the sense of urgency has been lost, but then Diligence replies:

> "With al myn hert," quod she, "I gre me wele;
> Moche better shul we spede whan we have done." (225-26)

The sense of urgency has not been forsaken at all; the delay is tolerated only so that it may result in still greater speed! The need for urgency is never explained and actually results in the narrator and Diligence arriving before the other women. Speed is certainly identifiable as a measurable concept, a way of knowing the world, but in this instance it seems to be a folly. There is no obvious benefit from such haste; it does not result in a better understanding of the world.

The narrator and Diligence encounter a "hospital" along the route to Pleasaunt Regarde in which a gentlewoman known to the narrator is waiting with the narrator's blue dress. This is perhaps one of the more unusual events in the poem, as the gentlewoman has suddenly appeared without any introduction and is apparently fully informed of the narrator's journey. The gentlewoman explains:

> "I herd Perseveraunce,
> How she warned youre felawes everichone,

And what array that ye shal have upon." (236-38)

The appearance of the gentlewoman is a patent shift between narrative frames. Perseveraunce had appeared to the narrator within the third frame of the dream, and miraculously, all of her companions have now been transported into the dream as well, including this particular gentlewoman. It is not stated, however, if this gentlewoman is one of the four mentioned at the beginning of the poem as part of the narrator's "felawship," and after dressing the narrator in her blue dress, the gentlewoman disappears as suddenly as she has arrived. Even the narrator is surprised, saying her presence is a "mervaile" (234), a word that elicits connotations of a supernatural world. A supernatural world would be difficult to argue in this instance, but it does seem relevant to note that the word "mervaile" is another reminder of the multiple narrative frames functioning simultaneously in *The Assembly of Ladies*.

On arrival at Pleasaunt Regarde the narrator discovers her companions have not preceded her and she sits and waits for them to arrive. She notes carefully the dress of Contenaunce, but a significant break occurs in the description that hints at the existence of a narrative frame which, so far, has not been considered. The narrator notes Contenaunce's motto: "The whiche saide thus, as my penne can endite, / *A moy que je voy*, writen with lettres white" (308-09). Scholars have noted with some criticism that the poet of *The Assembly of Ladies* frequently uses proverbs and tags in constructing the second part of a line of verse.[72] Pearsall notes:

> The handling of the verse in [*The Assembly of Ladies*] is assured if monotonous. The author knows well how to economise in effort by the use of tags and tautological expressions, how to spin out a thought to the end of the stanza, and how to find rhymes in an easy way.[73]

In this example, the poet has added the expression "as my penne can endite" to the end of line 308, which could well be regarded as no more than an attempt to complete the line and provide an appropriate rhyme; certainly the description of the dress is not aided by the reference. This is, however, an example of another framing narrative operating underneath all those discussed so far. Until this point in the poem there has been no reference whatsoever to the narrator being the author of a poem—this is revealed only at the end of the poem. The narrator-as-poet is a frame that can be seen to encompass the entire poem, acting as a meta-frame in which all the other frames exist. The narrator, then, reveals here for the first time that she is the authority behind the poem. The narrator uses the theories of linear perspective to display each scene before the reader, but that view is controlled and directed by her; our view is limited. Similarly, the narrator uses the theories of *Perspectiva* to control our ability to measure and understand the world. This meta-frame will be examined in greater detail shortly, but it is significant to note that the example in line 308 is not isolated. Throughout the presentation of the bills of complaint the narrator shifts between describing the oral presentation of the bills to describing the bills as written documents, a shift that occurs so frequently it is hard to consider it an error.

The stories on the internal walls of Pleasaunt Regarde are, of course, very obvious examples of frames within frames. As has been discussed in Chapter Three, the stories of the women are intended to signify the way women's voices are stifled in literature; these stories are literally stifled behind the covering of umple. One of the reasons given for the covering of the pictures, however, is particularly significant and unusual. The narrator states:

> And bicause the wallis shone so bright
> With fyne umple they were al over-spredde
> To that entent folk shuld nat hurt theyr sight. (470-72)

According to Holley, both Witelo and Grosseteste made several claims for an association between light and the soul, and even went so far as to suggest that people with a mental affliction should not look at bright light.[74] The inference is that light penetrates to the soul and will harm the viewer if he or she does not have the capacity, knowledge, or strength to bear it. Chaucer uses this suggestion in *Troilus and Criseyde* when Pandarus departs from the bedside of Troilus and Criseyde:

> For aught I kan aspien,
> This light, not I, ne serven here of nought.
> Light is nought good for sike folkes yen!   (III, 1135-37)

Holley notes that Chaucer draws together both light and narrative in this instance, equating Pandarus' narrative-like effort to bring Troilus and Criseyde together with the effect of light on the soul. At this point in the poem, neither is appropriate. Pandarus' story draws to its climax, he must depart from the scene for to remain would be harmful, just as the effect of light on a sick person.[75]

The implication of light being harmful is that light is regarded in *Perspectiva* as a source of truth. To look at a bright light when one is mentally ill is to risk the revelation of this state in the viewer. By covering the pictures with umple, the "truth" that the pictures contain will not be able to harm anyone; in fact, the pictures become benign and totally ineffectual.

The third frame of *The Assembly of Ladies* is certainly the most substantial frame of the poem, and would seem to be the easiest for the reader to judge because it is so clearly defined by the dream. Yet here, too, the reader has difficulty passing judgment because so many events are seemingly without meaning or reason. We cannot understand the need for urgency by Diligence and the narrator, indeed their haste provides no obvious benefit. The sudden appearance of the gentlewoman and her equally sudden disappearance is not explained and creates an overlap between the second and third narrative frames. The narrator's defiant behaviour in Pleasaunt Regarde is difficult to understand unless we are prepared to consider that the boundaries and regulations of the castle, like the boundaries of the narratives, are too restrictive for her. Our attempt to measure and judge the third frame will be an impossible task if we remain restricted by the boundaries of the frame. The narrator, through her erratic behaviour and her jumps from one frame to another, indicates to the reader that the only way to judge the poem is to shift from one point of view to another. Recalling Dieric Bouts' painting of *The Last Supper*, the preliminary framework of that painting used linear perspective, but the artist then shifted to several different points of view in order to make his intention clear.[76] Here in *The Assembly of Ladies* the narrator traverses the narrative frames, always pointing to the possible presence of other frames and other worlds just beyond our view. To be able to judge the poem and to measure and understand the worlds presented by the narrator successfully, the reader must abandon the restrictive, limiting frameworks, or at least be prepared to shift from a single point of view to multiple points of view in order to discern the new ways of speaking that the narrator is attempting to show.

The final three stanzas of *The Assembly of Ladies* shift through several frames in quick succession. In lines 736-42, the narrator awakens into the second frame in which she is still in the arbour at the centre of the maze, but what is particularly peculiar is she then says:

> With that anon I went and made this booke,
> Thus simply rehersyng the substaunce
> Because it shuld nat out of remembraunce.   (740-42)

The reference to having written her story down is a shift into another frame, that of the first frame in which she is speaking to the inquisitive knight. The narrator explains to him that she wrote the story down, but it is particularly significant that she says she rehearsed the "substaunce" of the story "because it shuld nat out of remembraunce." To have used the word "substaunce" suggests that she rehearsed the main points of the tale only, some details were omitted as insignificant. She has tailored the story to suit her own purposes, she has not attempted to memorise accurately all that occurred in the dream.

The inquisitive knight responds immediately to her, suggesting the story was told very well since it was of "none encombraunce" (746) for him to stand for such a long time listening to her. The story's apparent benign impact is what the knight applauds. Yet even the inquisitive knight's language is somewhat confusing. He indicates he has been standing listening to her story, yet he then asks "what ye the booke do cal" (748); suddenly the story is a written document. The narrator responds to tell him the book is called "La semble de Dames" (752), a punning title in which the word "semble" may mean "assembly" or "semblance."[77] The narrator even seems to invite the inquisitive knight to consider the pun when she asks "How think ye that the name is?" (753), but the joke is lost on him, he replies simply that the title is "Goode, parde!" With a little confusion between the oral and written status of the story, the narrative frames have worked in reverse order in the final stanzas. The dream has reverted to the arbour, which in turn reverts to the maze and the knight.

The final line of the poem, however, raises further issues about the narrative frame in *The Assembly of Ladies*. "Red wele my dreame, for now my tale is done" (756), are the narrator's final words, but they are not addressed to the inquisitive knight, whom she has already dismissed. The final line of the poem is a new frame altogether, although it was briefly mentioned earlier in this chapter. The final line of the poem is addressed directly to the reader, so that we now know (if we had not already guessed) that the poem we are reading is the very same "booke" that she has written; *The Assembly of Ladies* is the text she was "rehersyng" "because it shuld nat out of remembraunce" (742). The effect of the final line is that it appears as a challenge to the reader. Having mocked the inquisitive knight for his inability to understand her pun on the title of the book, she now challenges the reader to understand the title, and to understand the book. The poem may be entitled *The Assembly of Ladies,* but we are to understand it as "the semblance of ladies;" the narrator encourages the reader to uncover the falsities within the text, the elements that do not seem logical and indicate that the "truth" of the text is more likely to lie in what has been omitted from the narrative. The reader cannot possibly judge the poem as "virtuous" because it does not conform consistently to the limitations of the narrative frames, but rather shifts through and between the frames. The narrator rather nonchalantly says she simply included the parts she could remember, but she always remembers to point out that there is more to this story than what is immediately visible. Just around the edges of the frame is another story, a new way of speaking, but the poetic conventions do not allow us read it.

Conclusions

Perspectiva and perspective can both be seen to advance methods of understanding the world, but both methods simultaneously reveal their own limitations because each method inherently draws attention to its incompleteness. The flaws of both of these methods signal the narrator's inability to find an effective means of communication within the masculine conventions that *Perspectiva* and perspective represent. The narrator's gender causes the reader to consider *Perspectiva* and perspective as masculine and to correlate social conventions with literary conventions. Just as *Perspectiva* describes the limits of physical vision, and perspective describes the limits of painting, *The Assembly of Ladies* asserts the limits of literary participation for women, indicating that the effective means of communication sought by the narrator cannot be achieved within masculine literary conventions.

CHAPTER SIX

MANUSCRIPT AGENCY IN THE THREE MANUSCRIPTS OF *THE ASSEMBLY OF LADIES*

There are three extant manuscripts that contain *The Assembly of Ladies*: Cambridge, Trinity College MS R.3.19, Warminster, MS Longleat 258, and London, British Library MS Additional 34360.[1] These manuscripts will be examined here in some detail as I will argue that the organisational properties of each manuscript reflects the different ways that the poem was interpreted in fifteenth-century England. This strongly corroborates the approach taken in this book, which asserts a deliberate correlation between the literary conventions used in the poem and broader social conventions of fifteenth-century England.

Much of the following analyses chime clearly with Stephen G. Nichols' "New Philology," although I have not attempted a "New Philological" analysis with any deliberation. This examination is presented as a support to the focus on the narrative voice because, as I will show, the manuscript context of *The Assembly of Ladies* draws attention to the issue of gender and language constructions in a similar manner to the narrator of the poem.

Nichols states that "In medieval studies, philology is the matrix out of which all else springs,"[2] in his introduction to the January 1990 *Speculum* devoted entirely to "New Philology," and indeed the following analyses are grounded in a philological account of the manuscripts in order that they may contribute to the broader argument concerning the fifteenth-century reception of *The Assembly of Ladies*. As Nichols point out, philology ultimately underpins all theoretical analyses of medieval texts and if there is anything new in "New Philology," it is the call to reaffirm manuscript study as a valid enterprise that is accepting of the variability inherent in manuscripts, as opposed to earlier nineteenth-and twentieth-century views of philology that sought to stabilise manuscripts artificially through the production of printed critical editions. In this earlier understanding, Nichols says, "Philology sought a fixed text as transparent as possible, one that would provide the vehicle for scholarly endeavour but, once the work of editing accomplished, not the focus of inquiry. It required, in short, a printed text."[3] While I am not attempting to reduce the value of the recent excellent editions of *The Assembly of Ladies* by Derek Pearsall and more recently by Julia Boffey, there remains much to be learned from returning to the three manuscripts to consider how they may contribute to our understanding of how the poem fitted into its fifteenth-century context.

As Paul Strohm points out, "A necessary task of theory is precisely to provoke a text into unpremeditated articulation, into the utterance of what it somehow contains or knows but neither intends nor is able to say."[4] Texts, according to Strohm, when considered in their manuscript contexts, can be seen to have an unarticulated unconscious level. For *The Assembly of Ladies*, that unconscious level is contained within the female narrative voice and the relationship between that voice and manuscript contexts in which it is positioned.

Often very little information about a medieval text exists, and many scholars have acknowledged the necessity for manuscript study under such circumstances. J. A. Burrow highlights the difficulties of literary analysis for medievalists in his article "Poems without Contexts," in which he draws attention to the way the study of literature from recent periods is able to take for granted the context from which a text may derive, and that this is a luxury not always available in the study of medieval literature:

> By comparison with their modern colleagues, mediaevalists generally know rather little about the contexts of the works they study. Many surviving works are anonymous; and we often do not know exactly when they were written, or with what purpose, or for what audience.[5]

Julia Boffey draws attention to Burrow's article in order to suggest that, in the absence of clear contextual information such as authorship, date, and intended audience, we can examine texts within their manuscript contexts to begin to be able to discover such information. With specific reference to Middle English lyrics, Boffey wonders if, on the one hand, the anthologising of such texts, the removal of lyrics from their manuscript contexts, results in an implied "homogeneity of genre and function"[6] that may not be apparent when seen in the manuscript contexts and, on the other hand, if the "manuscripts suggest in any way that the poems were seen as serving similar purposes or fulfilling similar needs."[7] Without manuscript study, Boffey implies, particular meanings created by texts may go unnoticed.

Rosemary Woolf also remarks on the value of manuscript study with regard to the study of medieval lyrics:

> The reading of lyrics in their manuscripts is a valuable exercise, for they often then give an impression very different from that which they give in modern anthologies. The manuscript context of the lyrics is one of the clearest indications of how they were regarded in the Middle Ages.[8]

While I would be cautious of suggesting manuscript study allows for the recovery of a lost history, which is the implication from Woolf's comment here, there is certainly an important concept suggested. Since one of the difficulties with the study of medieval literature is that texts do not always exist in such stable forms as modern printed texts, the possibility of considering texts within their literary contexts, as Boffey reiterates, allows us to glean meanings that would not otherwise be visible.

In *The Whole Book,* Nichols describes manuscript study as important because it demands that the relationship between the text and its historical context be scrutinised. According to Nichols, "materialist philology seeks to analyze the consequences of this relationship on the way these texts may be read and interpreted."[9] Nichols suggests this leads to an understanding of how a manuscript may be organised: "it postulates the possibility that a given manuscript, having been organized along certain principles, may well present its text(s) according to its own agenda, as worked out by the person who planned and supervised the production of the manuscript."[10] Of course in the production of a manuscript the organising principles may change and vary according to circumstances, but the importance of Nichols' comments here is the suggestion that a manuscript may have its own discernible agenda: "The manuscript agency–manuscript kind or identity—can thus offer social or anthropological insights into the way its texts were or could have been read by the patron or public to which it was diffused."[11] Once again one must be cautious not to extend this to suggest that it is possible to recover history from such research, which would be to impose an artificial stability on to a manuscript. Nichols' comment, however, is valuable for recognising the way a manuscript may well give some indications as to its use and value during different time periods.

Derek Pearsall gives a broader consideration of the impact of the relationship between a manuscript and the modern reader than Nichols, demonstrating a broader consideration of the impact a reader may have on a text. He says, on the one hand:

> The methods of compilers and manuscript editors of all kinds, whether professional or amateur, need to be studied, if we are to understand the reception and readership assumed for the literary works contained in [manuscripts].

On the other hand, however, Pearsall reminds us that:

> Reading is always an act in which we share with the writer in the making
> of meaning. Attention to the activities of the scribes, compilers, editors,
> decorators and illustrators of our fifteenth-century manuscripts helps to
> ensure that the reader's share is fairly apportioned.[12]

The balance Pearsall suggests is that in examining a text within its
manuscript context we may be able to discern some of the scribal and/or
authorial intentions in the composition, as well as acknowledging the
meanings generated by the reader. This view, it seems to me, tempers the
suggestions of Woolf and Nichols in which they seem to seek to recover a
lost history within manuscripts, as if such a definable concept of history
exists. Pearsall cautions this attitude with the reminder of the impact we,
the modern reader, have on a text or manuscript, and the meanings that we,
ourselves, generate as reflective of our contemporary setting.

In another article, Pearsall also reminds us of the fluidity of medieval
texts. In criticising the modern critical editions of medieval texts, Pearsall
points out that such editions posit an artificial stability on to texts. As
examples, he cites *The Canterbury Tales* and *Piers Plowman*; the former,
he reminds us, is a clearly unfinished, unordered collection of stories, but
is presented in modern editions as a complete, unified text. He says:
"There is no authorized order [of the *Canterbury Tales*]; but editors have
to print the tale in some order, and the order they print them in comes to
have a specially privileged status."[13] With reference to *Piers Plowman*,
Pearsall draws our attention to the intentional ambiguities within the
manuscripts, in which the lack of a clear practice with regard to
capitalisations deliberately blurs any attempt to know with certainty
whether an abstract noun is actually a personification, or where the lack of
speech marks deliberately blurs the distinction between a character's
speech and the narrator's speech. Pearsall cites the speech of
Rechelesnesse, in which

> ...it is not entirely clear where he starts and stops talking. This expresses
> very effectively that manner in which he both is and is not a representation
> of the divided will of the narrator: the blurring, shiftiness is essential, and
> yet the modern editor has to remove it.[14]

Modern editions of *Piers Plowman*, Pearsall points out, remove these
ambiguities, thus creating an artificial stability that was never originally
there. This is a significant point because, while Pearsall regards
manuscript study as a vitally important tool, he cautions against the notion

that manuscript study will necessarily reveal any sense of certainty about a text.

In the case of *The Assembly of Ladies*, it will also be significant to examine the manuscript evidence for the ways its different readers have used and valued the manuscripts over time. The idea of manuscript agency as presented by Nichols and the caution of Pearsall that the reader's impact must also be considered imply a wide division, both psychologically and in time, between the composition of a manuscript and the modern reader. It must be remembered, however, that the manuscripts being considered here were probably compiled over a long period of time, and have been read and used throughout the intervening five hundred or so years. As such, it is possible for the agency of a manuscript to change over time, and certainly for the reader's impact to vary over such a wide time period. The organisational properties of MS Longleat 258, for example, can be seen to have been valued in different ways at different time periods. At the time of its compilation there seems to be a general organisational principle of collecting courtly love poetry into a single volume, yet some fifty years later the manuscript was valued by William Thynne not for this organisational property but for its collection of Chaucerian texts.[15] The implication of this is that the organisational principles of manuscripts may be many and varied and different aspects may be valued at different times; essentially it may well be possible to discern several agendas within a single manuscript pertaining to different time periods and psychological understanding.

The Miscellany

In the facsimile edition of Trinity College Manuscript R.3.19, the editor, Bradford Y. Fletcher, introduces the manuscript as "a fascicular miscellany of generally secular Middle English verse,"[16] and all three of the manuscripts in which *The Assembly of Ladies* appears could be broadly described in these terms. Such a description, however, is problematic and in some instances far too simplistic to adequately encompass the content of each of the manuscripts. The term "miscellany" in Fletcher's introduction implies a random collection of texts; manuscripts in which no particular organising principle is visible, and yet in all of the manuscripts to be discussed here, discernible patterns and systems of organisation are visible. Nichols points out the potentially misleading implications in the term "miscellany": "*Miscellany*...sheds little light on the relationship of the texts to their codicological context, and it may even be misleading, suggesting, as it does, an arbitrary principle of organization for manuscripts in which there may be a perfectly clear organizing principle."[17] The fact that such organising principles are visible makes these manuscripts of interest here, as the different ways in which the three manuscripts are organised suggests each included *The Assembly of Ladies* for different reasons.

The *Oxford English Dictionary* cites Wentworth's 1615 edition of *The Miscellanie* as the earliest known use of the term "miscellany" to refer to a codex of various, unrelated written material.[18] Certainly the word itself existed long before this, being derived from the Latin *miscellanea*, but it does not appear to have been a term used in medieval writing to apply, in the modern sense, to an arbitrary collection of written material. These findings suggest the use of the term "miscellany" is a modern over-simplification for the kind of manuscript whose organising principle may be difficult, at first glance, to discern and for which there is little other contextual information readily available to indicate its purpose.

Julia Boffey and John J. Thompson prefer the term "anthology" in their chapter from *Book Production and Publishing in Britain 1375-1475*,[19] in which they use "anthology" as a generic term that may be applied to any codex, with or without an clearly noted organising principle, which contains a variety of texts. The vagueness of this definition is deliberate on their part, as it necessitates that every such manuscript be examined on its own merits rather than being diminished by an all-encompassing label. They further consider the term "commonplace book" as being another expression for describing a book containing many different texts, but they also point out the difficulty this presents, with numerous examples of books that have clearly different and varied organising principles, but which are all frequently labelled as "commonplace books." They point out the contradictions in this definition by referring to specific examples:

> Commonplace books, it is argued, are rather haphazard, amateur productions which have been compiled over a period according to the whims of their owners...The term is broad enough to embrace most privately produced books and some institutional products, but frequently quoted examples which have been used to define this type of book include the mainly literary collection of Latin and English items in Trinity College Cambridge MS O.9.38; the collection of mainly historical and political writings in Latin and English in Trinity College Dublin MS 516, and the rather more heterogeneous collection in Trinity College Cambridge O.2.53.[20]

The point Boffey and Thompson make here is that the clear structural and thematic distinctions of many manuscripts are ignored when they are labelled as "commonplace books;" such a term cannot accurately reflect the contents of a manuscript.

Siegfried Wenzel also highlights the difficulties presented by the term "miscellany," demonstrating the way the term actually fails to distinguish between manuscripts that clearly have different organising principles. Wenzel does concede, however, that "miscellany" is better than nothing, and if its inadequacies force us to constantly refer back to the manuscripts themselves, then all the better.[21] Despite this, it seems more appropriate for this study not to regard the manuscripts under consideration as miscellanies in order to avoid reducing their individual characteristics. It is the unique organising principles of each manuscript that are of importance here, because they indicate a wider range of meanings for *The Assembly of Ladies* than would otherwise be discernible. In the absence of a named author for the poem, the contextual information provided by the manuscripts highlights the way the poem focuses in numerous ways on varying aspects of gender difference in the fifteenth century.

Cambridge, Trinity College MS R. 3.19

The most striking feature of Cambridge, Trinity College MS R. 3.19 (hereafter T) in its current form is its collation. Comprised of thirteen booklets each separately foliated by the same fifteenth-century hand, the manuscript is now clearly misbound. A paper manuscript of 254 leaves measuring 265 x 195 mm, the foliation and the textual content both indicate the fascicles are in the wrong order, although there is no evidence to state exactly what the correct order may have been.[22] Many of the outer leaves of the fascicles are worn and dirty, indicating a time-lapse between composition and being bound into a single volume, yet there is some evidence to suggest that the fascicles were associated together in some form before binding, primarily based on the fact that the foliation is in a single hand, and on the association between this manuscript and Cambridge, Trinity College R.3.21, which is also a collection of booklets. It has been conjectured by scholars that these two manuscripts may have once formed a pair—T a selection of secular verse, Trinity R.3.21 of religious verse: "perhaps [T's] component parts were designed to complement the religious bias of the booklets making up MS R.3.21."[23] A single scribe is responsible for the majority of the texts in both manuscripts.

T contains a total of forty-seven texts and appears to have at least passed through the hands of John Stow as he is responsible for the copying of some of Lydgate's fables on folios 235r-236r. Four other hands are discernible; the main scribe, as mentioned, was responsible for most of the copying, of some 203 folios. Fletcher indicates that T contains almost no evidence of scribal supervision, but does note that the main scribe is remarkably accurate and thus may well have been responsible in some way for the overall production. Of particular significance to this study are the frequent emendations made by later unidentified hands, which suggest the ways in which the manuscript may have been used and the way its use changed over time.

The fact that the manuscript is comprised of a series of booklets demands further attention, as scholars have suggested that the booklet was an independent written form in the medieval period.[24] P. R. Robinson describes the booklet as an independent unit and contrasts it with the forms of quire and *pecia*, both of which, while identifiable as discrete parts, serve primarily to form the components of a complete codex. The booklet, according to Robinson, "originated as a small but structurally independent production containing a single work or a number of short works."[25] The booklets of T, and of Trinity R.3.21 can both be regarded in this way, as Boffey and Thompson argue: "The outer leaves of some of the booklets are grubby and worn, as if the different parts did in fact remain in an unbound state for some time."[26] This feature suggests to Boffey and Thompson that, generally, the: "production and circulation of material in booklets seems to have been a reality."[27]

Robinson identifies some particularly significant identifying features of booklets that will be useful in this study. The size of a booklet was generally determined by its content, and so may range from a single quire to several gatherings. As few independent examples survive, Robinson describes the nature of booklets as found bound into larger collections, and she identifies ten relevant features of the booklet as related to its manuscript:

- The dimensions of its leaves may differ from those of other parts of the manuscript.
- Its handwriting may differ.
- Its style of decoration or illustrations may differ.
- Its catchwords may run only within the "booklet," there being no catchword at the end of its last gathering it link it with the first quire of the next booklet.
- It may have its own series of quire signatures.
- Its outer leaves may be soiled or rubbed, suggesting that the booklet circulated independently for some time before being bound up with others.
- Its number of leaves to a quire may differ from the number(s) in other parts of the manuscript.

- A scribe may have had difficulty in fitting a text into the quire structure of a "booklet" and, consequently, have modified that structure.
- The last page (or pages) of a "booklet" may have been left blank because the text did not fill the "booklet."
- Sometimes text has been added on an originally blank endleaf (or leaves) by the scribe, collector or later owner.[28]

Some of these features may well seem self-evident, such as a difference in handwriting or ornamentation, but when all ten of these elements are considered together they can highlight some unusual aspects within a manuscript. Within T, for example, some of these ten elements are present, such as the worn outer leaves and the presence of several blank leaves at the end of some of the booklets, suggesting independent circulation of the booklets. Yet it is significant in T that the main scribe has copied nine of the thirteen booklets, and this same scribe is responsible for the foliation of all of the booklets. Clearly, then, it is difficult to conclude with certainty that the booklets of T circulated as independent units; if they did so, their circulation must have been limited enough that the main scribe was able to exert a certain amount of supervisory control over the booklets, including over the four booklets copied by other scribes.

It is possible that the main scribe of T had available to him manuscripts written by John Shirley. This is based on two pieces of conjectural evidence. First, the main scribe of T collaborated with the so-called "Hammond scribe" on Trinity College R. 3.21, as has already been noted. The "Hammond scribe" has been identified as being responsible for the copying of parts of BL Additional 34360 (another of the manuscripts to contain the *Assembly of Ladies*), BL Harley 2251, Trinity College R.3.21, BL Arundel 59, BL Royal 17 D. XV, and several others, and, there seems little doubt, had access to manuscripts written by John Shirley.[29] Second, according to Fletcher, T contains distinct Shirlean spellings:

> Since the heading of at least one poem in [T] is decidedly Shirlean and since there are occasional Shirlean spellings, it is fair to suppose that [T] was the product of scribes who operated John Shirley's "scriptorium" and "lending library" after his death in 1456.[30]

Certainly such evidence is thin, but it does suggest the copying of T occurred in the general milieu of urban commercial manuscript copying of the late fifteenth century.

Boffey and Thompson cite a specific example from T that further illustrates the manuscript tradition of this time period, focusing on the English version of Alain Chartier's *La Belle Dame Sans Merci*, translated by Sir Richard Roos. The text appears in five other manuscripts besides T but the textual affiliations of these six copies suggest to Boffey and Thompson "the co-existence of different manuscript traditions of single works among the material available to related London scribes".[31] The six manuscripts divide into two groups, as noted by Skeat: Group A consisting of Trinity R.3.19, CUL Ff.1.6 (the Findern manuscript), Longleat 258 (which also contains *The Assembly of Ladies*), and Sloane 1710. Group B consists of Fairfax 16 and Harley 372. These groupings are determined by the fact that the Group B texts were clearly copied from an exemplar in which several leaves were missing.[32] The point that Boffey and Thompson illustrate is that, despite these groupings that indicate the use of different exemplars, T and Harley 372, each from different groups, have a third manuscript in common. Part of the Harley manuscript is copied by the "Hammond scribe," who, as has been noted, collaborated with the main scribe of T on Trinity R.3.21. According to Boffey and Thompson:

> That two scribes possibly related to the same commercial concern should have access to such very different versions of the same text can only confirm suspicions that the organisation which supported them was a relatively informal, flexible one.[33]

The main scribe of T and the "Hammond scribe" collaborated together on Trinity R. 3.21 and yet it appears that each had access to different versions of *La Belle Dame Sans Merci*. This is an indication of the wider commercial context in which these manuscripts were produced and suggests a greater freedom of availability of texts than is generally presumed for this time period.

A comparison between *La Belle Dame Sans Merci* and *The Assembly of Ladies* can be made here, in terms of the length of each of the poems. Boffey and Thompson describe the length of *La Belle* (749 lines) as "too small to form a complete volume on its own account, and yet too long to be categorised as mere makeweight."[34] The six manuscripts in which it appears suggest that the poem, because of its length, was regarded in several different ways: "as one of a series of items, or as a part of a small collection, as well as in some independent form."[35] The same could be said of *The Assembly of Ladies* (756 lines), that it is of a sufficient length that could see it circulate as part of a series of texts (as it appears to in Additional 34360), as part of a small collection (as in Longleat 258), or independently. Within T the poem appears as a single booklet and so may have circulated independently, yet its current existence in the manuscript gives the poem further significance in relation to the other texts in the manuscript.

The date of T is relatively straightforward to determine from three pieces of evidence. First, Fletcher notes the four dated watermarks visible are particularly unusual, and all suggest a date after the second half of the 1470s.[36] Second, according to Manly and Rickert, the portion of the manuscript containing 720 lines from Chaucer's *Monk's Tale,* ff. 179r-184r and 184v-188r, appears to have been copied from Caxton's 1478 edition of *The Canterbury Tales.*[37] Third, the final item in the manuscript, a prose piece entitled *The Petigrew of England,* ff. 247r-251r, contains a reference to Edward IV that suggests it would be unlikely for the manuscript to be dated after Edward's death in 1483.

To discuss any sense of overall thematic unity within T might seem inappropriate given its probable early state as a series of independent booklets. It must be acknowledged, however, that even if its circulation as booklets did occur, it was then collated into a single volume at some stage, and it is this collation that is of interest here. Whoever was responsible for the collation into a single codex, whether it was the main scribe or someone later, it remains likely that the booklets, when combined, were intended as a single collection. As such, it is appropriate to consider the texts in relation to each other, although with the added caution that since the original order of the booklets is unknown, the original ordering of the texts also remains unknown unless they occur within a single booklet.

Fletcher regards the contents of T as evidence of "a taste that may perhaps most safely be called eclectic."[38] At best, the only consistent feature he finds throughout the manuscript is "the overwhelmingly Chaucerian nature of the collection."[39] There are, however, finer details to be found within the content of T that indicate particular themes which shed significant light on the inclusion of *The Assembly of Ladies* within the collection. Julia Boffey indicates some of these themes in her examination of the lyrics within the manuscript.

The lyrics of T are found predominantly within booklets one and ten, with a particularly large number, thirteen, found within booklet one. That the poems in booklet one are all courtly love poems would suggest a consistent tone and theme, yet, as Boffey indicates, this is not the case: "Interposed among them, however, and shattering any impression of homogeneity of subject or tone, are some other short poems of rather different kinds."[40] The poems she refers to are two anti-feminist poems by Lydgate (*Bycorne and Chychevache* and an extract from *The Fall of Princes* concerning the virtue of chastity), a lyric against hypocritical women, and *The Craft of Lovers*, of which Boffey says: "contrives simultaneously to expose the fatuity of conventional courtly language and to condemn the frailty of female virtue."[41] Despite having suggested these poems destroy any sense of thematic unity within the booklet, I would suggest that Boffey's description actually reveals another pattern altogether. The combination of the courtly love lyrics with the anti-feminist poems shows a trend of diminishing both the sentiment and the florid language of the courtly love lyrics. This suggests an overt awareness of the conventional language of courtly lyrics, which is metonymically highlighted by the positioning of the lyrics among the anti-feminist poems. Booklet ten contains a combination of the courtly love lyrics with *O Mossy Quince*, *The Describing of a Fair Lady*, a lyric warning against deceitful women, and Lydgate's *Horn's Away*. Here again the courtly tone and language is undercut by the humorous poems interspersed through the booklet.

The texts by Chaucer are noticeably isolated from the other texts in the manuscript, being found only in two booklets, three and eight. Booklet three contains only the one item, the *Parliament of Fowls*, and booklet eight contains the *Legend of Good Women* and the *Complaint unto Pity*. The isolation of the Chaucer texts within the manuscript suggests they need not be compared directly with any particular texts found elsewhere within T, but that in terms of general themes of secular love, attitudes to women, and the heightened awareness of the linguistic conventions used to convey these themes, these three texts can be considered as contributing to both a theme of courtly love and to the undercutting of that theme, particularly in a text such as the *Legend of Good Women*.

Booklet seven appears to reiterate this theme, containing *La Belle Dame Sans Merci*, the *Ten Commandments of Love*, and the *Nine Ladies Worthy*. As has been mentioned, *La Belle* is of sufficient length that it could occupy a booklet on its own, but here it is accompanied by two short poems. *La Belle* is a dialogue between a lover and a woman in which the woman rejects the lover, and the lover subsequently dies. The two short accompanying poems could each be said to complement the speech of the two characters in *La Belle*. The *Ten Commandments of Love* contains advice in the form of a list of suitable and appropriate behaviour for a man to follow when pursuing a woman, such as Faith, Intention, Discretion, Patience, and Prudence. The presence of this poem alongside *La Belle* draws attention to the courtly love conventions being employed by the lover in his pursuit of the woman. Similarly, *The Nine Ladies Worthy* could be said to correspond to the independent attitude displayed by the woman in *La Belle*. Skeat remarks on this poem for its unusual choice of women: Sinope, Hippolyta, Deipyle, Teuta, Penthesilea, Tomyris, Lampeto, Semiramis, and Menalippe, who are generally associated with battle or warfare.[42] The presence of these two poems within the booklet gives rise to a comparison between the language and intention employed by each of two characters of *La Belle*. The lover uses the tactics suggested by the *Ten Commandments of Love*, such as Intention and Perseverance, when he states clearly:

> What ever it be that me hath thus purchased,
> Wening hath nat disceyved me, certain,
> But fervent love so sore that me y-chased
> That I, unware, am casten in your chayne;
> And sith so it is, as Fortune list ordayne,
> Al my welfare is in your handes falle,
> In eschewing of more mischevous payn;
> Who sonest dyeth, his care is leest of alle. (ll.285-292)

The woman, in response, gives a reply that replicates the description of the behaviour of the *Nine Ladies Worthy*, arguing with strategic reason and logic when she says:

> This sicknesse is right esy to endure,
> But fewe people it causeth for to dy;
> But what they mene, I know it very sure,
> Of more comfort to draw the remedy.
> Such be thee now, playning ful pitously,
> That fele, god wot, nat alther-grettest payne;
> And if so be, love hurt so grevously,
> Lesse harm it were, oon sorowful, than twayne. (ll. 293-300)

The effect is to demonstrate the way the male and female characters within *La Belle* fail to communicate effectively; they employ different strategies in their language and each has their own particular goal in mind. Thus the two poems effectively undercut the courtly love tone of *La Belle* by overtly drawing attention to the mechanics of the language being used.

It must be stated that many of the booklets within T do not conform to the theme of courtly love or its ridicule. Booklet thirteen contains a single prose text entitled the *Petigrew of Englond*, booklet nine contains an unusual composite text made up of 240 stanzas from Lydgate's *Fall of Princes* and 90 stanzas from Chaucer's *Monk's Tale*, and booklet five contains two Lydgate texts, the *Four Complexions* and an extract from the *Four Seasons*. Despite the lack of a homogeneous and consistent theme throughout the entire manuscript, the courtly love theme is a clear and discernible concept that can be seen in eight of the thirteen booklets, which seems to be sufficiently substantial to acknowledge it as the dominant theme of the manuscript.

It has been acknowledged already that *The Assembly of Ladies* inhabits a single booklet, booklet six, and so may have circulated independently. In light of the dominant theme of courtly love and it refutation, however, it is possible to see its inclusion within T as entirely predictable. Rather than allowing the poem to exist solely as an example of courtly love poetry, the presence of the other poems within the manuscript helps to raise the presence of the artificiality of the courtly language employed in the poem, and by highlighting this, suggest its subversion. *The Assembly of Ladies,* as we have seen, utilises poetic conventions in order to emphasise their shortcomings, and it would seem that the placement of the poem within T corresponds to this interpretation.

Warminster, MS Longleat 258

MS Longleat 258 (L) is a predominantly paper codex of 215mm x 137mm, with slightly smaller vellum leaves acting as covers to the paper quires. In its current state the manuscript consists of 147 leaves and is evidently missing a quire of sixteen leaves.[43] Bradshaw's certainty of the missing texts is based on a table of contents on the verso of the final leaf written by the main scribe of the manuscript. The table of contents reads as follows:

Littera directa cupidinis amatoribus
Vnum carmen
Templum vitreum
De folio et flore
Exclamacio Martis
Exclamacio de morte pietatis
Congregacio dominarum
Exclamacio Annelide contra Arcite
Parliamentum auium
De oculo et corde
La bele dame sans mercy
De rustico et aue

In addition to this list, there is an inscription beneath that reads:

Maister Willm thyne
clerke of the kechin
to our soueraigne lorde
King henry the viii[th]
Thomas Godfray.[44]

This inscription is important as it is the main piece of evidence that the manuscript was at one time owned by William Thynne, and that portions of it were used by Thynne in preparation for his 1532 edition of Chaucer's works. As is well known, the practice of early editors such as Thynne and Stow of including as many "new" texts as possible in their printed editions of Chaucer led to the inclusion of a large number of texts clearly written by other authors. It is largely due to this practice that texts such as *The Assembly of Ladies* and *The Floure and The Leafe* are known today. *The Floure and The Leafe* is particularly interesting in this respect, as this is one of the missing texts from the L and there are no other manuscript versions known to be extant; Speght's 1598 edition of the poem is the earliest surviving.[45] Derek Pearsall speculates at some length on a possible link between the missing Longleat version of *The Floure and The Leafe* and Speght's edition of the poem, in which he suggests that perhaps the missing quire, once separated from the manuscript, passed through the hands of John Stow and thence on to Speght.[46]

According to James E. Blodgett, the Longleat version of *The Assembly of Ladies* was provided by Thynne as a printer's copy to Thomas Godfrey for the 1532 edition of Chaucer's Works. Blodgett says parts of L

> are counted off in marks characteristically used by Tudor printers to prepare copy... The relationship between these printer's marks and the corresponding texts proves that Thomas Godfrey used [Longleat] as his copy of *The Assembly of Ladies*.[47]

Blodgett also notes markings in the manuscript that indicate how the poem is to be arranged on the printed page.

The manuscript is collated into sixteen quires, most of which consist of eight folios, although towards the end of the manuscript the quires are not as regular with some containing nine and ten folios. Despite each of the quires being contained within vellum "covers," many of the texts run on from one quire to the next, uninterrupted, thus it seems unlikely the manuscript ever existed as a series of independent booklets. Unlike Trinity R.3.19, L appears to be a homogenous collection of poetry, very likely to have been bound soon after compilation. The existence of the vellum "covers" around each of the quires seems unusual in a manuscript that is so cohesive. Referring back to Robinson's list of features of the booklet, evidence of such covers is more in keeping with the booklet format rather than of a single large manuscript. It is only possible to speculate on this matter, that perhaps the quires were once intended for independent use, but were then required for the purpose of a larger single volume.

Pearsall notes the manuscript was probably written for private purposes,[48] and Hammond suggests that the uniformity of the collection indicates that perhaps "the copyist was also the owner,"[49] and both of these possibilities deserve some further consideration here. There is no record of ownership of L prior to William Thynne, and thus its original purpose and use cannot be known with any certainty. In addition to suggesting the manuscript was written for private purposes, Pearsall also suggests the scribe was "neat but inaccurate and unprofessional"[50] and it would seem that it is primarily on the nature of the handwriting that Pearsall suggests its private use. Although not stated, Pearsall's understanding seems to be that a scribal hand that is inaccurate and unprofessional would only occur in a manuscript written by the person who is to use the codex. This is certainly a possibility but there is another feature of L that may suggest another reason for the apparent inaccuracies and lack of scribal professionalism. Pearsall seems not to have considered the fact that the manuscript is clearly unfinished. From observation of the manuscript there are indications throughout of initial decorations that were never completed, thus it is not impossible that the manuscript may have been a working copy.[51] This possibility would correspond with Hammond's suggestion that the copyist was also the owner of the manuscript. With regard to the unfinished state of the manuscript, there is no indication that the supposed missing quires ever existed. While the scribal note at the end of the manuscript may suggest texts that are now missing from the manuscript, we do not know if they ever were included or if they were proposed for inclusion but later omitted.

Pearsall's suggestion of L being an unprofessional production is puzzling. The layout of the manuscript is quite uniform, written almost entirely by one scribe with three stanzas to a page. The only other hands visible include the running titles inserted by a sixteenth-century hand; this scribe is also responsible for a small number of corrections throughout the manuscript.[52] According to J. Schick, Sir John Thynne inserted a three-stanza poem by Richard Hattfeld on folio 32r,[53] and three stanzas of the last poem in the manuscript, Lydgate's *Churl and Bird*, have been written by still another hand. Hammond notes that at the top of folio 1r is written "Constat John Thynne," which is presumably where Schick identifies John Thynne's handwriting for the poem of Richard Hattfeld, although this is not stated. There is nothing significant, however, to suggest a lack of professionalism in the execution of the manuscript. One wonders if perhaps Pearsall's comment is more a reference to the rural setting in which the manuscript was composed, suggesting the unlikelihood of the availability of professional scribes, yet even this is untenable given that clearly exemplars of well-known texts were clearly available in such a rural setting and thus one need not assume that professional scribes were not available also.

The only indications of the date of the manuscript are suggested by Boffey and Thompson (late fifteenth century), Pearsall (about 1500), and Hammond (late fifteenth or early sixteenth century). There is nothing within the manuscript itself to indicate the date of composition, although a further examination of the watermarks may prove useful.

An interesting feature of L is Hammond's view that it is related to the so-called Oxford group of texts that she identified in *Chaucer: A Bibliographical Manual*.[54] Hammond considered that L was related to the better-known manuscripts of Fairfax 16, Tanner 346, and Bodley 638 and speculated that they may have been copied from the same or related exemplars. While this type of speculation can never be verified, it would suggest, like Trinity R.3.19, the type of literary milieu in which the manuscript was created. The circulation of manuscripts for copying and the ready access to different exemplars of the same texts further emphasises the general social context in which manuscripts were compiled in the late fifteenth century. What is interesting about this in regard to L is that, as indicated above, the manuscript is evidence of the circulation of texts in a rural setting and in particular the compiler clearly had access to Shirlean manuscripts as exemplars.

Boffey suggests the general organising principle behind L is essentially a collection of Chaucer and Chaucerian secular love poems. I would suggest, however, there is another organising principle that defines the manuscript contents even further. As well as being a collection of secular love poems, the texts in L also show a strong relationship to legal literature of the period.

Each text, to varying degrees, displays a formality in which complaints are expressed, clearly and succinctly, in support of particular viewpoints. It is notable too that in all instances the complaints are expressed orally by the characters, which is a feature of medieval legal complaints. Thus it would appear that L is not only a collection of secular love poetry, but the texts also contain particular references to legal complaints as well. This is an organisational property not seen in the other manuscripts containing *The Assembly of Ladies*, and has the effect of shifting our focus to emphasise the bills of complaint that feature in the poem above the other aspects of the poem.

One of the difficulties scholars have had with *The Assembly of Ladies* is that the bills of complaint seem rather tedious and drawn out, apparently unnecessarily so. Yet when the bills of complaint are seen in light of the entire contents of L, the importance of the bills becomes apparent. Where Pearsall suggests the bills indicate the poet was not in control of the allegory, I would suggest that the poet was not attempting to sustain the allegory. In representing nine bills of complaint in quite a detailed manner, the poet of the *Assembly of Ladies* seems to be emphasising the necessity of the accurate and detailed recording of events for the purpose of later recollection. This is further emphasised by the fact that the narrator of the poem actually states this as her purpose at the end of the poem. Once she awakens from her dream she says:

> With that anon I went and made this booke,
> Thus symply rehersyng the substaunce
> Because it shuld nat out of remembraunce.   (740-42)

Scholars have criticised negatively the ending of the poem, describing it as unfinished, dissatisfying, and abrupt. These comments are made simply because scholars have not been able to deduce any reason behind the nature of the ending, and are perhaps swayed by similar endings in other allegories. Yet in this instance I would suggest that the narrator's sudden shift from narrating a story orally to then recording the story as the written text is a deliberate emphasis on the legal necessity for recording events for posterity. The compiler of L clearly regarded the poem as contributing to literature that displays knowledge of legal language.

London, British Library MS Additional 34360

Like the Trinity manuscript, British Library MS Additional 34360 (A) is known to have been in the possession of John Stow. Containing twenty-nine separate texts, this manuscript does not demonstrate the same thematic coherence as Longleat 258, nor does it appear to have been a series of independent booklets like Trinity R.3.19; it appears to be an attempt to collect texts written by John Lydgate. The poems range in subject matter from Lydgate's interpretations of Aesop's fables, to interpretations of the Psalms and, item 18, an appeal to the Duke of Gloucester for money. There are some anonymous items, and a few items by Chaucer, including the *Complaint unto Pity,* the only text to be found along with the *Assembly of Ladies* in all three of the manuscripts under examination here.

Dated as being compiled in the late fifteenth century, the manuscript consists of 116 folios written on paper and measures approximately 260mm x 190mm. There are two scribal hands visible that Eleanor

Prescott Hammond identifies as the same scribes who worked on British Library MS Harley 2251, and this is a feature that requires further examination here.[55] Hammond identifies the first scribe of A as having written folios 1r-58r and 78r-116v, and the second scribe as having written folios 58v-77v. The items written by the first scribe are also written by this scribe in Harley 2251 along with a large numbers of other texts, folios 144r-293v. The items written by the second scribe in A, fifteen items, are identical to the items written by the same scribe in the Harley manuscript, and, with the exception of two entries, are arranged in the same order (folios, 1r-143v). An explanation of the scribal hands of the two manuscripts is as follows:

Additional 34360
ff. 1-58r   scribe one
ff. 58v-77v   scribe two
ff. 78r-116v   scribe one

Harley 2251
ff. 1-143v   scribe two
ff. 144r-293v scribe one

Scribe two is the aforementioned "Hammond scribe" identified by Hammond as responsible for a large number of late fifteenth-century manuscripts and who clearly had access to the manuscripts of John Shirley.

The relationship of A to Harley 2251 helps to indicate the conditions under which the manuscript was produced in the late fifteenth-century. That the two scribes are known to have collaborated on both manuscripts and that one of the scribes is known to have contributed to a large number of other manuscripts suggests some sort of an organised commercial enterprise. The other important suggestion these manuscripts indicate is in their content, which shows a concerted effort to create a volume of a single author's work. This would suggest a demand in the late fifteenth century for such codices and testifies to the popularity of both Chaucer and Lydgate. Julia Boffey discusses this popularity at some length with reference to those manuscripts "whose status lies somewhere between that of a verse anthology and that of an edition of the works of a single author."[56] As Boffey notes, there seems to be a distinct group of manuscripts that appear to be attempts at collating a single author's works, and yet will also contain many anonymous and wrongly attributed texts as well. Boffey suggests that perhaps this indicates a coherence now lost in these manuscripts:

In view of the carefree fifteenth-century confusion of canonical works with those which we now more scrupulously deem to be apocryphal, rigid dividing lines are hard to draw, and in many ways superfluous…it is perhaps worth bearing in mind that certain significances which originally gave coherence to the conjunction of items in a manuscript may now be totally hidden from the modern reader.[57]

Such is the case with A, which contains a large number of texts now attributed to Lydgate, but which in the manuscript are attributed to Chaucer, as well as texts, like the *Assembly of Ladies*, whose authorship is unknown.

Boffey also mentions the manuscripts of John Shirley and the later manuscripts based on them as an independent group, highlighting the impact that Shirley seems to have had on manuscript production in the fifteenth century: "Many manuscripts which were demonstrably produced after his death 1456 reflect his own personal style."[58] In this category, Boffey classes A, Harley 2251, and Trinity R.3.19, among others.

The manuscript is clearly unfinished, containing spaces available for ornamented initial letters throughout the manuscript, none of which were completed. Boffey has suggested this lack of completion may have been at least partially deliberate, as the lack of completed rubrication may have made the manuscript a more saleable item. It was common that many early print manuscripts were often only partially complete in their ornamentation, and could be completed by their subsequent owners. Features such as spaces left for the inclusion of coats of arms were common in these circumstances.

A is clearly not a thematic collection of texts, but rather a collection of texts mostly attributable to Lydgate. Of the twenty-nine texts in the manuscript, twenty-one appear to be by Lydgate, two are by Chaucer, one is attributed to the William de la Pole, and five are anonymous. In light of Boffey's reminder that the organizing principle behind a manuscript may no longer be visible to a modern reader, it is too much of an assumption to suggest that the compiler mistakenly thought the *Assembly of Ladies* was written by Lydgate.[59] A more likely possibility is that the compiler considered the *Assembly of Ladies* to continue the general tone and style of the other courtly love poems within the manuscript, such as the *Craft of Lovers*. The similarity does not necessarily indicate Lydgatian authorship, but does suggest the author of the *Assembly of Ladies* was familiar with the literary conventions in use in the fifteenth-century.

In his edition of the *Assembly of Ladies* Pearsall uses the text in A as his base text. He describes the text in A as "carelessly copied" (8) and lists the omissions and mistakes made by the scribes, yet he lists certain points about the text valuable and thus regards it as a more suitable text for editing. He rather broadly describes his edition from A as "the authentic text of the *Assembly of Ladies*" (8), and indicates his system of modernising the spelling of the text.

Bradford Y. Fletcher presents perhaps the only examination of the three manuscript editions of the *Assembly of Ladies*, and suggests that more is now known about the manuscript production process allowing some of Pearsall's assumptions to be questioned. In particular, Fletcher discusses the fact that Thynne's edition of the *Assembly of Ladies* is now widely thought to have been set up from the Longleat manuscript, of which Pearsall was not aware. As Fletcher points out, this is clear from observation of the manuscript which contains printer's markings in it. Fletcher's argument is to suggest that Pearsall's argument for the choice of A as a base text is somewhat flawed. Pearsall bases his choice primarily on the fact that there are far more independent readings within the manuscript, whereas Trinity, Longleat and Thynne's edition all show similar errors. While Fletcher generally concurs with this, he indicates that the independent readings within A are not necessarily better.

Conclusions

The three manuscripts examined here have, not surprisingly, many features in common. With all three having been produced in late fifteenth-century, it is not remarkable to discover that they share many of the same texts, that many of the same scribal hands are visible, and they may have been copied from the same or similar exemplars. What is significant about each of the manuscripts is the subtle way in which they differ from each other. By examining the way each of the manuscripts visually presents its texts, and, in particular, how each presents the *Assembly of Ladies*, it is possible to see that in each case a slightly different point of view is given of the texts. The Trinity manuscript can be regarded in two different states, as separate booklets and as a single codex. As the contents of an independent booklet, the *Assembly of Ladies* was clearly regarded as a significant enough courtly love poem in its own right to circulate separately from the rest of the manuscript, and yet as part of the whole manuscript it can be seen in a much more complex position, where, along with the other texts in the manuscript, the emphasis is on the undercutting of courtly love by drawing attention to the literary devices used to create the poems. The Longleat manuscript is by far the most homogeneous collection of texts, with its focus on debate poetry. While many of the poems in Longleat are courtly love poems, they do not form the same kind of group as the texts of the Trinity manuscript. Many of the texts in the Trinity manuscript, particularly the short lyrics, consist of a lover's lament, whereas in the Longleat manuscript most of the poems present both sides of a complaint, or, if not, they remain focused on the idea of debate per se rather than focused on love. Such is the case with the *Assembly of Ladies,* where specific legal terms are used in the presentation of the complaints, sometimes at the expense of narrative movement, suggesting that the linguistic structure of the argument is of greater importance than the nature of the complaint itself. BL Additional 34360 presents a different focus again. In a manuscript that is concerned principally to gather together works of a particular author, without any obvious thematic focus, the *Assembly of Ladies* can be seen most clearly as making use of standard fifteenth-century literary conventions. Its presence in the Additional manuscript highlights the way its themes, conventions and structures are part of the literary tradition of the period.

It is clear, then, that the benefit of a manuscript examination allows the multiple meanings of the text to be seen, and it is also possible that the meanings discovered in a manuscript analysis may well begin to indicate the ways in which the poems were regarded and valued at the time of their inclusion in the manuscripts. Of this we can never be certain, but it is most useful to note here that the three different presentations of the *Assembly of Ladies* reinforce the instability of the text rather than reduce it to a single interpretation.

CHAPTER SEVEN

THE FEMALE VOICE: FUTURE DIRECTIONS

The most visible and significant feature of *The Assembly of Ladies* that sets it apart from nearly all other fifteenth-century literature is the existence of the female narrator. It is this single feature that has dominated previous scholarship on the poem, and it has been the point of departure for this book. Where previous scholars have equated the narrator with the author, the result has been to assume female authorship for the poem. The question of authorship, however, has not been the focus of this book. Rather, the book has been concerned with exploring the meaning of the poem as generated by the overarching presence of the female narrator.

It is the presence of the female narrator that has determined the approach taken in this book. The gender issues in *The Assembly of Ladies* are presented to the reader by coupling social conventions with literary conventions. Extensive recourse to contemporary literature has made clear how and when *The Assembly of Ladies* has conformed to and deviated from literary conventions, and, in addition, shown how *The Assembly of Ladies* has drawn together social and literary conventions. The social restraints imposed on the women in the poem are replicated by the literary restraints imposed on the narrator, the result of which demonstrates how the female voice is marginalised in social and literary contexts.

Yet this analysis raises a number of questions for future research. The anonymity of the author, which I have argued here is deliberate, ought to cause scholars to question the emphasis on the need to know an author's identity. While the attribution to Chaucer has allowed *The Assembly of Ladies* a certain level of circulation, it has also resulted in the poem being regarded only in relation to Chaucer, even when finally rejected from the Chaucer canon. The shift away from Chaucer as the author resulted in a vacuum in scholarship on the poem, soon replaced with the assumption that the author must be a woman. There are two points this raises. The first is that, in the search for the author's identity, previous scholarship on *The Assembly of Ladies* has ignored the possibility that the anonymous author may be a necessary feature of the poem, as I have argued here, and the second point this leads to is that, in the midst of the author debate, very little previous scholarship has examined the poem in itself and regarded what meanings it may contain. This book has attempted to offer here a detailed analysis of *The Assembly of Ladies* in order to elevate for the reader how the contents of the poem situate the poem within its fifteenth-century context, and that this positioning draws the readers' attention to its fundamental question: how can a woman participate in literature? It is this question that I believe will provide a productive avenue of scholarly research in the future, and which will help us to reassess the significance women in literature.

APPENDIX

THE CONTENTS OF THE MANUSCRIPTS[1]

Cambridge, Trinity College, MS R.3.19

Booklet 1.
1. *Festum Natalis Domini*
ff. 1r-1v
IMEV 3807
Incipit: Tronos celorum continens…
Explicit: Yet to yo hyghnes hit myght be plesyng.

2. Lyric
ff. 2r-2v
Suppl. 2384.8
Incipit: O beauteuous braunche floure of formosyte…
Explicit: my in to your presence hastyly he bring.

3. Extract from *The Fall of Princes*–Lydgate
(4.2374-87, 3.1373-1421, 3. 77-84)
ff. 2v-3r
IMEV 1592
Incipit: In womanhede as Auctours all wryte…
Explicit: Byn euer redy to helpe hem and releue.

4. Lyric
f. 3v
Suppl. 2588.5
Incipit: O ye alle that ben or haue byn in dyssease…
Explicit: Euery trew louer to sle and to deuoure.

5. Lyric
ff. 3v-4r
Suppl. 190.5
Incipit: All lust and lykyng I begyn to lede (*above*, leue)…

Explicit: And let pyte comfort your dannghesse.

6. Lyric
ff. 4r-6v
Suppl. 2478.5
Incipit: O lady myne to whom thys boke I sende…
Explicit: But yef your womanhede rewarde my trew seruice.

7. Lyric
ff.7r-8v and 154r
Suppl. 928.5
Incipit: Go lytyl boke for dredefull ys thy message…
Explicit: With trew loue a thousand fold.

8. *The Craft of Lovers*
ff. 154v-156r
IMEV 3761
Incipit: Moralyse a similitude who lyst theyr balades sew…
Explicit: And graunt hem thy region and blysse celestiall.

9. Lyric
f. 156v
IMEV 2661
Incipit: Of theyre nature they gretly theym delyte…
Explicit: Wretyn in the lusty season of May.

10. Lyric
ff. 157r-157v
IMEV 2311
Incipit: Now fresshe floure to me that ys so bryght…
Explicit: My soule to god standeth in dyspeyre.

11. *Bycorne and Chychevache*–Lydgate
ff. 157v-159r
IMEV 2541
Incipit: O prudent folkes taketh hede…
Explicit: Lynked in a double chayne.
(In margin, seven glosses relating to text, and a hand pointing)

12. Lyric
f. 159v

IMEV 1238
Incipit: Honour and Joy helthe and prosperyte...
Explicit: Without your comfort but neuereylese to dy.

13. Lyric
f. 160r
IMEV 267
Incipit: Alone walking, in thought pleynynge ...
Explicit: Doth me auaunce, and thus an ende.

14. Lyric
f. 160r
IMEV 1562
Incipit: In the season of ffeuere when hyt was full colde...
Explicit: Graunt euery trew louer yo haue ioy of his.

15. Lyric
f. 160v
IMEV 1838
Incipit: Lady of pite for þy sorowes þat þou haddest...
Explicit: Yet wold I submit me in your remembraunce.

16. Lyric: 13 stanzas, 1-4 are from the *Court of Sapience*, 9 is from the *Craft of Lovers*, the remainder are unique
f. 161r-161v
IMEV 2510
Incipit: O merciful and o mercyable...
Explicit: God graunt hym blysse in heuen to haue a place.

17. *Pallas loquitur ad parisium de Troia*
f. 161v
IMEV 3197
Incipit: Son of Priamus Gentyll paris of Troy...
Explicit: Yeue hit me I am to haue hit able.

18. *Testament of Lydagte* (parts 2-4)
ff. 162r-169r
IMEV 2464
Incipit: The yeres past of my tendyr youthe...
Explicit: Thys lytyll dyte thys compilacion.

Booklet 2.
19. *The Fall of Princes*–Lydgate
(1.3522-28, 3795-3801)
f. 67r
IMEV 3493
Incipit: The vnware woo that commeth on gladnesse...
Explicit: Better ys to dy then lyue in suche penaunce.

20. *The Assembly of Gods*–attributed to Lydgate
ff. 67v-97v
IMEV 4005
Incipit: Here foloweth the Interpretacion of the names of goddys and
goddesses as ys rehersyd in þis tretyse folowyng as poetis write...
Explicit: Graunt eternall ioy aftyr thy last sentence.

21. *Churl and Bird*–Lydgate
ff. 9r-11v
IMEV 2784
Incipit: The tale of þe byrde and the chorle...
Explicit: With supportacion of your benygnyte.

22. Aesop's Fables–Lydgate
IMEV 4178
The Tale of the Cock
ff. 12r-13v
Incipit: The tale of the cok...
Explicit: Whyche ys conclusion of þys lytyll fable.

The Wolf and the Lamb
ff. 13v-14v
Incipit: The tale of the wolfe and the lambe...
Explicit: The wolfe rebuked for rauenous felnes.

The Frog and the Mouse
ff. 14v-15v
Incipit: The tale of the ffrogge and þe mowse
Explicit: Who vseþ frande with frande shalbe quyt.

The Hound and the Sheep
ff. 15v-16r

Incipit: The tale of þe Hownde and the Shepe
Explicit: Constreynyd by force to apere afore a juge...

Booklet 3.
23. *The Parliament of Fowls*–Chaucer (contains 1 extra stanza)
ff. 17r-25r
IMEV 3412, 2128
Incipit: So short þe lyfe, þe craft so long to lerne.
Explicit: In to euerythyng...thorow hys excellence.

Booklet 4.
24. *Guystard and Seiesemonde*–Boccaccio
ff. 26r-40v
IMEV 3258
Incipit: Tancret that was prynce of salern...
Explicit: Graunt these louers wy, and thus endeth my tale.

25. *Reflections of a Prisoner*–George Ashby
ff. 41r-45v
IMEV 437
Incipit: At the ende of somer when wynter began...
Explicit: Lackyng volunte for theyr dew penaunce.

Booklet 5.
26. *The Four Seasons*–Lydgate
ff. 49r-52r
IMEV 935
Incipit: What tyme the season of the yere...
Explicit: Dethe all consumythe which may not be denyed.

27. *The Four Complexions*–Lydgate
ff. 52v-53r
IMEV 2624
Incipit: Sanguineus. Natura þingues isti sunt atque jocantes.
Explicit: Thou shall hym know bi visage pale and wan.

Booklet 6.

28. *The Assembly of Ladies*
ff. 55r-65v
IMEV 1528
Incipit: In Septembre at the falling of the leef...
Explicit: Rede well my dreme for now my tale ys doon.

Booklet 7.
29. *La Belle Dame Sans Mercy*–Richard Roos
ff. 98r-108v
IMEV 1086
Incipit: Halfe in a dreme not fully well awakyd...
Explicit: I pray god sende hem bettyr auenture.

30. *The Ten Commandments of Love*
ff. 109r-110r
IMEV 590
Incipit: Certes fer extendeth yet my Reason...
Explicit: And call hym in to your Remembraunce.

31. *The Nine Ladies Worthy*
ff. 110v-111r
IMEV 2767
Incipit: Prefulgent in pretyousnes O synope the quene...
Explicit: Ouercame and venquysshed theym in batayle.

Booklet 8.
32. *The Legend of Good Women*–Chaucer
ff. 114r-150v
IMEV 100
Incipit: A thousand tymes haue I herd men tell...
Explicit: Thys tale ys sayde for thys conclusyoun.

33. *The Complaint unto Pity*–Chaucer
ff. 151r-152v
IMEV 2756
Incipit: Pyte that I haue sought so yore ago...
Explicit: With hert sore and full of besy payn.

Booklet 9.
34. A combination of 28 extracts from Lydgate's *Fall of Princes* and 2
extracts from Chaucer's *Monk's Tale*
ff. 170v -202r
IMEV 4231, 3983
Incipit: Worshipfull and dyscrete that here present be...
Explicit: When humble request your yre may nat aswage.

Booklet 10.
35. Lyric
ff. 205r-205v
IMEV 1300
Incipit: I haue a lady where so she be...
Explicit: For were she wele of me I dyd no cure.

36. Lyric
ff. 205v-206r
IMEV 2524
Incipit: O mosy quince hangyng by youre stalke...
Explicit: Of all wemen I loue yow best a thousand tymes fy.

37. *Horn's Away*–Lydgate
ff. 206r-207r
IMEV 2625
Incipit: Of God and kynde procedeth all Beawte...
Explicit: By example of hyr your hornys to cast away.

38. Lyric
ff. 207r-207v
IMEV 1944
Incipit: Looke well about ye that louers be...
Explicit: Beware therfore the blynde eteth many a fly.

39. Lyric
ff. 208r-208v
IMEV 2148
Incipit: Men may leue all gamys...
Explicit: A man were as good to be dede,
as smell therof þe stynk.

40. Lyric
f. 208v
Suppl. 1172.5
Incipit: He that wyll in Eschepe ete a goose so fat…
Explicit: Be the nyght neuer so long,

41. Lyric
ff. 209r-209v
IMEV 55
Incipit: A knyght that ys as hardy as a lyon…
Explicit: Of kyndly ryght may long endure.

42. Lyric
ff. 209v-211r
IMEV 3502
Incipit: The wyseman sayd vnto hys sonne…
Explicit: To day a man to morow no one.

43. *What the Good Wyfe Taught her Daughter*
ff. 211r-213r
IMEV 671
Incipit: The good wyfe taught hyr dowghtere…
Explicit: Her blessyng not þou haue and well not þou thryue.

Booklet 11.
44. *The Court of Love*
ff. 217r-234r
IMEV 4205
Incipit: With tymoros hert and tremlyng hand of drede…
Explicit: And Venus yet I thank I am alive.

45. Aesop's Fables–Lydgate
IMEV 4178
The Hound and the Sheep
ff. 235r-236r
Incipit: Thys ffable is of þe hound that bare the shep…
Explicit: Fesyryd twyne bothe he dyd lese.

How the Wolf deceived the Crane
Incipit: How the wolffe diseyvyd the crane…

Explicit: This tall applyinge agayn folke that be unkynde.

Booklet 12.
46. Piers of Fullham
ff. 240r-244v
IMEV 71
Incipit: Loo Worshipfull Sirs here after followeth a gentylmanly Tretyse...
Explicit: In oure tonge callede Culrage.

Booklet 13.
47. *The Petigrew of Englond*
ff.247r-251r
Prose
Incipit: This short tretise ys complied for to bryng the people oute of doubte that haue not hard of the Cronycle...
Explicit: The iij Son of Philippe labele – that ben ordeyned for thaym that occupie suche maner of open wronges.

Warminster, Longleat MS 258

1. *The Temple of Glas*–Lydgate
ff. 1r-32r
IMEV 851
Incipit: For thouht constreint and greuous heuines...
Explicit: Nou go þi way and put þe in hir grace.

2. Three stanzas by "Rycharde Hattfeld"
f. 32r
IMEV 232
Incipit: All women have vertues noble & excelent...
Explicit: They lak pride all lewdnes as I ye se.

3. *The Complaint of Mars*–Chaucer
ff. 49r-54v
IMEV 913
Incipit: Gladeth ye foules of the morowe gray...
Explicit: Kytheth therefore on her sum kyndenesse.

4. *Complaint unto Pity*–Chaucer
ff. 55r-57v
IMEV 2756
Incipit: Pite that I have sought so yore agoo...
Explicit: With herte sore and ful of besy peyne.

5. *The Assembly of Ladies*
ff. 58r-75v
IMEV 1528
Incipit: In Septembre at the falling of the leef...
Explicit: Rede well my dreme for now my tale ys doon.

6. *Anelida and Arcite*–Chaucer
ff. 76r-84r
IMEV 3670
Incipit: Thou ferse god of armes Mars the rede...
Explicit: That shapen was as ye shal after here.

7. *The Parliament of Fowls*–Chaucer
85r-101r
IMEV 3412

Incipit: The lyf so short the craft so long to lerne...
Explicit: The bet and thus to rede I nyl nat spare.

8. *The Eye and the Heart*
ff. 102r-119r
IMEV 1548
Incipit: In the first weke of the saison of May...
Explicit: That to al his desires he may attayne.

9. *La Belle Dame sans Mercy*–trans. Richard Roos
ff. 120r-136v
IMEV 1086
Incipit: Halfe in a dreme not fully well awakyd...
Explicit: I pray god sende hem bettyr auenture.

10. *Churl and Bird*–Lydgate
ff. 137r-147r
IMEV 2784
Incipit: Problemys liknessis and figures...
Explicit: With supportacioun of your benyngnyte.

London, British Library Additional MS 34360

1. *Fabula Duorum Mercatorum*–Lydgate
ff. 4r-18v
IMEV 1481
Incipit: In egipt whilom, as I rede and fynde...
Explicit: That in so be I pray yow sey al amen.

2. *Complaint unto his Purse*–Chaucer
f. 19r
IMEV 3787
Incipit: To yow, my purse, and to non other wight...
Explicit: Bieth heby ageyne or ellis must I dye.

3. *Complaint against Fortune*–attributed to Lydgate
ff. 19r-21v
IMEV 860
Incipit: Allas, fortune, allas, what haue I gilt...
Explicit: But reave on me and help me whan I dey. Amen.

4. Three stanzas entitled: "Balade that Chauncier made"
ff. 21v -22r
IMEV 3164
Incipit: So hath my hert caught in remembraunce...
Explicit: Yowre beaute hole, your stidefast gouernaunce.

5. "The question of halsam"–attributed to Lydgate
f. 22r
IMEV 3504
Incipit: The world so wide the heyre so remouable...
Explicit: May stidfast be as here in his liuyng.

6. Three Roundels–William de la Pole
ff. 22v-23v

     1.   Incipit: Lealement a tous jours mais...
            Explicit: Or serount nor coloaisirs perfais.

     2.   Incipit: Face vo coer tout ce que ly plerra...
            Explicit: Je bons regnere tant je pins.

3.   Incipit: Je vous salue ma maystresse...
     Explicit: Et me fait vro sy mayt dueux.

7. *The Order of Fools*–Lydgate
ff. 24r-26v
IMEV 3444
Incipit: The order of folis ful yore ago bigonne...
Explicit: Noon of this ordre is neuer lyk to the.

8. *The Horse, the Sheep, and the Goose*–Lydgate
ff. 27r-36v
IMEV 658
Incipit: Controuersies pleys and al discordis...
Explicit: For no prerogatiff his neyhbour shal dispise.

9. *The Assembly of Ladies*
ff. 37r-49r
IMEV 1528
Incipit: In Septembre at fallyng of the leef...
Explicit: Rede wele my dreame for now my tale is done.
10. *Complaint unto Pity*–Chaucer
ff. 49r-52v
IMEV 2756
Incipit: Pite whiche that I have sought so yoer...
Explicit: Ye dwelle withyn my trouble careful hert.

11. Paraphrase of Psalm cii–Lydgate
ff. 53r-57r
IMEV 2572
Incipit: Thow my soule gif laude unto the lord...
Explicit: for other sanstondnyt haue I non for me.

12. Paraphrase of Psalm lxxxvi–Lydgate
ff. 57r-57v
IMEV 2688
Incipit: In holy hillis whiche bien of grete renoun...
Explicit: How glorious thynges bien sunge and sayde of the.

13. Poem on the virtue of stone
ff. 58r-59r

IMEV 904
Incipit: Gentilnesse and curtese wold be rewarded...
Explicit: Super hanc petram, a verray stidefast stone. Amen.

14. *Hymn to Jesus Christ*–Lydgate
ff. 59r-59v
IMEV 1682
Incipit: Jhesu Crist kepe oure lyppes from pollucions...
Explicit: Or that the swerd be whet of vengeaunce.

15. *Hymn to the Virgin*–Lydgate
f. 60r-60v
IMEV 183
Incipit: All hayle Mary ful of grace...
Explicit: Such aungelis and devils knele therto.

16. *The Kings of England from William I to Edward IV*–Lydgate
ff. 60v-62v
IMEV 3632
Incipit: This myghti William [?] of Normandy...
Explicit: And that seynt George be with hym in his eight.
17. *Dietary*–Lydgate
ff. 63r-64r
IMEV 824
Incipit: For helth of body couer for col thyn hede...
Explicit: To al indifferent richest dietorye.

18. Lydgate's appeal to the Duke of Gloucester
ff. 64v-65v
IMEV 2825
Incipit: Right myghti prince and it be your wille...
Explicit: With a chere sowne of place and of coyngnage.

19. "Epitaphium eiusedem Ducis Glowcestrie"–Lydgate
ff. 65v-67v
IMEV 3206
Incipit: Souerayne immortal euerlastyng god...
Explicit: To the erth my body as for my sepulcure.

20. On outward acts of devotion–Lydgate
f. 68r-68v

IMEV 4245
Incipit: Ye devoute peple whiche kepe on obseruaunce...
Explicit: Whiche for thi sake wered a crowne of thorn.

21. *Hymn to the Virgin*–Lydgate
ff. 68v-68r
IMEV 3673
Incipit: Thow heuenly qwene of grace oure lodesterre...
Explicit: Save al thy seruantis from stroke of pestilence.

22. *Hymn to Jesus Christ*–Lydgate
ff. 69r-70v
IMEV 2218
Incipit: Most souerayne lord o blisful crist Jhesu...
Explicit: Hym and his moder, his peple and his land.

23. *Consulo Quisquis Eris*–Lydgate
ff. 70v-72v
IMEV 1294
Incipit: I counceile whatsoeuer thow be...
Explicit: To his plesaunce to utter his langage.

24. *Horn's Away*–Lydgate
f. 73r-73v
IMEV 2625
Incipit: Of god and kynd procedith al beaute...
Explicit: Theyre beaute to shewe though hornes were awey.

25. *The Craft of Lovers*
ff.73v-77r
IMEV 3761
Incipit: To moralise asimilitude who list þese balettes some...
Explicit: Traewe hert of me shal have his wyll.

26. *On Worldly Worship*–Lydgate
f. 77r
IMEV 4228
Incipit: Worldly worship is joye transitory...
Explicit: In most ensuerte perilously endureth.

27. "Of wyne awey the moles may ye wash"

f.77v
IMEV 2668
Incipit: Of wyne awey the moles may ye wash...
Explicit: But these in clensith wyne mylk and bone.

28. "There is none so wise a man / But he may wisdom lere"
f.77v
IMEV 3538
Incipit: There is none so wise a man...
Explicit: But sum man may hym greve.

29. *Secreta Secretorum*–Lydgate/Burgh
ff. 78r-116r
IMEV 935
Incipit: God almighty save and conserue oure kyng...
Explicit: Wher thou fayllest that men shal the correcte.

NOTES

Chapter One

[1] W. W. Skeat, ed., *Chaucerian and Other Pieces* (Oxford: Clarendon Press, 1897), lxix-lxx; W. W. Skeat, *The Chaucer Canon* (Oxford: Clarendon Press, 1900); Walter W. Skeat, "The Authoress of 'The Flower and the Leaf'," *Modern Language Quarterly* 3 (1900), 111-12.

[2] Ruth M. Fisher, *The Flower and the Leaf and The Assembly of Ladies: A Study of Two Love-Vision Poems of the Fifteenth Century* (unpublished doctoral thesis, Columbia University, 1955).

[3] Ethel Seaton, *Sir Richard Roos, Lancastrian Poet* (London: Rupert Hart-Davis, 1961).

[4] G. L. Marsh, "Authorship of The Floure and The Leafe," *JEGP* 6 (1906-7), 373-94; G. L. Marsh, "Sources and Analogues of The Flower and the Leaf," *MP* 4 (1906-7), 121-68, 281-328.

[5] Alexandra A. T. Barratt, "'The Flower and the Leaf' and 'The Assembly of Ladies': Is There a (Sexual) Difference?," *PQ* 66.1 (1987), 1-24.

[6] Julia Boffey, ed., *Fifteenth-Century English Dream Visions* (Oxford: Oxford University Press, 2003). All subsequent references to the text of *The Assembly of Ladies* are taken from this edition and will be referred to by line number only. The poem is extant in three manuscripts, Cambridge, Trinity College MS R.3.19, Warminster, MS Longleat 258, and London, British Library MS Additional 34360. These manuscripts are considered in detail in Chapter Six.

[7] Alexandra Barratt discusses the dearth of medieval literature written either by or about women. One reason for this, she suggests, is the lack of access women had to the means to write and to express themselves in literature. See Alexandra Barratt, ed., *Women's Writing in Middle English* (London: Longman, 1992), 2-7.

[8] The gender of the narrator in *The Assembly of Ladies* is considered by Ann McMillan, "'Fayre Sisters Al': The Flower and the Leaf and The Assembly of Ladies," *Tulsa Studies in Women's Literature* 1 (1982), 27-42; and Barratt (1987), 1-24.

[9] Luce Irigaray, *Speculum de l'autre femme* (Paris: Minuit, 1974), 227-40; I have used Margaret Whitford's edition of this text in which she translates "Incontournable volume" as "Volume without contours"; see Margaret Whitford, ed., *The Irigaray Reader* (Oxford: Blackwell, 1992), 53-67.

[10] Elaine Showalter, "American Gynocriticism," *American Literary History* 5.1 (1993), 111-28; Patricia Ticineto Clough, *Feminist Thought* (Oxford: Blackwell, 1994).

[11] See Ralph Hanna III, *Pursuing History: Middle English Manuscripts and their Texts* (Stanford, CA: Stanford University Press, 1996), particularly the chapter entitled "Authorial Versions, Rolling Revision, Scribal Error? Or, The Truth about *Truth*," 159-73.

[12] Barratt (1987), 2.

[13] These issues are considered in Charles Moorman, *Editing the Middle English Manuscript* (Jackson: University Press of Mississippi, 1975); and Vincent P. McCarren and Douglas Moffat, eds., *A Guide to Editing Middle English* (Ann Arbor: University of Michigan Press, 1998).

[14] McMillan, 27-42, considers the reasons for the foregrounding of gender, albeit by coupling *The Assembly of Ladies* with another fifteenth-century poem, *The Floure and the Leafe*.

Chapter Two

[1] For historical information about mazes, see Sir Frank Crisp, *Mediaeval Gardens* (New York: Hacker Art Books, 1966); Penelope Reed Doob, *The Idea of The Labyrinth: From Classical Antiquity through the Middle Ages,* (Ithaca, NY: Cornell University Press, 1990); Hermann Kern, *Through the Labyrinth: Designs and Meanings over 5000 years* (Munich: Prestel, 2000); W. H. Matthews, *Mazes and Labyrinths: Their History and Development* (New York: Dover, 1970); Craig Wright, *The Maze and the Warrior,* (Cambridge, MA: Harvard University Press, 2001). Wright suggests it is possible that there may have been hedge mazes earlier than the sixteenth century but that there is no remaining evidence to confirm this, 224. See also Fisher and Seaton who attempt to identify the exact location of the maze and to associate the characters from the poem with actual historic figures. Other scholars such as Pearsall in his edition of *The Assembly of Ladies* also rely heavily on historic evidence for their analysis of the maze. See D. A. Pearsall, ed., *The Floure and the Leafe and The Assembly of Ladies* (London: Thomas Nelson, 1962)

[2] Ruth Evans and Lesley Johnson, "The Assembly of Ladies: A Maze of Feminist Sign Reading?," in *Feminist Criticism: Theory and Practice*, ed. by Susan Sellers (Hemel Hempstead: Harvester Wheatsheaf, 1991), 171-96.

[3] Sources for architectural spatial theories are derived from Hanno-Walter Kruft, *A History of Architectural Theory: From Vitruvius to the Present* (New York: Princeton Architectural Press, 1994); Wim Swaan, *The Late Middle Ages: Art and Architecture from 1350 to the advent of the Renaissance* (London: Elek, 1977); John Harvey, *The Master Builders: Architecture in the Middle Ages* (London, Thames & Hudson, 1971); Xavier Barral i Altet, *The Early Middle Ages: From Late Antiquity to A.D. 1000* (New York: Taschen, 1997).

[4] Nancy Y. Wu, ed., *Ad quadratum: The Practical Application of Geometry in Medieval Architecture* (Aldershot: Ashgate, 2002).

[5] A notable example of this is offered by Carol Herselle Krinsky, "Seventy-Eight Vitruvius Manuscripts," *Journal of the Warburg and Courtauld Institutes* 30 (1967), 36-70, in which she argues that the *Ten Books on Architecture* by Vitruvius

was known during the Middle Ages, but not as a construction manual as it was later used during the Italian Renaissance, but as a literary and theoretical work considering spatial theories.

[6] It is coincidental but interesting to note that one of the manuscripts containing George Ashby's "Reflections of a Prisoner" is Cambridge, Trinity College R.3.19, which also contains *The Assembly of Ladies*.

[7] J. A. Burrow, ed., *Thomas Hoccleve's Complaint and Dialogue*, EETS o.s. 313 (Oxford: Oxford University Press, 1999), 3.

[8] The narrator of Chaucer's *The House of Fame* describes the dream he had on "The tenthe day now of Decembre;" this date is clearly not arbitrary as it is mentioned twice in the poem; see *The House of Fame*, in Larry D. Benson, ed., *The Riverside Chaucer* (Oxford: Oxford University Press, 1987), lines 63 and 111. All subsequent references to Chaucer are from this edition and will be referred to by line number only. The narrator of Dunbar's *In Wyntir* states that in winter "My hairt for languor dois forloir, / For laik of symmer with his flouris," lines 9-10; James Kinsley, ed., *The Poems of William Dunbar* (Oxford: Clarendon Press, 1979), 191-93. For *The Testament of Cresseid*, see Denton Fox, ed., *Robert Henryson: Testament of Cresseid* (London: Nelson, 1968), 61, lines 1-2, "Ane doolie sessoun to ane cairfull dyte / Suld correspond and be equivalent."

[9] Kern notes that the uni-cursal maze requires no effort on the part of walker, one arrives at the centre of the maze at the will of the architect. We do not know with certainty whether or not this maze is uni-cursal, but the movement of the women in the maze and their subsequent confusion, would suggest they are working in opposition to a greater force than their own. See Kern, 316.

[10] Pearsall, 154; and John Stephens, "The Questioning of Love in the Assembly of Ladies," *Review of English Studies* 24 (1973), 132.

[11] The terms "labyrinth" and "maze" are essentially interchangeable. "Labyrinth" is the earlier of the two terms and thus has been generally applied to the earlier uni-cursal mazes, that is, those with a single route to the centre. "Maze" is a later derivative of the word "amazed," and purely because it is a later development has been applied to the later multi-cursal mazes, that is, those with several routes in which one can become lost, or "amazed." In this book the term "maze" is used throughout; where necessary the expressions "uni-cursal" and "multi-cursal" will be employed for further clarity.

[12] This is a feature of much dream-vision literature. Consider Chaucer's narrator of *The House of Fame* and *The Book of the Duchess*, as examples.

[13] Walter Scheps, "A Climatological Reading of Henryson's Testament of Cresseid," *Studies in Scottish Literature* 15 (1980), 82.

[14] Many other medieval poems span several seasons, but none that I am aware of change as abruptly as *The Assembly of Ladies*. For further information regarding seasonal qualities of literature, see Rosemond Tuve, *Seasons and Months: Studies in a Tradition of Middle English Poetry* (Paris: Librairie Universitaire, 1933).

[15] Seaton, 295, and Stephens, 131.

[16] Pearsall, 155-56.

[17] For an examination of the types and uses of plants in Medieval gardens, see Sylvia Landsberg, *The Medieval Garden* (London: British Museum Press, 1995).

[18] Pearsall, *The Floure and the Leafe*, lines 158-61.
[19] Laurel was symbolic of endurance and purity; Woodbine was symbolic of faithful attachment, and Agnus Castus was a symbol of chastity.
[20] Fisher, 181.
[21] Seaton, 298.
[22] Pearsall (1962), 155.
[23] Robert Fabyan, *The chronicle of Fabian, whiche he nameth the concordaunce of histories, newly perused and continued form the beginnyng of Kyng Henry the seventh, to thends of Queens Mary* (London: Thon Kyngston, 1559), 350.
[24] *Thomas Usk: The Testament of Love*, ed. by R. Allen Shoaf (Kalamazoo: TEAMS, 1998), 12.
[25] *The House of Fame*, lines 1920-1921.
[26] Kern discusses the name "Domus Dedaly" in relation to the maze once found on the floor of Amiens cathedral and suggests that later hedge mazes dating from the sixteenth-century in France that also bear the name "Domus Dedaly" are probably derived from the Amiens example. See Kern, 148.
[27] Kern notes that the uni-cursal maze requires no effort on the part of walker, one arrives at the centre of the maze at the will of the architect. See Kern, 316.
[28] Piero Boitani, *Chaucer and the Imaginary World of Fame* (Cambridge: Brewer, 1984), 210.
[29] Boitani, 210.
[30] Doob, 328-29.
[31] Nicholas R. Havely, ed., *Chaucer: The House of Fame* (Durham: Durham Medieval Texts, 1994), 185.
[32] Boitani, 210.
[33] Doob, 329.
[34] See Scott D. Westrem, *The Hereford Map* (Turnhout: Brepols, 2001), 408-09.
[35] Fabyan, 351.
[36] Frank Justus Miller, ed., *Ovid: Metamorphoses* (Cambridge, MA: Harvard University Press, 1984), Book XII, lines 62-3.
[37] Pierre Bersuire, *Metamorphosis Ovidiana Moraliter Explanata, 1509*, ed. Stephen Orgel (New York: Garland, 1979), Book VIII, lxii.
[38] Doob, 152.
[39] Carolyn Dinshaw, *Chaucer's Sexual Poetics* (Madison: University of Wisconsin Press, 1989), 79.
[40] Susan Gubar, "'The Blank Page' and the Issues of Female Creativity," in *Writing and Sexual Difference*, ed. Elizabeth Abel (Brighton: Harvester, 1982), 74.
[41] Dinshaw, 79.
[42] Florence Percival, *Chaucer's Legendary Good Women* (Cambridge: Cambridge University Press, 1998), is doubtful of the sexual connotations seen by some scholars in Chaucer's tale of Ariadne. Referring to both Caroline Dinshaw and Sheila Delany, Percival accepts that one cannot discount such readings of the text, but considers it more likely that this is not the focus of the tale: "It must be acknowledged that the sexual innuendo in *Ariadne* is not so compelling that it is unable to be denied, and it may always have been conceived as a kind of optional extra," 193.

[43] See Dinshaw, 28-64, "Reading like a Man." Dinshaw discusses the occurrence of women internalizing masculine conventions in order to be able to function in society. Without this, she argues, women become marginalised and excluded.
[44] Tauno Nurmela, ed., "Giovanni Boccaccio: Il Corbaccio," *Annales Academiae Scientiarum Fennicae* Series B 146 (Helsinki: Suomalainen Tiedeakatemia, 1968); Anthony K. Cassell, ed., *The Corbaccio* (Urbana: University of Illinois Press, 1975).
[45] Nurmela, 45-6.
[46] Cassell, 6.
[47] Nurmela, 52.
[48] Cassell, 10.
[49] Nurmela, 57.
[50] Cassell, 14.
[51] Cassell, 140.
[52] Nurmela, 113-14.
[53] Cassell, 55-6.
[54] The bills of complaint in *The Assembly of Ladies* are considered in detail in Chapter Four.
[55] Pearsall, 167-8.

Chapter Three

[1] Jane Chance, "Christine de Pizan as Literary Mother: Women's Authority and Subjectivity in The Floure and the Leafe and the Assembly of Ladies," in *The City of Scholars: New Approaches to Christine de Pizan*, ed. Margarete Zimmermann and Dina De Rentiis (Berlin: Walter de Gruyter, 1994), 258.
[2] Barratt (1987), 15-16. Barratt argues that the narrator has an ambivalent attitude towards her companions: "she competes with them and yet is, literally and metaphorically, lost without them."
[3] See C. S. Lewis, *The Allegory of Love* (Oxford: Oxford University Press, 1936), 249, and Pearsall, 57.
[4] As will be discussed, the medieval concept of female honour is bound together with the household, reinforcing the separation of male and female spaces. See Ffiona Swabey, *Medieval Gentlewoman: Life in a Widow's Household in the Later Middle Ages* (Stroud: Sutton, 1999), for a discussion of "inner" and "outer" households for women and men, 15.
[5] Although Boffey's edition, quoted here, is based primarily on London, British Library MS Additional 34360, this manuscript does not contain the word "bay" in line 163; the word is taken from Cambridge, Trinity College MS R.3.19. Seaton has made much of the description of the bay windows, using their mention to support her theory that Pleasaunt Regarde refers to the residence of Margaret of Anjou at Plesaunce in Greenwich. According to renovation records, Plesaunce was notable for "the thousands of Flanders tiles bought for paving the queen's room, the dais in the great hall, two bay-windows, and especially a parlour in the little garden," 298.

[6] See Elizabeth Grosz, "Bodies-Cities," in *Sexuality & Space*, ed. Beatriz Colomina (Princeton, NJ: Princeton University Press, 1992), 241-254. Grosz considers the paradox that while cities are created by individuals, the city space as a collective entity also subsumes the individual at the same time, rendering the individual powerless.

[7] It is helpful to consider Gaston Bachelard, *The Poetics of Space*, trans. Maria Jolas (Boston, MA: Beacon Press, 1969), in which he compares interior space with the home, as a place of security and comfort, 6. The interior space of *The Assembly of Ladies* is similarly conceived as a protected environment but the narrator's response to it is to feel entrapped and oppressed by the space rather than secure and protected.

[8] For a consideration of the concept of gendered space, see Mark Wigley, "Untitled: The Housing of Gender," in *Sexuality & Space*, ed. Beatriz Colomina (Princeton, NJ: Princeton University Press, 1992), 327-389.

[9] The nostalgia for a past time is considered in the chapter concerning enclosed gardens, in which the narrator sits in the centre of the maze and, "remembryng of many dyvers cace" (75), begins to dream. The inference from the narrator's words is that she is recalling to mind a former time in which life was better. See Chapter Two.

[10] Clear comparisons can be made here with the enclosed space of the convent, a topic to be discussed shortly.

[11] All references to this text are taken from Earl Jeffrey Richards, ed., *The Book of the City of Ladies: Christine de Pizan* (New York: Persea Books, 1982).

[12] Richards, 10.

[13] Richards, 10-11.

[14] Sheila Delany is cautious about scholarship that promotes Christine as a proto-feminist. Delany notes that despite Christine's intention to create a new literary tradition for women, she is frustrated by Christine's "self-righteousness, her prudery, and the intensely self-serving narrowness of her views." Sheila Delany, "Mothers to Think Back Through: Who are they? The Ambiguous Example of Christine de Pizan," in *Medieval Texts and Contemporary Readers*, ed. Laurie A. Finke and Martin B. Schichtman (Ithaca, NY: Cornell University Press, 1987), 186.

[15] The divisions of social class are noted by Judy Chicago in her artwork *The Dinner Party*. The artwork consisted of a series of dinner-table settings specifically created for famous women through history, including Christine de Pizan. "As I worked on research for *The Dinner Party* and then on the piece itself, a nagging voice kept reminding me that the women whose plates I was painting, whose runners we were embroidering, whose names we were firing on to the porcelain floor were primarily women of the ruling classes." Judy Chicago, *The Dinner Party: A Symbol of Our Heritage* (New York, NY: Doubleday, 1979), 56; The entry on Christine de Pizan is 78-9.

[16] Richards, 10.

[17] See Jean Le Fèvre, *Le Livre de Mathéolus: poème français deu XIVe siècle* (Brussels, Imprimerie de A. Mertens et fils, 1846-64)

[18] See Maureen Quilligan, *The Allegory of Female Authority: Christine de Pizan's Cité des Dames* (Ithaca, NY: Cornell University Press, 1991), particularly her chapter entitled "Rewriting Tradition: The Authority of Female Subjectivity," 69-103; Quilligan makes the association between textuality and misogyny in Christine's use of the story of Semiramis. Boccaccio's version of the story condemns Semiramis for incest with her son, but Christine positions Semiramis' story as existing prior to the existence of written law, thus absolving her of the charge of incest. The suggestion is that it is the written text that condemns her, even though Christine justifies Semiramis' actions according to common sense and reason.

[19] See Glenda McLeod, "Poetics and Antimisogynist Polemics in Christine de Pizan's *Le Livre de la Cité des Dames*," in *Reinterpreting Christine de Pizan*, ed. Earl Jeffrey Richards (Athens, GA: University of Georgia Press, 1992), 37-47; McLeod discusses Christine's manipulation of poetic conventions to create an alternative female literary tradition.

[20] Richards, 41.

[21] Richards, 40.

[22] Richards, 41.

[23] Richards, 10.

[24] Grosz, 241-53.

[25] Grosz, 245.

[26] The narrator's difficulty in negotiating the regulations of Pleasaunt Regarde can, of course, be compared to the convoluted pathways of the maze in the poem, but the difference is that the narrator had no difficulty in reaching the centre of the maze.

[27] Lewis sees this as a fault in the poem, suggesting that "what the writer really wants to describe is no inner drama with loyalty as its heroine, but the stir and bustle of an actual court, the whispered consultations, the putting on of clothes, and the important comings and goings," 250.

[28] See Jean-Pierre Foucher and Andre Ortais, ed., *Chrétien de Troyes: Perceval ou le Roman du Graal* (Paris: Gallimard, 1974), and Burton Raffel, ed., *Perceval: The Story of the Grail by Chrétien de Troyes* (New Haven: Yale University Press, 1999).

[29] *IMEV* 671. The manuscripts containing *What the Good Wife taught her Daughter* are as follows: Cambridge, Emmanuel College, MS 106; London, Lambeth Palace Library, MS 853; San Marino, California, Huntingdon Library MS HM128; Cambridge, Trinity College MS R.3.19; Oxford, Bodleian Library, MS Ashmole 61. Printed editions of the poem: F. J. Furnivall, ed., *A Booke of Precedence*, EETS e.s. 8 (London: Trübner, 1869), 44-51; Frederick J. Furnivall, ed., *The Babees Book*, EETS o.s. 32 (London: Trübner, 1868), 36-47; Tauno Mustanoja, ed., "The Good Wife Taught her Daughter, The Good Wyfe Wold a Pylgremage, The Thewis of Gud Women," *Annales Academiae Scientiarum Fennicae* B 61/2 (Helsinki: Suomalainen Tiedeakatemia, 1948). See also the Appendix for its location in the Trinity manuscript.

[30] Pearsall, lines 579-80.

[31] Felicity Riddy, "Mother Knows Best: Reading Social Change in a Courtesy Text," *Speculum*, 71 (1996), 66-86.
[32] Riddy, 74.
[33] Riddy, 76.
[34] Riddy, 81-2.
[35] Aberystwyth, National Library of Wales, MS Porkington 10, f. 135^r; this poem is printed in Furnivall (1869), 39-43.
[36] Simone Marshall, ed., "An abstracte owte of a boke þat is callid *Formula Nouiciorum*," *Mystics Quarterly* 29.3-4 (2003), 102.
[37] Lina Eckenstein, *Woman Under Monasticism: Chapters on Saint-Lore and Convent Life between A.D.500 and A.D.1500* (New York: Russell and Russell, 1963), 378-79.
[38] See also Berenice M. Kerr, *Religious Life for Women* (Oxford: Clarendon Press, 1999), 101-128, where the hierarchical nature of the religious house is discussed further.
[39] Swabey, 21.
[40] The exact distinction between Lady and Gentlewoman is not clear and at times in scholarship the two terms have been used interchangeably. Ffiona Swabey, in discussing the household of Alice de Bryene, describes her as the "lord" of her household since she is a widow, yet in the title of her book, Swabey uses the phrase "Gentlewoman." See also Kate Mertes, *The English Noble Household 1250-1600* (Oxford: Blackwell, 1988). Mertes states that "in most cases 'the ladies of the lady' were her social equals or nearly so," 58. The distinction seems to indicate more who was serving whom, rather than one's class or social standing.
[41] Jennifer C. Ward, *English Noblewomen in the Later Middle Ages* (London: Longman, 1992), 143-63. Ward discusses the prevalence of noblewomen becoming nuns in later life and of the likely existence of female lay orders in England, both clear indications of an overlap between the lay and religious worlds. See also Mertes, who examines the lay household as a religious community, 139-60.
[42] Eckenstein, 376-77.
[43] Swabey, 15.
[44] Charity Cannon Willard, ed., *A Medieval Woman's Mirror of Honor: The Treasury of the City of Ladies* (New York, NY: Persea Books, 1989).
[45] Willard, 180.
[46] Willard, 92-4; "Sobriety also should be evident in all the lady's senses...Chastity will direct her to such purity that her word, deed, appearance, dress, countenance, bearing, status, and high regard will be unreproachable."
[47] Willard, 180.
[48] Cambridge, Queens' College, MS 31. See P. S. Jolliffe, "Middle English Translations of *De Exterioris et Interioris Hominis Compositione*," *Mediaeval Studies* 36 (1974), 268.
[49] Bella Millet and Jocelyn Wogan-Browne, *Medieval English Prose for Women: Selections from the Katherine Group and Ancrene Wisse* (Oxford: Clarendon Press, 1990), xx.

[50] James Dean, ed., *Six Ecclesiastical Satires* (Kalamazoo, MI: TEAMS, 1991), 227-46. This poem is found in London, British Library, Cotton Vespasian MS D. ix, fols 177^r-182^v, 190^r-190^v.

[51] Dean, 228.

[52] Eileen Power, *Medieval English Nunneries, c. 1275-1535* (Cambridge: Cambridge University Press, 1922). See 545-49 for a discussion of *Why I Can't Be a Nun*, and 604-21 for a discussion of the genre of *chanson de nonne*.

[53] Power, 604.

[54] Of course, Chaucer's Wife of Bath notes that her education is from experience, lines 1-2.

[55] Pearsall (1962), 58; Stephens, 137.

[56] Fisher examines the mottoes of the women in *The Assembly of Ladies* in great detail and, in personal correspondence with Joan Evans, notes that mottoes and devices sewn on to dresses were almost unknown in England in the fifteenth century but common in France. She also states that, while mottoes and devices were generally an extension of the family crest, in the later medieval period they became increasingly personalised and obscure in their meaning. Fisher, 192-200. The only other example of a personal motto used in fifteenth-century poetry to my knowledge occurs in Lydgate's *Temple of Glas*, in which the woman in the poem bears the motto *De mieulx en mieulx* [better and better]. See Julia Boffey, ed., "The Temple of Glas," in *Fifteenth Century English Dream Visions* (Oxford: Oxford University Press, 2003). Lydgate's poem seems to have had a large influence on the poet of *The Assembly of Ladies*, a feature that is noted by Stephens, 129-140.

[57] The colour blue is, of course, a symbol of loyalty and it could be argued that the narrator does not wish her loyalty to be obscured by a device or motto. See Jean Chevalier and Alain Gheerbrant, *A Dictionary of Symbols* (Oxford: Blackwells, 1994).

[58] Lewis, 250.

[59] Rozsika Parker, *The Subversive Stitch* (London: The Women's Press, 1984), 11.

[60] Susan Crane, *The Performance of Self: Ritual, Clothing, and Identity During the Hundred Years War* (Philadelphia: University of Pennsylvania Press, 2002), 86.

[61] Joan Evans, *Dress in Mediaeval France* (Oxford: Clarendon Press, 1952).

[62] Ruth Marie Fisher, *The Flower and the Leaf and the Assembly of Ladies: A Study of Two Love-Vision Poems of the Fifteenth Century* (unpublished doctoral thesis, Columbia University, 1955).

[63] Boffey (2003), 15-89.

[64] Barratt (1992), 8-10.

[65] Joan Evans, *A History of Jewellery 1100-1870* (London: Faber and Faber, 1970), 45.

[66] *English Medieval Lapidaries*, ed. Joan Evans and Mary S. Serjeantson, EETS o.s. 190 (London: Oxford University Press, 1933), 28.

[67] Evans and Serjeantson, 37.

[68] Other texts with painted murals include Chaucer's *The Book of the Duchess* and *The Parliament of Fowls*, Lydgate's *The Assembly of Gods* and *The Temple of Glas*, *The Court of Love*, and Stephen Hawes' *The Pastime of Pleasure*.

[69] See John V. Fleming, *The Roman de la Rose: A Study in Allegory and Iconography* (Princeton, NJ: Princeton University Press, 1969), 31-34, for a detailed examination of the vices painted on the exterior walls of Deduit.

[70] Grant Showerman, ed., *Ovid: Heroides and Amores* (London: Heinemann, 1914), 23.

[71] Harold Isbell, ed., *Ovid: Heroides* (London: Penguin, 1990), 11.

[72] *The Legend of Phyllis*, lines 2394-2561.

[73] Percival, 286-88.

[74] Percival, 287.

[75] Percival, 288.

[76] The story of Pyramus and Thisbe is part of the thirteenth-century interpretation of Ovid found in Pierre Bersuire, Book 4, ll. 55-166. It is also useful to consider George Sandys, *Ovids Metamorphoses Englished, Mythologized, and Represented in Figures, 1632* (New York, NY: Garland, 1976), 114-117, for an early English translation of the story of Pyramus and Thisbe.

[77] *The Legend of Thisbe*, lines 706-923.

[78] Elaine Tuttle Hansen, *Chaucer and the Fictions of Gender* (Berkeley: University of California Press, 1992), 4.

[79] Scholarship suggests Giovanni Boccaccio's *De Casibus illustrium virorum,* Book 6, and *De Claris Mulieribus*, may, in part, have been sources for Chaucer's "Legend of Cleopatra;" John Gower's retelling of the tale in the *Confessio Amantis*, 8.2571-77 is thought to have been based on Chaucer. See Benson, 1066, and Beverly Taylor, "The Medieval Cleopatra: The Classical and Medieval Tradition of Chaucer's Legend of Cleopatra," *Journal of Medieval and Renaissance Studies* 7 (1977), 249-69.

[80] Percival, 237.

[81] Percival, 224-28; Dinshaw, 70.

[82] Louis Strouff, ed., *Mélusine: Roman du XIVe Siècle* (Geneva: Slatkine Reprints, 1974).

[83] London, British Library, MS Bibl. Reg. 18.B. ii, printed in A. K. Donald, ed., *Mélusine*, EETS e.s. 68 (London: Trübner, 1895); and Cambridge, Trinity College, MS R. 3.17, printed in W. W. Skeat, ed., *Romans of Partenay*, EETS o.s. 22 (London: Trübner, 1866).

[84] See, in particular, Sara Sturm-Maddox, "Crossed Destinies: Narrative Programs in the Roman de Mélusine," in *Mélusine of Lusignan: Founding Fiction in Late Medieval France,* ed. Donald Maddox and Sara Sturm-Maddox (Athens, GA: University of Georgia Press, 1996), 12-31.

[85] Gabrielle M. Spiegel, "Maternity and Monstrosity: Reproductive Biology in the Roman de Mélusine," in *Mélusine of Lusignan: Founding Fiction in Late Medieval France,* ed. Donald Maddox and Sara Sturm-Maddox (Athens, GA: University of Georgia Press, 1996), 103.

[86] Christine, notably, uses Semiramis as a precedent for women building cities, although she equally could have used Mélusine. See Richards, 38-40.

[87] Kevin Brownlee, "Mélusine's Hybrid Body and the Poetics of Metamorphosis," in *Mélusine of Lusignan: Founding Fiction in Late Medieval France,* ed. Donald

Maddox and Sara Sturm-Maddox (Athens, GA: University of Georgia Press, 1996), 76-99.

[88] Brownlee, 77.

[89] The earliest citation in the *MED* for the word "umple" is c.1426.

[90] Alastair J. Minnis, *Lifting the Veil: Sexual/Textual Nakedness in the Roman de la Rose* (London: King's College London, Centre for Late Antique and Medieval Studies, 1995), 2.

[91] William Harris Stahl, ed., *Commentary on the Dream of Scipio by Macrobius* (New York, NY: Columbia University Press, 1990), 86-7.

[92] Peter Dronke, *Fabula: Explorations into the Uses of Myth in Medieval Platonism* (Leiden: E. J. Brill, 1974), 48.

[93] James J. Sheridan, ed., *Alan of Lille: Anticlaudianus or The Good and Perfect Man* (Toronto: Pontifical Institute of Mediaeval Studies, 1973), 40.

Chapter Four

[1] This difference is explicitly stated by Gilbert and Gubar (1987), 21-48. Gilbert and Gubar highlight the masculinity of the alphabet, "the public character of the alphabet would seem to exclude women's historically privatized experience" (22), and "without the alphabet, women would seem to be without a history of their own" (23). In these examples, Gilbert and Gubar are correlating the written language with masculine power; this is opposed to feminine language which they equate with being primarily oral and experiential.

[2] See Walter J. Ong, *Orality and Literacy: The Technologizing of the Word* (London: Methuen: 1982), 72. Ong determines that "sight isolates, sounds incorporates," by which he suggests the written word can present only a limited point of view which may be misunderstood and misinterpreted at different times and on different occasions, whereas the spoken word is always all-encompassing, available simultaneously to all listeners and its meaning can be more certain because of its immediacy and its direct contact with the human "lifeworld." Ong describes the spoken word as homeostatic, "word meanings come continuously out of the present" (46-7), imbuing them with a stability not attainable by the written word, which may change its meaning over time.

[3] See M. T. Clanchy, *From Memory to Written Record* (Oxford: Blackwell, 1993), 253-95; David Mellinkoff, *The Language of the Law* (Boston, MA: Little, Brown, 1963), 92; and Frederick Pollock and Frederick William Maitland, *The History of English Law before the time of Edward I* (Cambridge: Cambridge University Press, 1898), 90, in which consideration is made of the performative, oral aspect of medieval law and legal agreements.

[4] Julia Boffey, ed, *The Temple of Glas*, in *Fifteenth-Century English Dream-Visions* (Oxford: Oxford University Press, 2003) and Walter Skeat, ed., *La Belle Dame Sans Merci*, in *Chaucerian and Other Pieces* (Oxford: Clarendon Press, 1897).

[5] Neil Cartlidge, ed., *The Owl and the Nightingale* (Exeter: University of Exeter Press, 2001), *The Parliament of Fowls*, in Larry D Benson, ed., *The Riverside*

Chaucer (Oxford: Oxford University Press, 1987), 383-394. Another example of a contemporary debate poem is Lydgate's *Churl and Bird*, a poem which appears in one of the manuscripts that contains *The Assembly of Ladies*, Cambridge, Trinity College, R.3.19, ff. 9^r-11^v.

[6] Similarities between Lydgate's *Temple of Glas* and *The Assembly of Ladies*, particularly the presence of Cupid's martyrs in both texts, have been noted by Marsh, 374.

[7] Compare Chaucer's *House of Fame*, on which Lydgate largely based his poem, where the Temple of Venus is also a venue for making complaints of love.

[8] The difference in points of view in medieval texts is considered by Sarah Stanbury in her article "Feminist Masterplots: The Gaze on the Body of Pearl's Dead Girl," in *Feminist Approaches to the Body in Medieval Literature*, ed. Linda Lomperis and Sarah Stanbury (Philadelphia, PA: University of Pennsylvania Press, 1993), 96-115, in which the direction of the eye, that is, the point of view, is directed and controlled. See also Linda Tart Holley, *Chaucer's Measuring Eye* (Houston, TX: Rice University Press, 1990); in which the artistic effect of perspective is seen to impact on the point of view of the narrator of a text. The perspective and the narrative frames of *The Assembly of Ladies* will be considered in greater detail in Chapter Five.

[9] According to Ong, words in a primary oral culture are an "event," and that generally language is a "mode of action and not simply a countersign of thought," 32, indicating that at its most basic level, and even in literate cultures that have only residual orality, language is always performative.

[10] The narrator of *La Belle Dame Sans Merci* displays a similar voyeuristic tendency by remaining hidden from the view of the lovers, not unlike the narrator of William Dunbar's poem *The Tretis of the Tua Mariit Wemen and the Wedo*, in *The Poems of William Dunbar*, ed. James Kinsley (Oxford: Clarendon Press, 1979), 42-59.

[11] The lovers in *La Belle Dame Sans Merci* seem to use two different literary conventions. The man's love complaint displays the conventions of the lover that one could find in Andreas Capellanus' *The Art of Courtly Love*, ed. and trans. John Jay Parry (New York, NY: Frederick Ungar, 1957) whereas the woman's rational and logical response bears more in common with Aristotle's *The Art of Rhetoric*, ed. and trans. H. C. Lawson-Tancred (London: Penguin, 1991).

[12] Reed, 46.

[13] Kathryn Hume, *The Owl and the Nightingale: The Poem and its Critics* (Toronto: University of Toronto Press, 1975), 131.

[14] See D. S. Brewer , ed., *The Parlement of Foulys* (London: Thomas Nelson, 1960), 1-64.

[15] Reed, 324.

[16] Pearsall says of the narrator at the end of the poem: "She seems to have forgotten that she is supposed to be telling her story orally," 171, n. 740. This is an unlikely conclusion as the narrator clearly directs her speech towards the inquisitive knight who is listening to the tale. It seems more likely to me that she is deliberately blurring the distinction between written and spoken communication, a point to be considered in more detail in Chapter Four.

[17] Clanchy, 275, considers the shifting between oral and written legal complaints when he cites a case from 1293 in which a defendant was required to read aloud his objections concerning certain jurors. Being unable to read the defendant's assistant whispered the written text to the defendant, who then orally spoke the complaints while appearing to read them from the text! Cases such as these, according to Clanchy, demonstrate the overlap between oral and literate cultures. See also Alan Harding, "Plaints and Bills in the History of English Law," in *Legal History Studies,* ed. by Dafydd Jenkins (Cardiff: University of Wales Press, 1975), 65-86, in which Harding says "The writing down of complaints and the presenting of petitions seems to have become widespread only in the second half of the thirteenth century," 74.

[18] I can find no literary or historic precedent for this use of a tapestry. Like the covering of the images of Cupid's Martyrs with gauze, this may be an original invention of the poet. The primary use for tapestries was as wall hangings, for both decoration and warmth, although they are known to have been used as curtains, cushions, and blankets. Immensely valuable, they were also important for the display of wealth, both in secular and religious settings. According to Adolfo Salvatore Cavallo, religious tapestries were used "either as devotional objects or as an aid in teaching Christian lessons to the illiterate." See Adolfo Salvatore Cavallo, *Medieval Tapestries* (New York: Metropolitan Museum of Art, 1993), 31. The stories depicted in tapestries, whether religious or secular, may well have had instructional purposes, although I do not think this is the purpose of the tapestries in *The Assembly of Ladies.* In this instance it seems more likely the tapestries, as examples of an activity primarily performed by women, are used in an exclusionary manner. Plesaunt Regarde is an enclosed space solely for women, and the tapestries complement this feminine space.

[19] See Seaton, 294-308. Seaton attempts to compare the assembly with the court of Margaret of Anjou and suggests the poem was occasional, probably written for an event now unknown. Any allegorical reference in the events at the assembly, she suggests, must have been of significance to that court.

[20] Richard Firth Green, *A Crisis of Truth: Literature and Law in Ricardian England* (Philadelphia: University of Pennsylvania Press, 1999), 41.

[21] André Salmon, ed., *Le Livre des Serfs de Marmoutiers* (Tours: Société archéologique de Touraine, 1864).

[22] Green, 41. See also Clanchy, 294-327.

[23] Green, 273.

[24] On the issue of memory in pre-literate societies, Ong comments that in order to be able to retrieve information in oral societies, "thought must come into being in heavily rhythmic, balanced patterns, in repetitions or antithesis, in alliterations and assonances...patterned for retention and ready recall," 34.

[25] Green, 50.

[26] Green, 273.

[27] See Clanchy in the section entitled "Symbolic Objects and Documents," 254-60.

[28] Green notes an example of a piece of parchment being worn as a protective talisman by an illiterate man to ward off illness. It was later discovered the

parchment contained nothing more than gibberish, indicating the value lay in the physicality of the item, not in the words it purportedly contained, 50.

[29] Clanchy notes an example of a book being used as a legal token, 256.

[30] See Ong, 34-5.

[31] *The Franklin's Tale*, l. 1622.

[32] For further consideration of the conclusion to *The Franklin's Tale*, see R. D. Eaton, "Narrative Closure in Chaucer's Franklin's Tale," *Neophilologus* 84.2 (2000), 309-21, and Timothy H. Flake, "Love, Trouthe, and the Happy Ending of the Franklin's Tale," *English Studies* 77.3 (1996), 209-26.

[33] R. W. Chambers and Marjorie Daunt, eds, *A Book of London English 1384-1425* (Oxford: Clarendon Press, 1931), 35.

[34] These two terms will be discussed in greater detail shortly.

[35] Green, 42-4.

[36] Mabel Day and Robert Steele, eds, *Mum and the Sothsegger,* EETS o.s. 199 (London: Oxford University Press, 1936).

[37] Ong describes spoken language as evanescent, "sound exists only when it is going out of existence," 32. Clanchy explains the sense of truthfulness of the spoken word versus the potential falseness of the written word: "The danger with writing was that it implanted forgetfulness in the soul, preventing people from recalling the truth from within themselves. Writing anything down externalized it and changed it and falsified it to some extent," 193.

[38] G. A. Lester, ed., *Mankind,* in *Three Late Medieval Morality Plays* (London: A & C Black, 1981), 1-57.

[39] *Piers the Plowman's Crede*, in James Dean, ed., *Six Ecclesiastical Satires* (Kalamazoo, MI: TEAMS, Western Michigan University, 1991), 1-50.

[40] A. V. C. Schmidt, ed., *William Langland: Piers Plowman* (London: Longman, 1995).

[41] See John A. Alford, "Literature and the Law," *PMLA* 92.1 (1977), 941-51. Alford examines several texts, including *Piers Plowman* and *The Assembly of Ladies*, in which he suggests the general trend in medieval literary texts that include legal themes is to display the degeneration in legal values.

[42] It is possible to compare these complaints with women's lament poems, such as those found in the Findern manuscript, Cambridge University Libraray MS Ff.1.6, in which the narrative voice of the poems laments the departure or absence of a lover, sometimes sorrowfully, angrily, or resignedly. See Sarah McNamer, "Female Authors, Provincial Setting: The Re-versing of Courtly Love in the Findern Manuscript," *Viator* 22 (1991), 279-310, and Simone Celine Marshall, "Notes of C.U.L. MS Ff.1.6: The Findern Manuscript," *NQ* 49.4 (2002), 439-42.

[43] *The Owl and the Nightingale* makes frequent use of proverbial statements which are used, as in this instance, as an oral authority.

[44] Ong comments on proverbs being used as aids for the memory in oral cultures and in societies with a strong oral residue, 35.

[45] See Jan Moore, ed., *Selected Middle English Lyrics* (Wellington: Victoria University Press, 1985), 303. Moore describes the Medieval tradition of using physical appearance to determine inner qualities.

[46] Ong refers to the importance of repetition in oral delivery, used as a method of emphasizing a single idea or concept, 39-40.

[47] Chambers and Daunt, 35.

[48] See Peter Coss, *The Lady in Medieval England 1100-1500* (Stroud: Sutton, 1998), 36, concerning the language of deference used to address a lady.

[49] See Mertes, 58.

[50] As far as I am aware this has not been noted in any previous scholarship on *The Assembly of Ladies*.

[51] Evans and Johnson, 3.

[52] See Paul Binski, *Medieval Death: Ritual and Representation* (London: British Museum Press, 1996), particularly chapter three, "The Macabre," 123-63.

[53] Boffey (2003) suggests a comparison between the nine women of *The Assembly of Ladies* and the nine muses of poetry or "the nine famous women of antiquity who were in later Middle Ages cited in association with the celebrated Nine (male) Worthies," 196. I would argue that this can only be regarded as a broad comparison because the women of *The Assembly of Ladies* are not specifically identified as a group of nine women, rather they are two groups: five ladies and four gentlewomen.

[54] Barratt (1987), 15.

[55] See Barratt (1987), 20, Lewis, 249, Pearsall, 169, n. 680, and Stephens, 137.

[56] Pearsall, 169-70, and Barratt (1987), 19-20.

[57] The three manuscripts that contain *The Assembly of Ladies* show no instances of emendation or erasure that might suggest errors have contributed to the unusual content of these two stanzas. Only the text from BL Additional MS 34360 contains any errors of significance: two stanzas (lines 549-532) have been omitted which consist of a description of Lady Loiaulte's dress, and, more significantly for the discussion here, two lines (563 and 578) have been emended by the scribe to change the tense. In line 563 the scribe has crossed out "hir" and replaced it with "oure": "In hir [oure] presence she rede hem euerychone." Interestingly Pearsall, despite using the Additional MS as the base text for his edition, does not adopt this reading. In line 578 the scribe has crossed out "we" and replaced it with "they": "Reason it wold that we [they] were sonnest spedde," a reading Pearsall does adopt in his edition.

[58] Helen Barr, *Signes and Sothe: Language in the Piers Plowman Tradition* (Cambridge: Brewer, 1994), 61.

[59] This seems rather drastic yet it provides an interesting comparison for complaints narrated by men. As has been shown in *La Belle Dame Sans Merci*, the male lover so often places his fate in the hands of the woman, should she show him mercy and agree to be wooed by him, he will live, but if she rejects him, he will surely die.

[60] Green, 14.

[61] Green, 14.

[62] *The Book of the Duchess*, l. 753.

[63] *Troilus and Criseyde*, 5, l. 1676.

[64] The *MED* defines "trouth" as "fidelity, faithfulness, honour, integrity, and honesty," whereas "sooth" is defined as "the truth of a situation, a true thing, a fact

or reality." The primary difference is that "trouth" is what a person knows internally, and "sooth" is an external judgment by others.

[65] Pearsall, 169, n. 680.

[66] Stephens, 137.

[67] Barratt (1987), 20.

[68] See Ong, 57-68, and Douglas Gray, "Notes on Some Middle English Charms," in *Chaucer and Middle English Studies*, ed. Beryl Rowland (London: Allen and Unwin, 1974), 56-71. Gray says "Charms have to be 'performed'. This implies a symbolic action, a ritual which is both efficacious and expressive," 61.

[69] Ong, 42.

Chapter Five

[1] See, in particular, David C. Lindberg, *Roger Bacon and the Origins of Perspectiva in the Middle Ages* (Oxford: Clarendon Press, 1996); *Studies in the History of Medieval Optics* (London: Variorum Reprints, 1983); and *Theories of Vision from Al-Kindi to Kepler* (Chicago, IL: University of Chicago Press, 1976).

[2] The limitations of *Perspectiva* are particularly considered by Holley, 25-26.

[3] Significantly, few early theorists seem to have been aware of the limitations of linear perspective, or if they were they chose to ignore the issue. Leon Battista Alberti appears not to have considered the limitations in his work *De Pictura* (1435), as did Lorenzo Ghiberti, despite drawing directly on the works of Vitruvius, Alhazen, Peckham, and Bacon for his manifesto on painting. Antonio Manetti, in his commentary on the *Life of Filippo Brunelleschi*, carefully side-steps potential difficulties by only using examples that comply completely with the rules of perspective. For further discussion on these three art-theorists, see John White, *The Birth and Rebirth of Pictorial Space* (Cambridge, MA: Belknap Press, 1987), 113-34. As will be discussed later in this chapter, many painters and artists were aware of the limitations of linear perspective and tended to "bend the rules" somewhat to suit their purposes.

[4] See *Le Roman de la Rose,* lines 18034-18290; *The Squire's Tale*, lines 9-670, and *The House of Fame*, lines 509-1090.

[5] Holley considers the dissemination and availability of optical texts to writers such as Chaucer, 30-31 and 41.

[6] David C. Lindberg notes briefly the epistemological association with *Perspectiva* in his article "The Science of Optics," in *Science in the Middle Ages*, ed. David C. Lindberg (Chicago, IL: University of Chicago Press, 1978), 338-68.

[7] The title *Perspectiva* has been used for the works of several notable early visual theorists, including John Pecham, *Perspectiva communis*; Witelo, *Perspectiva*; Alhazen, *Perspectiva*; and Roger Bacon, *Perspectiva*; for further information see Edward Grant, ed., *A Source Book in Medieval Science* (Cambridge, MA: Harvard University Press, 1974), 392-93.

[8] See Grant, 376-441, for a survey of the wide range of topics included in *Perspectiva*.

[9] Lindberg, 338.

[10] Hermann Gollancz, ed., *Dodi Venechdi* (London: Oxford University Press, 1920), 114-121.

[11] Robert Grinnell, "The Theoretical Attitude towards Space in the Middle Ages," *Speculum*, 21 (1946),148.

[12] Grinnell, 149.

[13] Grinnell, 148.

[14] Grant, 380-83.

[15] Clare C. Riedl, ed., *Robert Grosseteste: De Luce* (Milwaukee: Marquette University Press, 1942), 385.

[16] A. Mark Smith, ed., *Ptolemy's Theory of Visual Perception: An English Translation of the Optics* (Philadelphia: American Philosophical Society, 1996); A. I. Sabra, ed., *The Optics of Ibn Al-Haytham* (London: Warburg Institute, 1989).

[17] Grinnell, 149.

[18] Grinnell, 148.

[19] Holley, 24.

[20] Leon Battista Alberti, *De Pictura*, ed. and trans. Cecil Grayson (London: Phaidon, 1972).

[21] Consider, for example, Gerald of Wales' twelfth-century assessment of painting in John J. O'Meara, ed., "Giraldus Cambrensis in Topographia Hibernie," in *Proceedings of the Royal Irish Academy* 52.C (1949),151-52; and Jean Pucelle's fourteenth-century theories of manuscript illumination in L. F. Sandler, ed., "Jean Pucelle and the Lost Miniatures of the Belleville Breviary," *Art Bulletin* 66 (1984), 73-96.

[22] White, 122.

[23] Grayson, 54.

[24] White, 123.

[25] White, 125.

[26] David Hockney, *Secret Knowledge: Rediscovering the Lost Techniques of the Old Masters* (London: Thames and Hudson, 2001), 96-97.

[27] Grayson, 54.

[28] Charles Hope, "'Composition' from Cennini and Alberti to Vasari," in *Pictorial Composition from Medieval to Modern Art*, ed. Paul Taylor and François Quiviger (London: The Warburg Institute, 2000), 33.

[29] D. V. Thompson, ed., *Cennino Cennini: Il Libro dell'Arte* (London: 1933), cap. 1.

[30] Priscilla Heath Barnum, ed., *Dives and Pauper*, vol 1, part 1, EETS, o.s. 275 (1976).

[31] Barnum, 81.

[32] Barnum, 81.

[33] Barnum, 83.

[34] *The Book of Kells and the Art of Illumination* (Canberra: National Gallery of Australia, 2000), 67; Melbourne, National Gallery of Victoria, MS Felton 1072-3, fol 37v.

[35] Hockney, 86.

[36] Hockney, 87.

[37] Gollancz, 114.

[38] Grayson, 54.

[39] Reiss, 13.

[40] As will be discussed later, another, all-encompassing, frame surrounds the entire poem.

[41] Meyer Schapiro, "On Some Problems in the Semiotics of Visual Art: Field and Vehicle in Image-Signs," *Semiotica* I. 3 (1969), 241.

[42] Grayson, 54.

[43] Holley, 7.

[44] Holley, 28.

[45] Robert Belle Burke, ed., *Opus Majus of Roger Bacon* (Philadelphia: University of Pennsylvania Press, 1928), 234.

[46] Bacon preferences sight over all other senses, suggesting: "sed non possumus experiri que addiscimus nisi per visum. Si autem allegemus et tactum et olfactum, tunc induimus bestialem sapientiam." [but we cannot experientially test what we thus learn except through vision. However, if we adduce taste, touch, and smell as counter-examples, we are adopting a conception of wisdom applicable to animals.] Lindberg (1996), 4-5.

[47] See also Tuve for further examples of references to seasons and months in medieval poetry.

[48] Particularly Stephens, 131; and Pearsall, 169.

[49] See Barratt (1987), 12; and Chance, 245.

[50] Holley, 33.

[51] W. Beckett, *The Story of Painting* (Washington, DC: National Gallery of Art, 1994), 52.

[52] Holley, 25.

[53] This is also considered by Grinnell, 144.

[54] See Charles Muscatine, "The Canterbury Tales: Style of the Man and Style of the Work," in *Chaucer and the Chaucerians*, ed. D. S. Brewer (London: Thomas Nelson, 1966), 94-5.

[55] Compare with V. A. Kolve's analysis of the visual references in Chaucer. He says of the objects described in *The Canterbury Tales* that: "They do not call attention to themselves in specifically symbolic ways, but are instead discovered in-uncovered by-the narrative as it moves naturally from its beginning to its end, and the clue to their identity is the way they create a certain residue in the mind." Kolve's suggestion indicates a gradual and systematic placement of objects throughout the text, according to the flow of the narrative. V. A. Kolve, "Chaucer and the Visual Arts," in *Writers and their Background: Geoffrey Chaucer,* ed. Derek Brewer (London: Bell & Sons, 1974), 309.

[56] Holley, 13.

[57] Perhaps compare this to Dunbar's *The Tretis of the Tua Mariit Wemen and the Wedo* in which the narrator is an eager voyeur, waiting for the personal revelations of the three women.

[58] Burke, 234.

[59] See Stephens, 134.

[60] *Annunciation* (London: Phaidon, 2000), 77.

[61] The depiction of God's point of view is clear in another example of the Annunciation, by Jan Van Eyck. In this painting the words of Gabriel to the virgin, "Hail, thou art full of grace" emerge from his mouth in the direction of the Virgin. The Virgin's reply, however, "Behold the handmaid of the Lord," is written upside down, as if to be read by God above.

[62] As a comparison, consider Chaucer's *The Second Nun's Tale* in which the Nun retells the story of St Cecilia. Just as Cecilia's Christian life is contrasted with Roman pagan life, so too the Nun contrasts the chaste life of St Cecilia with the less-than-noble behaviour of the pilgrims on their way to Canterbury. In this way the frame of the story of Cecilia interacts with the frame of the pilgrimage.

[63] Kern, 207-36.

[64] Burke, 234.

[65] Holley, 24.

[66] Holley, 43.

[67] Holley, 24.

[68] See Samuel Y. Edgerton, Jr, *The Heritage of Giotto's Geometry: Art and Science on the Eve of the Scientific Revolution* (Ithaca, NY: Cornell University Press, 1991), 27-28. Edgerton gives a comprehensive explanation of the development of perspective.

[69] Stephens, 138.

[70] Pearsall, 156.

[71] Consider Mary Carruthers and Jan M. Ziolkowski, eds, *The Medieval Craft of Memory* (Philadelphia, University of Pennsylvania Press, 2002), 8. Carruthers says memory is strongly associated with emotion which is then often physically manifested: "each memory is thus to an important degree a physiological, bodily phenomenon." We may regard the narrator's sighs as such a physical enactment of her memories.

[72] See Lewis, 251.

[73] Pearsall, 64.

[74] Holley, 165, n. 11: "Witelo and Grosseteste comment on how painful light is to the unhealthy eye or to the eye unaccustomed to light. Grosseteste links the unhealthy mental sight with its analogue in the unhealthy physical sight weighed down by the body."

[75] Holley, 85.

[76] Hockney, 86.

[77] The *MED* contain entries for the word "semble" in two forms, as a noun: "The gathering together of persons for a particular purpose" and as an adjective: "similar, the same, in like manner."

Chapter Six

[1] A detailed list of the contents of these manuscripts is provided later; brief descriptions, however, may be found in Eleanor Prescott Hammond, "MS Longleat 258–A Chaucerian Codex," *Modern Language Notes* 20 (1905), 77-79; *Catalogue of Additions to the Manuscripts in the British Museum* (London: Longmans,

1894), 317-321, and Montague Rhodes James, *The Western Manuscripts in the Library of Trinity College, Cambridge* (Cambridge: Cambridge University Press, 1901), 69-74. James' description has now been superseded by that of Bradford Y. Fletcher, *Manuscript Trinity R.3.19: A Facsimile* (Norman, OK: Pilgrim Books, 1987), xvi-xx.

[2] Stephen G. Nichols, "The New Philology," *Speculum* 65 (1990), 1.

[3] Nichols, (1990), 3.

[4] Paul Strohm, *Theory and the Premodern Text* (Minneapolis: University of Minnesota Press, 2000), xiii.

[5] J. A. Burrow, "Poems without Contexts," *Essays in Criticism* 29 (1979), 6.

[6] Julia Boffey, "The Manuscripts of English Courtly Love Lyrics in the Fifteenth Century," in *Manuscripts and Readers in Fifteenth-Century England: The Literary Implications of Manuscripts Study*, ed. Derek Pearsall (Cambridge, D. S. Brewer, 1981), 3.

[7] Boffey, (1981), 3.

[8] R. Woolf, *The English Religious Lyrics in the Middle Ages* (Oxford: Oxford University Press, 1968), 376. See also Burrow, 6-32.

[9] Stephen G. Nichols, *The Whole Book: Cultural Perspectives on the Medieval Miscellany*, ed. Stephen G. Nichols and Siegfried Wenzel (Ann Arbor: University of Michigan Press, 1996), 2.

[10] Nichols, (1996), 2.

[11] Nichols, (1996), 2.

[12] Derek Pearsall, ed., *Manuscripts and Readers in Fifteenth-Century England: The Literary Implications of Manuscript Study* (Cambridge: D. S. Brewer, 1983), 1-2.

[13] Derek Pearsall, "The Uses of Manuscripts," *Harvard Library Bulletin* 4.4 (1994), 32.

[14] Pearsall, (1994), 33.

[15] For a discussion of the manuscripts used by William Thynne in the preparation of his edition of Chaucer's works, see James E. Blodgett, "William Thynne," in *Editing Chaucer: The Great Tradition,* ed. Paul G. Ruggiers (Norman, OK: Pilgrim Books, 1984), 35-52.

[16] Bradford Y. Fletcher, ed., *Manuscript Trinity R.3.19: A Facsimile* (Norman, OK: Pilgrim Books, 1987), xv.

[17] Nichols, (1996), 3

[18] *Oxford English Dictionary*, 2nd ed. (Oxford: Clarendon Press, 1989)

[19] Julia Boffey and John J. Thompson, "Anthologies and Miscellanies: Production and Choice of Texts," *Book Production and Publishing in Britain 1375-1475*, ed. Jeremy Griffiths and Derek Pearsall (Cambridge: Cambridge University Press, 1989), 279-316.

[20] Boffey and Thompson, (1989), 292.

[21] Siegfried Wenzel, "Sermon Collections and their Taxonom," in *The Whole Book: Cultural Perspectives on the Medieval Miscellany*, ed. Stephen G. Nichols and Siegfried Wenzel (Ann Arbor, MI: University of Michigan Press, 1996), 20-21.

[22] Fletcher discusses the misbound state of the manuscript, as does Julia Boffey, *Manuscripts of English Courtly Lyrics* (Cambridge: D. S. Brewer, 1985), 18, 34n.

Boffey suggests the original order of the booklets can be discerned from the foliation, but this is misleading. While the internal contents of each booklet can be determined from the foliation, this does not indicate the order in which the booklets might have been arranged in relation to each other.

[23] Boffey and Thompson, (1989), 288; see also B. Y. Fletcher, "Printer's Copy for Stow's Chaucer," *Studies in Bibliography* 31 (1978), 184-201.

[24] See P. R. Robinson, "The 'Booklet': A Self-Contained Unit in Composite Manuscripts," *Codicologica* 3 (1980), 46-69; and also Ralph Hanna, "Booklets in Medieval Manuscripts: Further Considerations," *Studies in Bibliography* 39 (1986), 100-11.

[25] Robinson, (1980), 46.

[26] Boffey and Thompson, (1989), 289.

[27] Boffey and Thompson, (1989), 289.

[28] This list is a summary of that provided by Robinson, (1980), 47-48.

[29] See Eleanor Prescott Hammond, "A Scribe of Chaucer," *Modern Philology* 27 (1929-30), 27-33 and "Two British Museum Manuscripts," *Anglia* 28 (1905), 1-28. See also Aage Brusendorff, *The Chaucer Tradition* (London: Oxford University Press, 1925), 181-198.

[30] Fletcher, (1987), xxvii.

[31] Boffey and Thompson, (1989), 283.

[32] Walter W. Skeat, *Chaucerian and Other Pieces* (Oxford: Clarendon Press, 1897), li-lv. Skeat was not aware of the existence of Longleat 258 or Sloane 1710, but the grouping he suggests here is still appropriate.

[33] Boffey and Thompson, (1989), 283.

[34] Boffey and Thompson, (1989), 283.

[35] Boffey and Thompson, (1989), 283.

[36] Fletcher, (1987), xxix, see also Fletcher's detailed analysis of the watermarks, xxii-xxvi.

[37] John M. Manly and Edith Rickert, eds, *The Text of the Canterbury Tales* (Chicago, IL: Chicago University Press, 1940)

[38] Fletcher, (1987), xv.

[39] Fletcher, (1987), xv.

[40] Boffey, (1985), 18.

[41] Boffey, (1985), 19.

[42] Skeat, (1897), xiii.

[43] Bradshaw notes: "a quire, here missing, consisted of sixteen leaves, three stanzas to the page. *The Flower and the Leaf* would begin on the first page, and end on the last leaf but one with one stanza only on the page, the rest of the page blank and the back of the leaf blank. The last leaf of the quire contained the first six stanzas of the *Complaint of Mars*." This is quoted by both Hammond, *MLN*, (1905), 78, and D. A Pearsall, *The Floure and the Leafe and The Assembly of Ladies* (London: Thomas Nelson, 1962), 3, but originally comes from a loose note inserted in the manuscript.

[44] This inscription is transcribed by Blodgett, (1984), 39-40.

[45] See Eleanor Prescott Hammond, *Chaucer: A Bibliographical Manual* (New York, NY: Peter Smith, 1933), 123-5 for a discussion and list of the contents of Speght's 1598 edition of Chaucer, and D. A. Pearsall, (1962), 79-80.

[46] Pearsall, (1962), 2-6.

[47] Blodgett, (1984), 39, Pearsall also notes this relationship, 7.

[48] Pearsall, (1962), 7.

[49] Hammond, *MLN*, (1905), 79. Boffey and Thompson, (1987), also make this suggestion, 282.

[50] Pearsall, (1962), 7.

[51] Boffey (1985), 43, notes the unfinished initial decoration of L but does not speculate about what this may indicate. In contrast to Pearsall, however, she regards the texts as having been professionally copied.

[52] Boffey and Thompson, (1987), 282.

[53] J. Schick, *Lydgate's Temple of Glas*, EETS o.s. 57, 59 (London: Kegan Paul, 1891), xxv.

[54] Hammond, (1933), 108.

[55] Hammond, *Anglia*, 28 (1905), 1-28.

[56] Boffey, (1985), 14.

[57] Boffey, (1985), 14.

[58] Boffey, (1985), 17.

[59] Interestingly, George L. Marsh argues for Lydgate as the author of the *Flower and the Leaf* in his article 'The Authorship of the Flower and the Leaf', *Journal of English and Germanic Philology*, 6 (1906-7), pp. 373-394.

Appendix

[1] I would like to thank the librarians of the Wren Library, Trinity College, Cambridge, Longleat House, Warminster, and the British Library, London, for allowing me to use their facilities in the preparation of these descriptions. The items in this appendix are accompanied by their corresponding listing in Carleton Brown and R. H. Robbins, *Index of Middle English Verse* (New York, 1943), and R. H. Robbins and J. L. Cutler, *Supplement to the Index of Middle English Verse* (Lexington, KY: 1965).

As is noted elsewhere, the Trinity manuscript has been misbound at a date after its composition, and so I have presented this description to correspond to Fletcher's arrangement of the texts, which is according to their apparent booklet format rather than their current foliation.

The description of Longleat 258 is based on personal examination of the manuscript, but some reference has been made to Eleanor Prescott Hammond's description provided in her article "MS Longleat 258–A Chaucerian Codex," *Modern Language Notes* 20 (1905), 77-9.

The description of BL Additional 34360 is based primarily on my own examination of the manuscript, but reference has been made, where appropriate, to the descriptions in the *Catalogue of Additions to the Manuscripts in the British*

Museum (1894), 317-21, and to Eleanor Prescott Hammond's article "Two British Museum Manuscripts," *Anglia* (1905), 1-28.

BIBLIOGRAPHY

Primary Sources

1. Manuscripts

Cambridge, Trinity College, MS R.3.19
Cambridge, Trinity College, MS R.3.21
Cambridge, University Library, MS Ff.1.6
London, British Library, MS Additional 34360
London, British Library, MS Arundel 197
London, British Library, MS Cotton Vespasian D. ix
London, British Library, MS Harley 2251
London, British Library, MS Harley 4431
Melbourne, National Gallery of Victoria, MS Felton 1072-3
Warminster, Longleat House, MS 258

2. Editions and Translations

Adelard of Bath. *Dodi Venechdi, the Work of Berachya Hanakdan, now edited from MSS at Munich and Oxford, with an English Translation, Introduction, etc., to which is added the first English Translation from the Latin of Adelard of Bath's Quaestiones Naturales*, edited by Hermann Gollancz. London: Oxford University Press, 1920.

Alan of Lille. *Anticlaudianus or The Good and Perfect Man*, edited and translated by James J. Sheridan. Toronto: Pontifical Institute of Mediaeval Studies, 1973.

Alberti, Leon Battista. *De Pictura*, edited and translated by Cecil Grayson. London: Phaidon, 1972.

Al-Haytham, Ibn. *The Optics of Ibn Al-Haytham*, edited and translated by A. I. Sabra. London: Warburg Institute, 1989.

Alighieri, Dante. *De Vulgari Eloquentia*, edited and translated by Steven Botterill. Cambridge: Cambridge University Press, 1996.

Aristotle. *The Art of Rhetoric*, edited and translated by H. C. Lawson-Tancred. London: Penguin, 1991.

Ashby, George. *George Ashby's Poems*, edited by Mary Bateson. EETS e.s. 76. London: Trübner, 1899.

Bacon, Roger. *Roger Bacon and the Origins of Perspectiva in the Middle Ages*, edited and translated by David C. Lindberg. Oxford: Clarendon Press, 1996.

——. *Roger Bacon's Philosophy of Nature*, edited and translated by David C. Lindberg. Oxford: Clarendon Press, 1983.

——. *The Opus Majus of Roger Bacon*, edited by J. H. Bridges. London: Williams and Norgate, 1900.

——. *The Opus Majus of Roger Bacon*, edited by Robert Belle Burke. Philadelphia: University of Pennsylvania Press, 1928.

Baird, Joseph L. and John R. Kane, eds. *La Querelle de la Rose: Letters and Documents*. Chapel Hill: North Carolina University Press, 1978.

Barnum, Priscilla Heath, ed. *Dives and Pauper*. vol 1, part 1, EETS o.s. 275. London: Oxford University Press, 1976.

Barr, Helen, ed. *The Piers Plowman Tradition: A Critical Edition of Pierce the Ploughman's Crede, Richard the Redeless, Mum and the Sothsegger and The Crowned King*. London: Dent, 1993.

Barratt, Alexandra, ed. *Women's Writing in Middle English*. London: Longman, 1992.

Beadle, Richard and A. E. B. Owen, eds. *The Findern Manuscript, C.U.L. MS Ff.1.6*. London: Scolar Press, 1977.

Bersuire, Pierre. *Metamorphosis Ovidiana Moraliter Explanata, 1509*, edited by Stephen Orgel. New York: Garland, 1979.

Biblia Sacra juxta Vulgatam Clementinam, nova editio. Madrid: Biblioteca de Autores Cristianos, 1985.

Boccaccio, Giovanni. "Il Corbaccio," In *Annales Academiae Scientiarum Fennicae*, Series B, 146, edited by Tauno Nurmela. Helsinki: Suomalainen Tiedeakatemia, 1968.

——. *Concerning Famous Women by Giovanni Boccaccio*, edited and translated by Guido A. Guarino. New Brunswick, NJ: Rutgers University Press, 1963.

——. *De Casibus illustrium virorum by Giovanni Boccaccio*, edited and translated by Louis B. Hall. Gainesville, FL: Scholars' Facsimiles and Reprints, 1962.

——. *Il Corbaccio*, edited by Giulia Natali. Milan: Mursia, 1992.

——. *The Corbaccio*, edited and translated by Anthony K. Cassell. Urbana: University of Illinois Press, 1975.

——. *Tutte le Opere di Giovanni Boccaccio*, edited by Vittore Branca. Florence: Arnoldo Mondadori, 1970.

Boethius. *The Consolation of Philosophy*, edited and translated by S. J. Tester. London: Heinemann, 1973.

—. *The Consolation of Philosophy*, edited and translated by Victor Watts. London: Penguin, 1999.

Boffey, Julia, ed. *Fifteenth-Century English Dream Visions*. Oxford: Oxford University Press, 2003.

Bokenham, Osbern. *A Legend of Holy Women: A Translation of Osbern Bokenham's Legends of Holy Women*, edited and translated by Sheila Delany. Notre Dame, IN: University of Notre Dame Press, 1992.

Brown, Carleton, ed. *Religious Lyrics of the XVth Century*. Oxford: Oxford University Press, 1962.

Capellanus, Andreas. *The Art of Courtly Love*, edited by Frederick W. Locke, translated by John Jay Parry. New York: Frederick Ungar, 1957.

Cartlidge, Neil, ed. *The Owl and the Nightingale*. Exeter: University of Exeter Press, 2001.

Casson, L. F., ed. *The Romance of Sir Degrevant: A Parallel-Text Edition from MSS Lincoln Cathedral A.5.2 and Cambridge University Ff.1.6*, EETS o.s. 221. London: Oxford University Press, 1949.

Chambers, R. W. and Marjorie Daunt, eds. *A Book of London English 1384-1425*. Oxford: Clarendon Press, 1931.

Charles d'Orleans. *The English Poems of Charles d'Orleans*, edited by Robert Steele, EETS o.s. 215. London: Oxford University Press, 1941.

Chaucer, Geoffrey. *A Parallel-Text Edition of Chaucer's Minor Poems*, edited by Frederick J. Furnivall, Chaucer Society no. 21. London: Trübner, 1871-79.

—. *Geoffrey Chaucer: The Works 1532*, edited by William Thynne. London: Scolar Press, 1974.

—. *More Odd Texts of Chaucer's Minor Poems*, edited by F. J. Furnivall, Chaucer Society no. 77. London: Trübner, 1886.

—. *Odd Texts of Chaucer's Minor Poems*, edited by Frederick J. Furnivall, Chaucer Society no. 23. London: Trübner 1868-80.

—. *The Canterbury Tales of Chaucer 1778*, edited by Thomas Tyrwhitt. London: Payne, 1778; repr. New York: AMS, 1972.

—. *The House of Fame*, edited by Nicholas R. Havely. Durham: Durham Medieval Texts, 1994.

—. *The Parlement of Foulys*, edited by D. S. Brewer. London: Thomas Nelson, 1960.

—. *The Riverside Chaucer*, edited by Larry D. Benson. Oxford: Oxford University Press, 1987.

—. *The Text of the Canterbury Tales*, edited by John M. Manly and Edith Rickert. Chicago: Chicago University Press, 1940.

Chrètien de Troyes. *Arthurian Romances*, edited and translated by D. D. R. Owen. London: J. M. Dent, 1987.

—. *Perceval ou le Roman du Graal*, edited by Jean-Pierre Foucher and Andre Ortais. Paris: Gallimard, 1974.

—. *Perceval: The Story of the Grail by Chrètien de Troyes*, edited and translated by Burton Raffel. New Haven: Yale University Press, 1999.

Christine de Pizan. *A Medieval Woman's Mirror of Honor: The Treasury of the City of Ladies*, edited and translated by Charity Cannon Willard. New York: Persea Books, 1989.

—. *The Book of the City of Ladies: Christine de Pizan*, edited and translated by Earl Jeffrey Richards. New York: Persea Books, 1982.

—. *The Selected Writings of Christine de Pizan*, edited and translated by Renate Blumenfeld-Kosinski and Kevin Brownlee. New York: Norton, 1997.

Clanvowe, John. *The Works of Sir John Clanvowe*, edited by V. J. Scattergood. Cambridge: Brewer, 1975.

Connolly, Margaret, ed. *Contemplations on the Dread and Love of God*. EETS o.s. 303. Oxford: Oxford University Press, 1993.

Copley, J., ed. *Seven English Songs and Carols of the Fifteenth Century*. 6. Leeds: University of Leeds Texts and Monographs, 1940.

Davies, R. T., ed. *Medieval English Lyrics: A Critical Anthology*. London: Faber and Faber, 1963.

Davis, Norman, ed. *Paston Letters and Papers of the Fifteenth Century*. Oxford: Oxford University Press, 1971-1976.

Day, Mabel and Robert Steele, eds. *Mum and the Sothsegger*. EETS o.s. 199. London: Oxford University Press, 1936.

Dean, James, ed. *Six Ecclesiastical Satires*. Kalamazoo: Western Michigan University Press for TEAMS, 1991.

Donald, A. K., ed. *Mélusine*. EETS e.s. 68. London: Trübner, 1895.

Dunbar, William. *The Poems of William Dunbar*, edited by James Kinsley. Oxford: Clarendon Press, 1979.

Evans, Joan and Mary S. Serjeantson, eds. *English Medieval Lapidaries*. EETS o.s. 190. London: Oxford University Press, 1933.

Fabyan, Robert. *The chronicle of Fabian, whiche he nameth the concordaunce of histories, newly perused and continued form the beginnyng of Kyng Henry the seventh, to thends of Queens Mary*. London: Thon Kyngston, 1559.

Fletcher, Bradford Y., ed. *Manuscript Trinity R.3.19: A Facsimile*. Norman, OK: Pilgrim Books, 1987.

Furnivall, F. J., ed. *A Booke of Precedence*. EETS e.s. 8. London: Trübner, 1869.

—. ed. *The Minor Poems of the Vernon MS*. EETS o.s. 117. London: Trübner, 1901.

—. ed. *Political, Religious and Love Poems*, EETS o.s. 15. London: Trübner, 1866.

—. ed. *The Babees Book*. EETS o.s. 32. London: Trübner, 1868.

Gerald of Wales. "Giraldus Cambrensis in Topographia Hibernie." In *Proceedings of the Royal Irish Academy*, edited and translated by John J. O'Meara. 52.C. (1949): 113-78.

Gower, John. *The Complete Works of John Gower*, edited by G. C. Macauley. Oxford: Clarendon Press, 1899.

Greene, R. L., ed. *The Early English Carols*. Oxford: Oxford University Press, 1977.

Guillaume de Lorris and Jean de Meun. *Le Roman de la Rose*, edited by Armand Strubel. Paris: Le Livre de Poche, 1992.

—. *The Romance of the Rose by Guillaume de Lorris and Jean de Meun*, edited and translated by Charles Dahlberg. Princeton, NJ: Princeton University Press, 1971.

Halliwell, J. O., ed. *The Thornton Romances*. Camden Society no. 30. London: Nichols, 1844.

Hawes, Stephen. *The Pastime of Pleasure by Stephen Hawes*, edited by William Edward Mead. EETS o.s. 173. London: Oxford University Press, 1928.

Henryson, Robert. *Testament of Cresseid*, edited by Denton Fox. London: Nelson, 1968.

—. *The Poems of Robert Henryson*, edited by Robert L. Kindrick. Kalamazoo: Western Michigan University Press for TEAMS, 1997.

Hoccleve, Thomas. *Hoccleve's Works: The Minor Poems*, edited by Frederick J. Furnivall. EETS e.s. 61. London: Trübner, 1892.

—. *Selections from Hoccleve*, edited by M. C. Seymour. Oxford: Oxford University Press, 1981.

—. *Thomas Hoccleve's Complaint and Dialogue*, edited by J. A. Burrow. EETS o.s. 313. Oxford: Oxford University Press, 1999.

Homer. *The Illiad*, edited and translated by Robert Fagles. Bath: The Softback Preview, 1997.

Inglis, Eric, ed. *The Hours of Mary of Burgundy: Codex Vindobonensis 1857 Vienna, Osterreichische Nationalbibliothek*. London: Harvey Miller, 1995.

Jacobus de Voragine. *The Golden Legend: Readings on the Saints*, edited and translated by William Granger Ryan. Princeton, NJ: Princeton University Press, 1993.

James I of Scotland. *The Kingis Quair*, edited by John Norton-Smith. Leiden: E. J. Brill, 1981.

John of Garland. *The Parisiana Poetria of John of Garland*, edited and translated by Traugott Lawler. New Haven: Yale University Press, 1974.

Langland, William. *Piers Plowman–A Parallel-Text Edition of the A, B, C and Z Versions*, edited by A. V. C. Schmidt. London: Longman, 1995.

Le Livre des Serfs de Marmoutiers. edited by André Salmon. Tours: Société archéologique de Touraine, 1864.

Lester, G. A., ed. *Three Late Medieval Morality Plays*. London: A & C Black, 1981.

Lydgate, John. *Lydgate and Burgh's Secrees of Old Philisoffres: A Version of the Secreta Secretorum*, edited by Robert Steele. EETS e.s. 66. London, Trübner, 1894.

—. *Lydgate's Temple of Glas*, edited by J. Schick. EETS e.s. 60. London: Trübner, 1891.

—. *The Assembly of Gods by John Lydgate*, edited by Oscar Lovell Triggs. Chicago: University of Chicago Press, 1895.

—. *The Minor Poems of John Lydgate*, edited by Henry Noble MacCracken. EETS o.s. 192. London: Oxford University Press, 1934.

Macrobius. *Commentary on the Dream of Scipio by Macrobius*, edited and translated by William Harris Stahl. New York: Columbia University Press, 1990.

Marshall, Simone, ed. "An abstracte owte of a boke þat is callid *Formula Nouiciorum*." *Mystics Quarterly* 29.3-4 (2003): 71-139.

Mathéolus. *Le Livre de Mathéolus: poème français deu XIVe siècle*, edited by Jean Le Fèvre. Brussels, Imprimerie de A. Mertens et fils, 1846-64.

Millet, Bella and Jocelyn Wogan-Browne, eds. *Medieval English Prose for Women: Selections from the Katherine Group and Ancrene Wisse*. Oxford: Clarendon Press, 1990.

Moore, Jan, ed. *Selected Middle English Lyrics*. Wellington: Victoria University Press, 1985.

Mustanoja, Tauno, ed. "The Good Wife Taught her Daughter, The Good Wyfe Wold a Pylgremage, The Thewis of Gud Women." In *Annales Academiae Scientiarum Fennicae*, Series B 61.2. Helsinki: Suomalainen Tiedeakatemia, 1948.

Ovid. *Heroides and Amores*, edited and translated by Grant Showerman. London: Heinemann, 1914.

—. *Heroides*, edited and translated by Harold Isbell. London: Penguin, 1990.

—. *Metamorphoses*, edited and translated by Frank Justus Miller. Cambridge, MA: Harvard University Press, 1984.

—. *Ovid's Heroines: A Verse Translation of the Heroides*, edited and translated by Daryl Hine. New Haven: Yale University Press, 1991.

—. *The Metamorphoses of Ovid*, edited and translated by Allen Mandelbaum. San Diego: Harvest, 1993.

Pearsall, D. A., ed. *The Floure and the Leafe and The Assembly of Ladies*. London: Thomas Nelson, 1962.

Pearsall, Derek, ed. *The Floure and The Leafe, The Assembly of Ladies, and The Isle of Ladies*. Kalamazoo: Western Michigan University Press for TEAMS, 1990.

Person, Henry A., ed. *Cambridge Middle English Lyrics*. Seattle: University of Washington Press, 1953.

Robbins, Rossell Hope, ed. *Secular Lyrics of the XIV and XV Centuries*. Oxford: Oxford University Press, 1955.

—. ed. *Secular Lyrics of the XIVth and XVth Centuries*. Oxford: Clarendon Press, 1952.

Sandys, George. *Ovids Metamorphoses Englished, Mythologized, and Represented in Figures, 1632*. New York: Garland, 1976.

Severs, J. B. and A. E. Hartung, eds. *A Manual of the Writings in Middle English 1050-1500*. New Haven: Connecticut Academy of Arts and Sciences, 1967.

Silverstein, Theodore, ed. *Medieval English Lyrics*. London: Edward Arnold, 1971.

Skeat, W. W., ed. *Romans of Partenay*. EETS o.s. 22. London: Trübner, 1866.

Skeat, Walter, ed. *Chaucerian and Other Pieces*. Oxford: Clarendon Press, 1897.

Steele, Robert, ed. *Three Prose Versions of the Secreta Secretorum*. EETS e.s. 74. London, Trübner, 1898.

Stevick, Robert D., ed. *One Hundred Middle English Lyrics*. Indianapolis, IN: Bobbs-Merrill, 1964.

Strouff, Louis, ed. *Mélusine: Roman du XIVe Siècle*. Geneva: Slatkine Reprints, 1974.

Thiebaux, Marcelle, ed. *The Writings of Medieval Women*. New York: Garland, 1994.

Usk, Thomas. *The Testament of Love*, edited by R. Allen Shoaf. Kalamazoo: TEAMS, 1998.

Weiner, Karl Luick, ed. *Sir Degrevant*. Beiträge zur englischen Philologie, Bd. 47. Vienna, Braumüller, 1917.

Westrem, Scott D. *The Hereford Map*. Turnhout: Brepols, 2001.

Wilson, Katharina M., ed. *Medieval Women Writers*. Athens: University of Georgia Press, 1984.

Wright, Thomas, ed. *Political Poems and Songs Relating to English History*. London: Longman, 1861.

Secondary Sources

Abel, Elizabeth, ed. *Writing and Sexual Difference*. Brighton: New Harvester, 1982.

Alford, John A. "Literature and Law in Medieval England." *PMLA* 92.1 (1977): 941-51.

—. *Literature and Law in the Middle Ages: A Bibliography of Scholarship*. New York: Garland, 1984.

—. *Piers Plowman: A Glossary of Legal Diction*. Cambridge: Brewer, 1988.

Annunciation. London: Phaidon, 2000.

Ayrton, Michael. *A Meaning to the Maze*. Abingdon-on-Thames: Abbey Press, 1974.

—. *The Rudiments of Paradise*. London: Secker and Warburg, 1971.

Bachelard, Gaston. *The Poetics of Space*, translated by Maria Jolas. Boston, MA: Beacon Press, 1969.

Barr, Helen. *Signes and Sothe: Language in the Piers Plowman Tradition*. Cambridge: Brewer, 1994.

Barratt, Alexandra A. T. "'The Flower and the Leaf' and 'The Assembly of Ladies': Is There a (Sexual) Difference?" *PQ* 66.1 (1987): 1-24.

Bartlett, Anne Clark. *Male Authors, Female Readers*. Ithaca, NY: Cornell University Press, 1995.

Baugh, Albert C., ed. *A Literary History of England*. London: Routledge, 1950.

Beckett, W. *The Story of Painting*. Washington, DC: National Gallery of Art, 1994.

Beer, Barrett L. *Tudor England Observed: The World of John Stow*. Stroud: Sutton, 1998.

Ben-Amos, Dan, ed. *Folklore Genres*. Austin: University of Texas Press, 1976.

Bennett, H. S. *Chaucer and the Fifteenth Century*. Oxford: Clarendon Press, 1961.

Bennett, J. A. W. *Chaucer's Book of Fame*. Oxford: Clarendon Press, 1968.

Berger, John. *Ways of Seeing*. London: Penguin, 1982.

Blamires, Alcuin. "The Limits of Bible Study for Medieval Women." In *Women, The Book, and the Godly*, edited by Lesley Smith and Jane M. Taylor, 1-12. Cambridge: Brewer, 1995.

Bloch, R. Howard. "New Philology and Old French." *Speculum* 65 (1990): 38-58.

Blodgett, James E. "William Thynne." In *Editing Chaucer: The Great Tradition*, edited by Paul G. Ruggiers, 35-52. Norman, OK: Pilgrim Books, 1984.

Bloom, Harold. *The Western Canon: The Books and School of the Ages*. New York: Harcourt Brace, 1994.

Boffey, Julia and John J. Thompson. "Anthologies and Miscellanies: Production and Choice of Texts." In *Book Production and Publishing in Britain 1375-1475*, edited by Jeremy Griffiths and Derek Pearsall, 279-315. Cambridge: Cambridge University Press, 1989.

Boffey, Julia. "The Manuscripts of English Courtly Love Lyrics in the Fifteenth Century." In *Manuscripts and Readers in Fifteenth-Century England: The Literary Implications of Manuscripts Study*, edited by Derek Pearsall, 3-14. Cambridge: Brewer, 1981.

—. "Women Authors and Women's Literacy in Fourteenth- and Fifteenth-Century England." In *Women and Literature in Britain, 1150-1500*, edited by Carol M. Meale, 159-82. Cambridge: Cambridge University Press, 1993.

—. *Manuscripts of English Courtly Lyrics*. Cambridge: Brewer, 1985.

Boitani, Piero and Anna Torti, eds. *Mediaevalitas: Reading the Middle Ages*. Cambridge: Brewer, 1996.

—. *Chaucer and the Imaginary World of Fame*. Cambridge: Brewer, 1984.

Bono, James J. *The Word of God and the Languages of Man: Interpreting Nature in Early Modern Science and Medicine*. Madison: University of Wisconsin Press, 1995.

The Book of Kells and the Art of Illumination. Canberra: National Gallery of Australia, 2000.

Borchert, Till-Holger. *The Age of Van Eyck: The Mediterranean World and Early Netherlandish Painting, 1430-1530*. London: Thames and Hudson, 2002.

Bossy, John, ed. *Disputes and Settlements: Law and Human Relations in the West*. Cambridge: Cambridge University Press, 1983.

Bradshaw, Henry. *Collected Papers*. Cambridge: Cambridge University Press, 1888.

Brewer, D. S., ed. *Chaucer and the Chaucerians*. London: Thomas Nelson, 1966.

Brewer, Derek, ed. *Writers and their Background: Geoffrey Chaucer*. London: Bell & Sons, 1974.

Brown, Carleton and Rossell Hope Robbins. *The Index of Middle English Verse*. New York: Columbia University Press, 1943.

Brown, Carleton. *Register of Middle English Religious and Didactic Verse*. Oxford: Oxford University Press, 1916.

Brownlee, Kevin. "Mélusine's Hybrid Body and the Poetics of Metamorphosis." In *Mélusine of Lusignan: Founding Fiction in Late Medieval France*, edited by Donald Maddox and Sara Sturm-Maddox, 76-99. Athens: University of Georgia Press, 1996.

Bruckner, Matilda Tomaryn. *Shaping Romance: Interpretation, Truth, and Closure in Twelfth-Century French Fictions*. Philadelphia: University of Pennsylvania Press, 1993.

Brusendorff, Aage. *The Chaucer Tradition*. London: Oxford University Press, 1925.

Burrow, J. A. "Poems without Contexts." *Essays in Criticism* 29 (1979): 6-28.

—. ed. *Middle English Literature: British Academy Gollancz Lectures*. Oxford: Oxford University Press, 1989.

Cameron, Deborah, ed. *The Feminist Critique of Language: A Reader*. London: Routledge, 1998.

Cannon, Christopher. "Enclosure." In *The Cambridge Companion to Medieval Women's Writing*, edited by Carolyn Dinshaw and David Wallace, 109-23. Cambridge: Cambridge University Press, 2003.

Carlson, Cindy L. and Angela Jane Weisl, eds. *Constructions of Widowhood and Virginity in the Middle Ages*. New York: St Martin's Press, 1999.

Carruthers, Mary and Jan M. Ziolkowski, eds. *The Medieval Craft of Memory*. Philadelphia, PA: University of Pennsylvania Press, 2002.

Carruthers, Mary. *The Craft of Thought: Meditation, Rhetoric, and the Making of Images, 400-1200*. Cambridge: Cambridge University Press, 1998.

Catalogue of Additions to the Manuscripts in the British Museum. London: Longmans, 1894.

Cavallo, Adolfo Salvatore. *Medieval Tapestries*. New York: Metropolitan Museum of Art, 1993.

Chamberlain, David, ed. *New Readings of Late Medieval Love Poems.*
    Lanham, MD: University Press of America, 1993.
Chance, Jane. "Christine de Pizan as Literary Mother: Women's Authority
    and Subjectivity in The Floure and the Leafe and the Assembly of
    Ladies." In *The City of Scholars: New Approaches to Christine de
    Pizan*, edited by Margarete Zimmermann and Dina De Rentiis, 245-59.
    Berlin: Walter de Gruyter, 1994.
Cherewatuk, Karen and Ulrike Wiethaus, eds. *Dear Sister: Medieval
    Women and the Epistolary Genre.* Philadelphia, PA: University of
    Pennsylvania Press, 1993.
Chevalier, Jean, and Alain Gheerbrant. *A Dictionary of Symbols.* Oxford:
    Blackwells, 1994.
Chewning, Susannah Mary. "The Paradox of Virginity within the
    Anchoritic Tradition: The Masculine Gaze and the Feminine Body in
    the Wohunge Group." In *Constructions of Widowhood and Virginity in
    the Middle Ages*, edited by Cindy L. Carlson and Angela Jane Weisl,
    113-34. New York: St Martin's Press, 1999.
Chicago, Judy. *The Dinner Party: A Symbol of Our Heritage.* New York:
    Doubleday, 1979.
Cixous, Hélène. *The Newly Born Woman*, edited and translated by Betsy
    Wing. Minneapolis: University of Minnesota Press, 1986.
Clanchy, M. T. *From Memory to Written Record: England 1066-1307.*
    Oxford: Blackwell, 1993.
Clanchy, Michael. "Law and Love in the Middle Ages." In *Disputes and
    Settlements: Law and Human Relations in the West*, edited by John
    Bossy, 47-68. Cambridge: Cambridge University Press, 1983.
Clough, Patricia Ticineto. *Feminist Thought.* Oxford: Blackwell, 1994.
Coleman, Joyce. *Public Reading and the Reading Public in Late Medieval
    England and France.* Cambridge: Cambridge University Press, 1996.
Colomina, Beatriz, ed. *Sexuality & Space.* Princeton, NJ: Princeton
    University Press, 1992.
Coss, Peter. *The Lady in Medieval England 1100-1500.* Stroud: Sutton,
    1998.
Crisp, Sir Frank. *Mediaeval Gardens.* New York: Hacker Art Books,
    1966.
Crombie, A. C. *Science, Optics and Music in Medieval and Early Modern
    Thought.* London: Hambledon Press, 1990.
Daiches, David. *A Critical History of English Literature.* London: Secker
    & Warburg, 1961.
Davis, Norman. "Style and Stereotype in Early English Letters." *Leeds
    Studies in English* 1 (1967): 7-17.

—. "The Language of the Pastons." In *Middle English Literature: British Academy Gollancz Lectures,* edited by J. A. Burrow, 45-70. Oxford: Oxford University Press, 1989.

—. "The *Litera Troili* and English Letters." *RES* 16 (1965): 233-44.

de Beauvior, Simone. *Deuxieme sexe.* Paris: Gallimard, 1949.

Deedes, C. N. "The Labyrinth." In *The Labyrinth: Further Studies In The Relation Between Myth And Ritual In The Ancient World,* edited by S. H. Hooke, 1-42. New York: Macmillan, 1935.

Delany, Sheila. "Mothers to Think Back Through: Who are they? The Ambiguous Example of Christine de Pizan." In *Medieval Texts and Contemporary Readers,* edited by Laurie A. Finke and Martin B. Schichtman, 177-97. Ithaca, NY: Cornell University Press, 1987.

—. *Chaucer's House of Fame: The Poetics of Skeptical Fideism.* Gainesville: University Press of Florida, 1972.

Dinshaw, Carolyn and David Wallace, eds. *The Cambridge Companion to Medieval Women's Writing.* Cambridge: Cambridge University Press, 2003.

Dinshaw, Carolyn. *Chaucer's Sexual Poetics.* Madison: University of Wisconsin Press, 1989.

—. *Getting Medieval: Sexualities and Communities, Pre- and Postmodern.* Durham, NC: Duke University Press, 1999.

Donnelly, Colleen. "'Withoute Wordes': The Medieval Lady Dreams in The Assembly of Ladies." *Journal of the Rocky Mountain Medieval & Renaissance Association* 15 (1994): 35-55.

Donovan, Mortimer J. *The Breton Lay: A Guide to Varieties.* Notre Dame, IN: University of Notre Dame Press, 1969.

Doob, Penelope Reed. *The Idea of The Labyrinth: From Classical Antiquity through the Middle Ages.* Ithaca, NY: Cornell University Press, 1990.

Douthwaite-Hodges, Melita. *"How wonnen was the regne of femenye"?: Re-presenting Women in Four Late Medieval Narratives.* Unpublished doctoral thesis, University of Wales, Cardiff, 2000.

Doyle, A. I. and M. B. Parkes. "The Production of Copies of the Canterbury Tales and the Confessio Amantis in the Early Fifteenth Century." In *Medieval Scribes, Manuscripts, and Libraries,* edited by M. B. Parkes and Andrew G. Watson, 163-210. London: Scolar Press, 1978.

Dronke, Peter. *Fabula: Explorations into the Uses of Myth in Medieval Platonism.* Leiden: E. J. Brill, 1974.

Eaton, R. D. "Narrative Closure in Chaucer's Franklin's Tale." *Neophilologus* 84.2 (2000): 309-21.

Eckenstein, Lina. *Woman Under Monasticism: Chapters on Saint-Lore and Convent Life between A.D.500 and A.D.1500.* New York: Russell and Russell, 1963.

Eco, Umberto. *The Search for the Perfect Language.* Oxford: Blackwell, 1995.

Edgerton, Samuel Y. *The Heritage of Giotto's Geometry: Art and Science on the Eve of the Scientific Revolution.* Ithaca, NY: Cornell University Press, 1991.

—. *The Renaissance Rediscovery of Linear Perspective.* New York: Basic Books, 1975.

Edson, Evelyn. *Mapping Time and Space: How Medieval Mapmakers viewed their World.* London: The British Library, 1999.

Evans, Joan. *A History of Jewellery 1100-1870.* London: Faber and Faber, 1970.

—. *Dress in Mediaeval France.* Oxford: Clarendon Press, 1952.

Evans, Mary, ed. *Feminism: Critical Concepts in Literary and Cultural Studies.* London: Routledge, 2001.

Evans, Ruth and Lesley Johnson. "The Assembly of Ladies: A Maze of Feminist Sign Reading?" In *Feminist Criticism: Theory and Practice,* edited by Susan Sellers, 171-96. Hemel Hempstead: Harvester Wheatsheaf, 1991.

Evans, Ruth and Lesley Johnson, eds. *Feminist Readings in Middle English Literature: The Wife of Bath and all her Sect.* London: Routledge, 1994.

Evans, Ruth. "Virginities." In *The Cambridge Companion to Medieval Women's Writing,* edited by Carolyn Dinshaw and David Wallace, 21-39. Cambridge: Cambridge University Press, 2003.

Eyler, Ellen C. *Early English Gardens and Garden Books.* Ithaca, NY: Cornell University Press, 1963.

Ferrante, Joan M. *To the Glory of her Sex: Women's Roles in the Composition of Medieval Texts.* Indianapolis: Indiana University Press, 1997.

Finke, Laurie A. and Martin B. Schichtman, eds. *Medieval Texts and Contemporary Readers.* Ithaca, NY: Cornell University Press, 1987.

Finke, Laurie A. *Women's Writing in English: Medieval England.* London: Longman, 1999.

Finnegan, Ruth. *Oral Poetry: Its Nature, Significance and Social Context.* Cambridge: Cambridge University Press, 1977.

Fish, Stanley. *The Trouble with Principle.* Cambridge, MA: Harvard University Press, 1999.

Fisher, Ruth Marie. *The Flower and the Leaf and the Assembly of Ladies: A Study of Two Love-Vision Poems of the Fifteenth Century.* Unpublished doctoral thesis, Columbia University, 1955.

Flake, Timothy H. "Love, Trouthe, and the Happy Ending of the Franklin's Tale." *English Studies* 77.3 (1996): 209-26.

Fleischman, Suzanne. "Philology, Linguistics, and the Discourse of the Medieval Text." *Speculum* 65 (1990): 19-37.

Fleming, John V. *Reason and The Lover.* Princeton, NJ: Princeton University Press, 1984.

—. *The Roman de la Rose: A Study in Allegory and Iconography.* Princeton, NJ: Princeton University Press, 1969.

Fletcher, Bradford Y. "Printer's Copy for Stow's Chaucer." *Studies in Bibliography* 31 (1978): 184-201.

—. "*The Assembly of Ladies*: Text and Context." *The Bibliographical Society of America* 82.2 (1988): 229-34.

Gardiner, Judith Kegan. "On Female Identity and Writing by Women." In *Writing and Sexual Difference*, edited by Elizabeth Abel, 177-91. Brighton: Harvester, 1982.

Gauthier, Xavière. "Is there such a thing as women's writing?" In *New French Feminisms*, edited by Elaine Marks and Isabelle de Courtivron, 161-64. Amherst: University of Massachusetts Press, 1980.

Gellrich, Jesse M. *The Idea of the Book in the Middle Ages: Language, Theory, Mythology, and Fiction.* Ithaca, NY: Cornell University Press, 1985.

Gilbert, Sandra and Susan Gubar. *The Madwoman in the Attic: The Woman Writer and the Nineteenth-Century Literary Imagination.* New Haven: Yale University Press, 1979.

Gilbert, Sandra Caruso Mortola and Susan Dreyfuss David Gubar. "Ceremonies of the Alphabet: Female Grandmatologies and the Female Autograph." In *The Female Autograph*, edited by Domna C. Stanton, 21-48. Chicago: University of Chicago Press, 1987.

Goffin, R. C. "Quiting by Tidings in the House of Fame." *Medium Aevum* 12 (1943): 40-4.

Goldsmith, Elizabeth, ed. *Writing the Female Voice: Essays on Epistolary Literature.* Boston, MA: Northeastern University Press, 1989.

Gousset, Marie-Thérèse. *Éden: Le jardin médiéval à travers l'enluminure XIIIᵉ-XVIᵉ siècle.* Paris: Bibliotheque Nationale de France, 2001.

Grant, Edward, ed. *A Source Book in Medieval Science.* Cambridge, MA: Harvard University Press, 1974.

Grant, Edward. *Planets, Stars, and the Orbs: The Medieval Cosmos, 1200-1687.* Cambridge: Cambridge University Press, 1994.

Gray, Douglas. "Notes on Some Middle English Charms." In *Chaucer and Middle English Studies*, edited by Beryl Rowland, 56-71. London: Allen and Unwin, 1974.

Green, Richard Firth. "Medieval Literature and Law." In *The Cambridge History of Medieval English Literature*, edited by David Wallace, 407-31. Cambridge: Cambridge University Press, 1999.

—. *A Crisis of Truth: Literature and Law in Ricardian England*. Philadelphia: University of Pennsylvania Press, 1999.

—. *Poets and Princepleasers: Literature and the English Court in the Late Middle Ages*. Toronto: University of Toronto Press, 1980.

Griffiths, Jeremy and Derek Pearsall, eds. *Book Production and Publishing in Britain 1375-1475*. Cambridge: Cambridge University Press, 1989.

Grinnell, Robert. "The Theoretical Attitude towards Space in the Middle Ages." *Speculum* 21 (1946): 141-57.

Grosz, Elizabeth. "Bodies-Cities." In *Sexuality & Space*, edited by Beatriz Colomina, 241-54. Princeton, NJ: Princeton University Press, 1992.

Gubar, Susan. "'The Blank Page' and the Issues of Female Creativity." In *Writing and Sexual Difference*, edited by Elizabeth Abel, 73-93. Brighton: Harvester, 1982.

Guddat-Figge, Gisela. *Catalogue of Manuscripts Containing Middle English Romances*. Munich: Wilhelm Fink Verlag, 1976.

Hammond, E. P. "Grass and Green Wool." *MLN* 40 (1925): 185-86.

—. *English Verse between Chaucer and Surrey*. Durham, NC: Duke University Press, 1927.

Hammond, Eleanor Prescott. "A Scribe of Chaucer." *MP* 27 (1929-30): 27-33.

—. "MS Longleat 258–A Chaucerian Codex." *MLN* 20 (1905): 77-79.

—. "Two British Museum Manuscripts." *Anglia* 28 (1905): 1-28.

—. *Chaucer: A Bibliographical Manual*. New York: Peter Smith, 1933.

Hanna III, Ralph. "Booklets in Medieval Manuscripts: Further Considerations." *Studies in Bibliography* 39 (1986): 100-11.

—. *Pursuing History: Middle English Manuscripts and their Texts*. Stanford, CA: Stanford University Press, 1996.

Hansen, Elaine Tuttle. *Chaucer and the Fictions of Gender*. Berkeley: University of California Press, 1992.

Hanson-Smith, Elizabeth. "A Woman's View of Courtly Love: The Findern Anthology Cambridge University Library MS. Ff.1.6." *Journal of Women's Studies in Literature* 1.3 (1979): 179-194.

Hanson-Smith, Elizabeth. "Computer Dialect Study: The Findern Anthology." *College Literature* 15.1 (1988): 47-56.

Harding, Alan. "Plaints and Bills in the History of English Law." In *Legal History Studies,* edited by Dafydd Jenkins, 65-86. Cardiff: University of Wales Press, 1975.

Hardwick, C. *A Catalogue of the Manuscripts Preserved in the Library of the University of Cambridge.* Cambridge, Cambridge University Press, 1856.

Harrington, David V. "The Function of Allegory in the 'Flower and the Leaf'." *NM* 71 (1970): 244-253.

Harris, Kate. "The Origins and Make-up of Cambridge University Library MS Ff.1.6." *Transactions of the Cambridge Bibliographical Society* 8.3 (1983): 299-333.

Harvey, P. D. A. *Mappa Mundi: The Hereford World Map.* Toronto: University of Toronto Press, 1996.

Helmholz, R. H. *Marriage Litigation in Medieval England.* London: Cambridge University Press, 1974.

Hermann, John P. and John J. Burke, eds. *Signs and Symbols in Chaucer's Poetry.* Alabama: University of Alabama Press, 1981.

Hockney, David. *Secret Knowledge: Rediscovering the Lost Techniques of the Old Masters.* London: Thames and Hudson, 2001.

Holley, Linda Tart. *Chaucer's Measuring Eye.* Houston, TX: Rice University Press, 1990.

Hooke, S. H., ed. *The Labyrinth: Further Studies In The Relation Between Myth And Ritual In The Ancient World.* New York: Macmillan, 1935.

Hope, Charles. "'Composition' from Cennini and Alberti to Vasari." In *Pictorial Composition from Medieval to Modern Art,* edited by Paul Taylor and François Quiviger, 27-44. London: The Warburg Institute, 2000.

Hornsby, Joseph Allen. *Chaucer and the Law.* Norman, OK: Pilgrim Books, 1988.

Hume, Kathryn. *The Owl and the Nightingale: The Poem and its Critics.* Toronto: University of Toronto Press, 1975.

Irigaray, Luce. "Le miroir, de l'autre cote." *Critique* 309 (1973): 179-88.

—. *Ce sexe qui n'en est pas un.* Paris: Minuit, 1997.

—. *Sexes and Genealogies,* edited and translated by Gillian C. Gill. New York: Columbia University Press, 1993.

—. *Speculum de l'autre femme.* Paris: Minuit, 1974.

—. *Speculum of the Other Woman,* edited and translated by Gillian C. Gill. Ithaca, NY: Cornell University Press, 1985.

James, Montague Rhodes. *The Western Manuscripts in the Library of Trinity College, Cambridge.* Cambridge: Cambridge University Press, 1901.

Jameson, Frederic. *The Political Unconscious: Narrative as a Socially Symbolic Act.* Ithaca, NY: Cornell University Press, 1981.

Jenkins, Dafydd, ed. *Legal History Studies.* Cardiff: University of Wales Press, 1975.

Jochens, Jenny. "Before the Male Gaze: The Absence of the Female Body in Old Norse." In *Sex in the Middle Ages*, edited by Joyce E. Salisbury, 3-29. New York: Garland, 1991.

Jolliffe, P. S. "Middle English Translations of *De Exterioris et Interioris Hominis Compositione.*" *Mediaeval Studies* 36 (1974): 259-277.

Kane, G. *Piers Plowman, The Evidence for Authorship.* London: The Athlone Press, 1965.

Kaplan, Cora. "Language and Gender." In *The Feminist Critique of Language: A Reader*, edited by Deborah Cameron, 54-64. London: Routledge, 1998.

Kee, Kenneth. "Two Chaucerian Gardens." *Mediaeval Studies* 23 (1961): 154-62.

Kern, Hermann. *Through the Labyrinth: Designs and Meanings over 5000 years.* Munich: Prestel, 2000.

Kerr, Berenice M. *Religious Life for Women c.1100-c.1350.* Oxford: Clarendon Press, 1999.

Kimmelman, Burt. *The Poetics of Authorship in the Later Middle Ages: The Emergence of the Modern Literary Persona.* New York: Peter Lang, 1996.

Kittredge, G. L. "Chaucer and Some of his Friends." *MP* 1.1 (1903): 1-18.

Kline, Naomi Reed. *Maps of Medieval Thought: The Hereford Paradigm.* Woodbridge: Boydell, 2001.

Kolve, V. A. "Chaucer and the Visual Arts." In *Writers and their Background: Geoffrey Chaucer,* edited by Derek Brewer, 290-320. London: Bell & Sons, 1974.

—. "From Cleopatra to Alceste: An Iconographic Study of The Legend of Good Women." In *Signs and Symbols in Chaucer's Poetry*, edited by John P. Hermann and John J. Burke, 130-78. Alabama: University of Alabama Press, 1981.

—. *The Play called Corpus Christi.* Stanford, CA: Stanford University Press, 1966.

Kristeva, Julia. "La femme, ce n'est jamais ça." *Tel quel* 59 (1974): 19-24.

Laing, Lloyd and Jennifer. *Medieval Britain.* London: Herbert, 1998.

Landsberg, Sylvia. *The Medieval Garden.* London: British Museum Press, 1995.

Lansdown, Richard. *The Autonomy of Literature.* London: Macmillan, 2001.

Larrington, Carolyne. *Women and Writing in Medieval Europe*. London: Routledge, 1995.

Lewis, C. S. *The Allegory of Love*. Oxford: Oxford University Press, 1936.

Lewis, Katherine J., Noël James Menuge, and Kim M. Phillips, eds. *Young Medieval Women*. Stroud: Sutton, 1999.

Lindberg, David C. "The Science of Optics." In *Science in the Middle Ages*, edited by David C. Lindberg, 338-68. Chicago: University of Chicago Press, 1978.

—. ed. *Science in the Middle Ages*. Chicago: University of Chicago Press, 1978.

Lindberg, David C. *Studies in the History of Medieval Optics*. London: Variorum Reprints, 1983.

—. *Theories of Vision from Al-Kindi to Kepler*. Chicago: University of Chicago Press, 1976.

Lomperis, Linda and Sarah Stanbury, eds. *Feminist Approaches to the Body in Medieval Literature*. Philadelphia: University of Pennsylvania Press, 1993.

Lynch, Kathryn L. *The High Medieval Dream Vision*. Stanford, CA: Stanford University Press, 1988.

Lyons, Thomas R. and Michael J. Preston. *A Complete Concordance to Two 'Chaucerian' Poems: 'The Floure and the Leafe' and 'The Assembly of Ladies.'* Ann Arbor: Xerox University Microfilms, 1974.

MacCracken, Henry Noble. "An English Friend of Charles of Orléans." *PMLA* 26 (1911): 142-80.

MacDougall, Elisabeth B., ed. *Fons Sapientiae: Renaissance Garden Fountains*. Washington, DC: Dumbarton Oaks, 1978.

Maddox, Donald and Sara Sturm-Maddox, eds. *Melusine of Lusignan: Founding Fiction in Late Medieval France*. Athens: University of Georgia Press, 1996.

Makowski, Elisabeth M. "The Conjugal Debt and Medieval Canon Law." *Journal of Medieval History* 3.2 (1977): 99-114.

Margherita, Gayle. *The Romance of Origins*. Philadelphia: University of Pennsylvania Press, 1994.

Marks, Elaine and Isabelle de Courtivron, eds. *New French Feminisims*. Amherst: University of Massachusetts Press, 1980.

Marsh, G. L. "Authorship of The Floure and The Leafe." *JEGP* 6 (1906-7), 373-94

—. "Sources and Analogues of The Flower and the Leaf." *MP* 4 (1906-1907): 121-68, 281-328.

Marshall, Simone Celine. "Notes on C.U.L. MS Ff.1.6: The Findern Manuscript." *NQ* n.s. 49.4 (2002): 439-42.

Mason, H. A. *Humanism and Poetry in the Early Tudor Period: An Essay.* London: Routledge, 1959.

Matthews, W. H. *Mazes and Labyrinths: Their History and Development.* New York: Dover, 1970.

McCarren, Vincent P. and Douglas Moffat, eds. *A Guide to Editing Middle English.* Ann Arbor: University of Michigan Press, 1998.

McLean, Teresa. *Medieval English Gardens.* New York: Viking, 1980.

McLeod, Glenda. "Poetics and Antimisogynist Polemics in Christine de Pizan's *Le Livre de la Cité des Dames.*" In *Reinterpreting Christine de Pizan,* edited by Earl Jeffrey Richards, 37-37. Athens: University of Georgia Press, 1992.

McMillan, Ann. "'Fayre Sisters Al': The Flower and the Leaf and The Assembly of Ladies." *Tulsa Studies in Women's Literature* 1 (1982): 27-42.

McNamara, Jo-Ann. "City Air makes Men Free and Women Bound." In *Text and Territory: Geographical Imagination in the European Middle Ages,* edited by Sylvia Tomasch and Sealy Gilles, 143-58. Philadelphia: University of Pennsylvania Press, 1998.

McNamer, Sarah. "Female Authors, Provincial Setting: The Re-versing of Courtly Love in the Findern Manuscript." *Viator* 22 (1991): 279-310.

McNamer, Sarah. "Lyrics and Romances." In *The Cambridge Companion to Medieval Women's Writing,* edited by Carolyn Dinshaw and David Wallace, 195-209. Cambridge: Cambridge University Press, 2003.

Meale, Carol M., ed. *Women and Literature in Britain, 1150-1500.* Cambridge: Cambridge University Press, 1993.

Medcalf, Stephen, ed. *The Later Middle Ages.* London: Methuen, 1981.

Mellinkoff, David. *The Language of the Law.* Boston, MA: Little, Brown, 1963.

Menuge, Noël James, ed. *Medieval Women and the Law.* Woodbridge: Boydell, 2000.

Menuge, Noël James. *Medieval English Wardship in Romance and Law.* Cambridge: Brewer, 2001.

Mertes, Kate. *The English Noble Household 1250-1600.* Oxford: Blackwell, 1988.

Middle English Dictionary. Ann Arbor, MI: University of Michigan Press, 1952-2001.

Miller, James. "How to See Through Women: Medieval Blazons and the Male Gaze." In *The Centre and its Compass,* edited by Robert A.

Taylor, 367-88. Kalamazoo: Western Michigan University Press, 1993.

Miller, Naomi. *Mapping the City: The Language and Culture of Cartography in the Renaissance.* London: Continuum, 2003.

Minnis, A. J. *The Medieval Theory of Authorship.* London: Scolar Press, 1984.

Minnis, Alastair J. *Lifting the Veil: Sexual/Textual Nakedness in the Roman de la Rose.* London: King's College London, Centre for Late Antique and Medieval Studies, 1995.

Moore, Arthur K. *The Secular Lyric in Middle English.* Lexington: University of Kentucky Press, 1951.

Moorman, Charles. *Editing the Middle English Manuscript.* Jackson: University Press of Mississippi, 1975.

Morrison, Tessa. "The influence of Pseudo-Dionysius on Gothic Basilicas and Mnemonic Patterns of the Ancient Mysteries." Forthcoming.

Mosser, Monique and Georges Teyssot, eds. *The Architecture of Western Gardens.* Cambridge, MA: MIT Press,1991.

Mueller, Janel. *The Native Tongue and The Word: Developments in English Prose Style 1380-1580.* Chicago: Chicago University Press, 1985.

Muscatine, Charles. "The Canterbury Tales: Style of the Man and Style of the Work." In *Chaucer and the Chaucerians,* edited by D. S. Brewer, 88-113. London: Thomas Nelson, 1966.

Nichols, Stephen G. and Siegfried Wenzel, eds. *The Whole Book: Cultural Perspectives on the Medieval Miscellany.* Ann Arbor: University of Michigan Press, 1996.

Nichols, Stephen G. "The New Philology." *Speculum* 65 (1990): 1-10.

Nicolaisen, W. F. H., ed. *Oral Tradition in the Middle Ages.* Binghamton, NY: Medieval and Renaissance Texts and Studies, 1995.

O'Neill, John. *Critical Conventions: Interpretation in the Literary Arts and Sciences.* Norman: University of Oklahoma Press, 1992.

Ong, Walter J. *Interfaces of the Word: Studies in the Evolution of Consciousness and Culture.* Ithaca, NY: Cornell University Press, 1977.

—. *Orality and Literacy: The Technologizing of the Word.* London: Methuen, 1982.

Orme, Nicholas. *English Schools in the Middle Ages.* London: Methuen, 1973.

Oxford English Dictionary. Oxford: Clarendon Press, 1989.

Pace, George B. "The Text of Chaucer's Purse." *Papers of the Bibliographical Society University of Virginia* 1 (1948): 103-121.

Parker, Rozsika. *The Subversive Stitch*. London: The Women's Press, 1984.

Parkes, M. B. and Andrew G. Watson, eds. *Medieval Scribes, Manuscripts, and Libraries*. London: Scolar Press, 1978.

Pearsall, Derek. "The Assembly of Ladies and Generydes." *RES* 12 (1961): 229-37.

—. "The English Chaucerians." In *Chaucer and Chaucerians: Critical Studies in Middle English Literature*, edited by D. S. Brewer, 201-39. London: Thomas Nelson, 1966.

—. "The Uses of Manuscripts." *Harvard Library Bulletin* 4.4 (1994): 30-6.

—. ed. *Manuscripts and Readers in Fifteenth-Century England: The Literary Implications of Manuscript Study*. Cambridge: Brewer, 1983.

Peck, Russell A. *Chaucer's Romaunt of the Rose and Boece, Treatise on the Astrolabe, Equatorie of the Planetis, Lost Works, and Chaucerian Apocrypha: An Annotated Bibliography*. Toronto: University of Toronto Press, 1988.

Pelikan, Jaroslav. *Mary Through the Centuries: Her Place in the History of Culture*. New Haven: Yale University Press, 1996.

Pennick, Nigel. *Mazes and Labyrinths*. London: Robert Hale, 1990.

Percival, Florence. *Chaucer's Legendary Good Women*. Cambridge: Cambridge University Press, 1998.

Peter, John. *Complaint and Satire in Early English Literature*. Oxford: Clarendon Press, 1956.

Piehler, Paul. *The Visionary Landscape*. London: Edward Arnold, 1971.

Pollock, Frederick and Frederick William Maitland. *The History of English Law before the time of Edward I.* Cambridge: Cambridge University Press, 1898.

Power, Eileen. *Medieval English Nunneries, c.1275-1535*. Cambridge: Cambridge University Press, 1922.

—. *Medieval Women*, edited by M. M. Poston. Cambridge: Cambridge University Press, 1975.

Quilligan, Maureen. *The Allegory of Female Authority: Christine de Pizan's Cité des Dames*. Ithaca, NY: Cornell University Press, 1991.

Quinn, William A., ed. *Chaucer's Dream Visions and Shorter Poems*. New York: Garland, 1999.

Quiviger, François. "Imagining and Composing Stories in the Renaissance." In *Pictorial Composition from Medieval to Modern Art*, edited by Paul Taylor and François Quiviger, 45-57. London: The Warburg Institute, 2000.

Reed, Thomas L. *Medieval Debate Poetry and the Aesthetics of Irresolution.* Columbia: University of Missouri Press, 1990.

Reiss, Athene. "Pictorial Composition in Medieval Art." In *Pictorial Composition from Medieval to Modern Art*, edited by Paul Taylor and François Quiviger, 1-26. London: The Warburg Institute, 2000.

Reiss, Timothy J. *The Meaning of Literature.* Ithaca, NY: Cornell University Press, 1992.

Renwick, W. L. *The Beginnings of English Literature to Skelton.* London: Cresset Press, 1966.

Richards, Earl Jeffrey, ed. *Reinterpreting Christine de Pizan.* Athens: University of Georgia Press, 1992.

Riddy, Felicity. "Mother Knows Best: Reading Social Change in a Courtesy Text." *Speculum* 71 (1996): 66-86.

Ritson, Joseph. *Ancient Songs and Ballads, from the reign of King Henry the Second to the Revolution*, edited by W.Carew Hazlitt. London: Reeves and Turner, 1877.

Robbins, Rossell Hope and J. L. Cutler. *Supplement to the Index of Middle English Verse.* Lexington: University of Kentucky Press, 1965.

Robbins, Rossell Hope. "The Findern Anthology." *PMLA* 69 (1954): 610-642.

Robertson, Jr, D. W. "The Doctrine of Charity in Mediaeval Literary Gardens: A Topical Approach through Symbolism and Allegory." *Speculum* 26 (1951): 24-49.

Robinson, P. R. "The 'Booklet': A Self-Contained Unit in Composite Manuscripts." *Codicologica* 3 (1980): 46-69.

Rowland, Beryl, ed. *Chaucer and Middle English Studies.* London: Allen and Unwin, 1974.

Ruggiers, Paul G., ed. *Editing Chaucer: The Great Tradition.* Norman, OK: Pilgrim Books, 1984.

Russell, J. Stephen. *The English Dream Vision.* Columbus: Ohio State University Press, 1988.

Salisbury, Joyce E., ed. *Sex in the Middle Ages.* New York: Garland, 1991.

Sandler, L. F., ed. "Jean Pucelle and the Lost Miniatures of the Belleville Breviary." *Art Bulletin* 66 (1984): 73-96.

Santarcangeli, Paolo and Umberto Eco. *Il Libro Dei Labirinti: Storia di un Mito e di un Simbolo.* Milan: Frassinelli, 1984.

Scattergood, V. J. "The Authorship of 'The Book of Cupid'." *Anglia* 82 (1964): 140-143.

Schacherl, Lillian. *Très Riches Heures: Behind the Gothic Masterpiece.* Munich: Prestel, 1997.

Schapiro, Meyer. "On Some Problems in the Semiotics of Visual Art: Field and Vehicle in Image-Signs." *Semiotica* I.3 (1969): 223-42.

——. *Words and Pictures: On the Literal and the Symbolic in the Illustration of a Text.* The Hague: Mouton, 1973.

——. *Words, Script, and Pictures: Semiotics of Visual Language.* New York: George Braziller, 1996.

Scheps, Walter. "A Climatological Reading of Henryson's Testament of Cresseid." *Studies in Scottish Literature* 15 (1980): 80-7.

Seaton, Ethel. *Sir Richard Roos, Lancastrian Poet.* London: Rupert Hart-Davis, 1961.

Sell, Roger D. *Literature as Communication.* Amsterdam: John Benjamins, 2000.

Sellers, Susan, ed. *Feminist Criticism: Theory and Practice.* Hemel Hempstead: Harvester Wheatsheaf, 1991.

Sharpe, J. A. *Defamation and Sexual Slander in Early Modern England.* York: York University Press, 1980.

Showalter, Elaine. "American Gynocriticism." *American Literary History* 5.1 (1993): 111-28.

——. *A Literature of Their Own.* Princeton, NJ: Princeton University Press, 1977.

Skeat, W. W. *The Chaucer Canon.* Oxford: Clarendon Press, 1900.

Skeat, Walter W. "The Authoress of 'The Flower and the Leaf'." *Modern Language Quarterly* 3 (1900): 111-12.

Smith, Julie Ann. *Ordering Women's Lives: Penitentials and Nunnery Rules in the Early Medieval West.* Aldershot: Ashgate, 2001.

Smith, Lesley and Jane M. Taylor, eds. *Women, The Book, and the Godly.* Cambridge: Brewer, 1995.

Snyder, Cynthia Lockard. "The Floure and the Leafe: An Alternative Approach." In *New Readings of Late Medieval Love Poems*, edited by David Chamberlain, 145-71. Lanham, MD: University Press of America, 1993.

Solterer, Helen. *The Master and Minerva: Disputing Women in French Medieval Culture.* Berkley: University of California Press, 1995.

Southern, R. W. *Robert Grosseteste: The Growth of an English Mind in Medieval Europe.* Oxford: Clarendon Press, 1986.

Spearing, A. C. *Medieval Dream-Poetry.* Cambridge: Cambridge University Press, 1976.

——. *The Medieval Poet as Voyeur.* Cambridge: Cambridge University Press, 1993.

Spiegel, Gabrielle M. "Maternity and Monstrosity: Reproductive Biology in the Roman de Mélusine." In *Mélusine of Lusignan: Founding*

Fiction in Late Medieval France, edited by Donald Maddox and Sara Sturm-Maddox, 100-24. Athens: University of Georgia Press, 1996.

Spurgeon, C. F. E. *500 Years of Chaucer Criticism and Allusion 1357-1890.* London: Kegan Paul, 1908-1917.

Stanbury, Sarah. "Feminist Masterplots: The Gaze on the Body of Pearl's Dead Girl." In *Feminist Approaches to the Body in Medieval Literature,* edited by Linda Lomperis and Sarah Stanbury, 96-115. Philadelphia: University of Pennsylvania Press, 1993.

—. "Regimes of the Visual in Premodern England: Gaze, Body, and Chaucer's Clerk's Tale." *New Literary History* 28 (1997): 261-89.

Stanton, Domna C. "Autogynography: Is the Subject Different?" In *The Female Autograph,* edited by Domna C. Stanton, 3-20. Chicago: University of Chicago Press, 1984.

—. ed. *The Female Autograph.* Chicago: University of Chicago Press, 1987.

Starkey, David. "The Age of the Household: Politics, Society and the Arts c. 1350-c.1550." In *The Later Middle Ages,* edited by Stephen Medcalf, 225-90. London: Methuen, 1981.

Stephens, John. "The Questioning of Love in the Assembly of Ladies." *RES* 24 (1973): 129-140.

Stevens, John. *Music and Poetry in the Early Tudor Court.* London: Methuen, 1961.

Strohm, Paul. *Theory and the Premodern Text.* Minneapolis: University of Minnesota Press, 2000.

Sturm-Maddox, Sara. "Crossed Destinies: Narrative Programs in the Roman de Mélusine." In *Mélusine of Lusignan: Founding Fiction in Late Medieval France,* edited by Donald Maddox and Sara Sturm-Maddox, 12-31. Athens: University of Georgia Press, 1996.

Swabey, Ffiona. *Medieval Gentlewoman: Life in a Widow's Household in the Later Middle Ages.* Stroud: Sutton, 1999.

Tachau, Katherine H. *Vision and Certitude in the Age of Ockham: Optics, Epistemology and the Foundations of Semantics, 1250-1345.* Leiden: E. J. Brill, 1988.

Taylor, Beverly. "The Medieval Cleopatra: The Classical and Medieval Tradition of Chaucer's Legend of Cleopatra." *Journal of Medieval and Renaissance Studies* 7 (1977): 249-69.

Taylor, Paul and François Quiviger, eds. *Pictorial Composition from Medieval to Modern Art.* London: The Warburg Institute, 2000.

Taylor, Robert A., ed. *The Centre and its Compass.* Kalamazoo: Western Michigan University Press, 1993.

Tomasch, Sylvia and Sealy Gilles, eds. *Text and Territory: Geographical Imagination in the European Middle Ages*. Philadelphia: University of Pennsylvania Press, 1998.

Tuve, Rosemond. *Allegorical Imagery: Some Mediaeval Books and their Posterity*. Princeton, NJ: Princeton University Press, 1966.

—. *Seasons and Months: Studies in a Tradition of Middle English Poetry*. Paris: Librairie Universitaire, 1933.

Utley, Francis Lee. "Oral Genres as a Bridge to Written Literature." In *Folklore Genres*, edited by Dan Ben-Amos, 3-16. Austin: University of Texas Press, 1976.

—. *The Crooked Rib*. New York: Octagon Books, 1970.

Wallace, David, ed. *The Cambridge History of Medieval English Literature*. Cambridge: Cambridge University Press, 1999.

Ward, Jennifer C. *English Noblewomen in the Later Middle Ages*. London: Longman, 1992.

Wenzel, Siegfried. "Reflections on (New) Philology." *Speculum* 65 (1990): 11-18.

—. "Sermon Collections and their Taxonomy." In *The Whole Book: Cultural Perspectives on the Medieval Miscellany*, edited by Stephen G. Nichols and Siegfried Wenzel, 7-21. Ann Arbor: University of Michigan Press, 1996.

White, John. *The Birth and Rebirth of Pictorial Space*. Cambridge, MA: Belknap Press, 1987.

Whitford, Margaret, ed. *Luce Irigaray: Philosophy in the Feminine*. London: Routledge, 1991.

—. ed. *The Irigaray Reader*. Oxford: Blackwell, 1992.

Wigley, Mark. "Untitled: The Housing of Gender." In *Sexuality & Space*, edited by Beatriz Colomina, 327-89. Princeton, NJ: Princeton University Press, 1992.

Winston-Allen, Anne. "Gardens of Heavenly and Earthly Delight: Medieval Gardens of the Imagination." *NM* 99.1 (1998): 83-92.

Wogan-Browne, Jocelyn, Nicholas Watson, Andrew Taylor, and Ruth Evans, eds. *The Idea of the Vernacular: An Anthology of Middle English Literary Theory, 1280-1520*. University Park: Pennsylvania State University Press, 1999.

Woolf, R. *The English Religious Lyrics in the Middle Ages*. Oxford: Oxford University Press, 1968.

Woolf, Virginia. *The Common Reader*. London: Hogarth Press, 1925.

The World Encompassed: An Exhibition of the History of Maps held at the Baltimore Museum of Art, 1952. Baltimore: Walters Art Gallery, 1952.

Wright, Craig. *The Maze and the Warrior*. Cambridge MA: Harvard University Press, 2001.

Wright, Lawrence. *Perspective in Perspective*. London: Routledge, 1983.

Yenal, Edith. *Christine de Pizan: A Bibliography*. Metuchen, NJ: Scarecrow Press, 1989.

Zimmermann, Margarete and Dina De Rentiis, eds. *The City of Scholars: New Approaches to Christine de Pizan*. Berlin and New York: Walter de Gruyter, 1994.

INDEX